The Lad from Garrison Lane

Peter Round

First Edition June 2017

Copyright © Peter Round

The right of Peter Round to be identified as the
author of this work has been asserted.

All right reserved. No part of this publication may be reproduced,
stored in a retrieval system, or transmitted, in any form or by
any means, electronic, mechanical, photocopying,
recording, or otherwise, without the prior permission
of the publisher.

Cover design by Lulu Publishing

Printed in English

This book is dedicated to my family,
with special thanks to my wife Joan
who has always believed in me.

Enjoy the read.

Chapter 1	Growing Up at Garrison Lane School
Chapter 2	Tilton Road School
Chapter 3	Moms New Job
Chapter 4	My first day out – Rhyl
Chapter 5	Ada Road School
Chapter 6	My Last Year in School
Chapter 7	My Introduction to Market Life

Chapter 1
Growing Up at Garrison Lane School

'I'm in no trouble with the police and that's the truth.'

In 1943, before I went to Tilton Road School, I attended the school at Garrison Lane. I was there with a mate of mine; his name was Johnny Mulrenan. Johnny lived in top home (South Holme) and, we didn't know it then, but we would become lifelong mates. He came calling for me every morning and off we went, running down to the canal bridge. We would watch the barges go by with the horses pulling them and wave at the men   onboard. We was always late for school and usually got a telling off.

One time towards the end of a school week, Johnny and I was really late watching four barges pass down the canal from the bridge. We jumped off the bridge ran across the horse road through the gates and ran down the slope. You had to watch how you ran down because there was bricks sticking up, used for the horses to grip on. If you tripped over them you would know all about it! We got near to the edge of the slope and shouted 'Give us ride mister!' to a man on a passing barge. As the barge moved slowly towards us the bloke grabbed hold of my hand to pull us aboard. He gave us a ride to the locks at the top of Garrison Street. When Johnny and I got there we jumped off and went to the railway crossing, but we had to wait for the train to pass over. As went through the gates on Garrison Street we saw a rag and bone man driving his horse and cart. We shouted to him give us a ride to Garrison Lane school and he shouted back 'Go on hop it!' Johnny and I carried on shouting back to him and he eventually he let us jump on the back of his cart, giving us ride to the bottom of Garrison Street.

We ask him if he wanted any help, but he told us to piss off and get to school. When Johnny and I got to school we went straight to the classroom. Our teacher stood there and she said, 'You know you're very late, I'm going to take you two to the headmistress.' When we got to the headmistress' office our teacher told her we was always late and this time we was *very* late having only just arrived. The headmistress said, 'I'm going to give you a letter to give to your parents.' Then Johnny and I started to laugh at her. 'You think it's very funny the letter I'm going to give for your parents? It's going to be a very strongly worded one.' We was still laughing as we went back to the classroom. Come four o'clock we went to run out of the classroom but our teacher stopped Johnny and I. 'Hold on you two, the headmistress wants to see you before you go home.' Our teacher took us to the office again and we were given the letter for our parents and we was told that the headmistress expected to see our parents when they read the letter.' On our home Johnny and I never spoke to one another. When we got to the canal bridge I threw my letter into the cut, but still Johnny never spoke. As we passed the canal we walked a little further and Johnny stopped. He looked back towards the canal bridge and he ran back to throw his letter into the cut too. Afterwards, we both ran all the way home laughing.

    I remember it was a Saturday when Johnny came calling for me. As usual he didn't knock the door but shouted up to me. I lifted my window and shouted back that 'I'd be down in a tick!' As I was going out the door my Mom asked where I was going off to play. I told her that I'd be out with Johnny and that I'd be home later. I got to the bottom of the stairs by our front door our neighbour, Mrs Price, came out asking me to go to Able's to order a loaf. I think the food was still on ration at the time. Together, Johnny and I ran over to Able's to order loaf for Mrs Price before we went off to play. When we was there Mrs Able asked if my Mom wanted a loaf too. I said that she probably did and asked if Mrs Able could put one aside for Mom. Johnny suggested we walk up to Bordesley Green. Once we got there we met three lads who Johnny knew. This is where my troubles started. I'm going to call the lads them Tom, Dick, and Harry. We started to walk down the Bordesley Green Road until we came to a building, Johnny stopped he said to me, 'I'm not going with them I'm going home.' Johnny left us and we went a little way down the road till we were towards Bordesley Green railway station. Tom, Dick, and Harry was older than Johnny and I and they came from Saltley area. They told me to keep a look out and went into the nearby building. All of a sudden they all came running back out and gave me three tins of meat and told me to go home. As I looked back I saw a bloke come running out of the out building. He hurried after Tom, Dick, and Harry but I don't think he ever caught them. When I got to the top of the road I saw a police car speeding round the corner. It went down Bordesley Green Road and it stopped when it reached the bloke from the building.

Not wanting to hang around anymore I ran home fast as I could go. I was out of breath as I went up the stairs to our front door. Suddenly another neighbour, Mrs Bloomer, came out and said to me, 'I saw you on Bordesley Green Road, I saw you going down there with those three lads. They looked older than you, what have you been up to?' I said nothing, but then she asked me where I got the tins meat from that I was holding. I replied that the lads had given them to me. Mrs Bloomer kept asking if I'd nicked them, what the lads' names were and where did they lived. I kept saying I didn't know anything, but she wasn't letting go. Mrs Bloomer came up with me to my house and as soon as we walked in the first thing she said to my Mom was, 'Mrs Round this little so and so been up to no good, I saw him with three older lads. He has nicked two tins of meat from somewhere on the green.' Mom started to shout at me asking where I'd got the tins from, I replied that a kid gave them to me. She just thought I was lying and told me go to my room and wait until my brother came home.

I knew one of my older brothers, Albert, was still in the army. When my other brother Tommy came home first thing Mom told him was that I'd been up to no good. He walked into my bedroom; 'Okay nip (my two brothers always call me the nipper) what's been going on?' I replied; 'Nothing's been going on, just some kid gave me the tins meat, honest.' Tommy said it was okay and then asked if I knew the kids name. I said I didn't and that all I knew was that I was walking down Bordesley Green Road when this kid come running out of building with tins of meat in his arms. He gave me the two tins then he told me to run so I did. Tommy got me by the collar and lifted me off the bed and asked again what the kid's name was. I told him again that I honestly didn't know. Then Tommy went to hit me but Mom came in, so he threw me back down onto the bed. Both of them left my room. They closed the door behind them I got up off the bed and stood by the door to try listen to what they were saying. I heard Tommy saying I think he is telling the truth mom and that next time this happened Mom had to call the police.

In my bedroom you could pull the window halfway and climb out onto the window ledge. I went to the window and pulled down it down, and then I climbed through and stood on the ledge to reach out to the drainpipe and slid down. All I had on my mind was Tommy going to get police. I ran down Garrison Lane going nowhere in particular and then got to Garrison Lane park. It was getting dark and I was getting really hungry, so I started to walk up Dartmouth Street by the side of the park. As I was crossing the horse road by Witton Street Mrs Cross came out of one of the houses. As I passed her she ask me if I was Peter I said yes - Mrs Cox's son Brian went to the same school has me. She asked me what I was doing down there. I replied that I was looking for my Mom but I was locked out and getting hungry. Mrs Cox kindly invited me inside for a sandwich. She cut the bread thickly and after I finished I thanked her for the food and said that I would go and look for my mom. She said that I was going nowhere and that Mr Cross would take me home. I told Mrs Cross that my Mom wasn't home but she told me 'Never you mind, your Mom might be home by now. Off you go with Mr Cross.' As Mr Cross and I was walking up Dartmouth Street towards Maxstoke Street we saw Tommy crossing the horse road. He looked towards us and shouted, 'Peter come here!' Mr Cross told Tommy that I'd been at his house, that I'd been looking for his Mom, and that Mrs Cross had given him a sandwich. Then Tommy told Mr Cross what I'd been up to, he thanked Mr Cross for looking after me, and we started to walk home. Tommy started to tell me off and asked me why I'd run away. I explained that I'd heard him say he was going to fetch the copper's to get me. He put his arm around my shoulder and said; 'Look here nip, I'm on your side if you keep out of trouble. You're going to make your Mom ill.' When we got home there was Mom standing by the kitchen door, I could tell she was angry. She was about to hit me, but Tommy stopped her. He told my Mom he'd keep me out of trouble. On the Sunday I had to stay in all day apart from running over to Able's to see if she saved Mom's bread. Mom was watching me from the veranda as I went round the back of the shop and knocked on the door. Mrs Able asked who it was and I replied that it's me Peter Round and that Mom wanted to know did she save her loaf. Mrs Able said that yes she has the loaf, but that I was to tell my mother when she ordered anything she had to fetch it on the day, that the shop was closed on Sundays, and that my Mom could pay her tomorrow. As I was leaving the backyard another lad appeared, he asked me if the old cow got anymore bread. I knew the kid, he came from Bottom Holme. As I was walking back home I could see Mom standing on the veranda talking to Mrs Fleetwood, so I ran home up the stairs. As I did Mrs Bloomer came out and said that she wanted to talk with me. I told her that Mom was waiting for her loaf and that I couldn't keep her waiting. Mrs Bloomer ignored me and asked if I'd told my Mom about three kids I was with. When I didn't reply she invited me into her house. Inside she kindly asked what this was all about and whether I had been in trouble again. 'No Mrs Bloomer', I replied. I told her that my Mom had got it all wrong and that I was only walking down to railway station to look at the trains. Mrs Bloomer could tell I was lying, she said she could see it written all over my face. I can vividly remember saying to her that I had a wash that morning and that I'd washed my face. Mrs Bloomer told me not to be cheeky with her and I replied that I wasn't. 'Come on

Peter, what was you doing with them three kids?' she had asked again. I told her 'Nothing honestly Mrs Bloomer'. Then she started to laugh, I look at her I ask her why she laughing. She didn't reply so I said that I had to go, that my Mom would be waiting. Mrs Bloomer came to the door with me: she was still laughing as she watched me go up the stairs. When I got in my Mom said that I'd better start behaving myself from now on or she would fetch the police to me have put away. 'Okay Mom!' I remember thinking.

Come Monday morning Mom said that she was taking me to school. I said that Johnny would be calling for me like he always did. This didn't put Mom off, she said she take him as well. Johnny shouted up to me as usual and I opened the window to shout that I won't be long. From behind Mom pulled me away from the window and down shouted down to Johnny that she was taking both of us to school. 'Why Mrs Round?' Johnny had complained. 'To make sure you two go in,' my Mom replied. Johnny looked clean and smart that day and I was in rags. Johnny and I was walking a little in front of my Mom when he leaned in and whispered to me, 'Does your mom know about the letters?' I said no and we carried on walking slowly in front. When Johnny and I got close to the school door we ran straight into playground and climbed up on the school gates. I saw Mom standing on the other side of the horse road further down Garrison Lane, I waved to her and she waved back. As Mom carried on walking down Garrison Lane, the bell rang and we had to get in line to go into the classroom. Our teacher said Johnny and I had to go report to the headmistress first. We went to the office, knocked on the door and walked straight in. The headmistress shouted at us that we should knock and wait till we are called to come in. Johnny and I started to laugh again. She asked what we thought was so funny and I replied 'You miss.' She wanted to see our parents and asked if they read the letters. I said that, 'Yes, of course my Mom had read it', but that now she'd gone to work that I heard my Mom say she got to get some money to pay the rent man. The headmistress demanded that she see our parents the next day as our behaviour had to stop and that we was both coming to school late every day. Johnny said, 'Not today though miss.' She sent us back to our classroom saying that she would deal with us later. Once back in class our teacher said, with a very loud voice, that we would be split up. Johnny was sent to sit at the back and I was put at the front by Nancy (who I think lived on nearby Witton Street). I can remember Nancy kicking me on the ankle saying that I wasn't going to get her into trouble. Come break time when we got into the playground Johnny and I was going to run out of school, but I remember it started to rain, so we went back into the classroom where had to start to do some writing. Nancy moaned that I was looking at her and I started to laugh. Our teacher heard us and came over, then she slapped me round the head. I got up in an attempt to run out of the class, but she caught me by the collar and demanded I go back and sit back down. I must have said something because the whole class started to laugh. Our teacher said that she was going to have to remove me from the class. I can remember Nancy standing up and saying, 'Miss, I will look after him, I'll keep him out of trouble, I know his mom.' I looked at Nancy and laughed again. She didn't know my Mom at all. When the bell rang we all went to the hall to get our dinner, it wasn't much but at least it was something to eat. Nancy came to sit by Johnny and I and she started to chat away. The two of us soon got up after we finished our dinner and went into the playground. We both saw that the gates were open. We looked at one another. And then we ran for our lives.

We didn't know where we was running to but we finished up by the railway crossing top of Garrison Street. We stop there for bit watching the goods trains go by. A little while later we started to walk back down towards Midland Street and who should be coming round corner from Landor Street but Tom, Dick, and Harry. They came up to Johnny and I asking us where we was going. We replied 'Nowhere', so the three lads asked us to come along with them. We all ended up back down Garrison Street walking alongside some houses. As we went Tom, Dick, and Harry kept trying the doors of the houses to see if they were open. When we got further down Garrison Street there was an old lady on the other side of the horse road watching us. She shouted out to us that we should all be in school. One of the three lads shouted back 'Go on you old bag!' We all started to run down Garrison Street to the bottom by Lawley Street where we stood for a bit. Johnny suggested we go back to school but I said 'Let's hang on bit longer.' There was few houses on Lawley Street. Tom, Dick, and Harry went down to them while Johnny and I stood and watched. Some bloke suddenly came out of one of the houses and so the three lads started to run back. Johnny and I ran too then, turning into a little winding, cobbled alley that led onto Lily Crescent then into Montague Street. Once we got to Derby Street Tom, Dick, and Harry was walking in front of us. I told Johnny that we should go our own way now, that we was going to get into trouble. Johnny replied no, we wasn't leaving yet. Johnny and I walked round the corner of Montague Street and the three lads were standing on the corner. As we went up to them a copper appeared over Great Barr Bridge. Tom, Dick, and Harry didn't hesitate and they all ran off, leaving Johnny and I there. The copper got to us and asked who the lads were. We said 'We don't know sir.' The copper asked which school we went to (there were a few schools in the area) and Johnny and I told him Garrison Lane. He got both of us by the arm and took us back to school, straight into the headmistress office. She told the officer that she was fed up with Johnny and I, that we came into to school every morning, played it up in the classroom, and that our teacher couldn't control us. She told the copper that she had sent letters to our mothers but hadn't had any responses. The copper sent us outside where Johnny and I stood opposite each other. A little while later the copper came out and said that he was going to take us both to Digbeth Police Station where we would wait till our parents came to fetch us. At hearing this I went to run but the copper was fast and he got hold of my jacket. The sleeve ripped off, hanging from the seams where he had grabbed me. On the walk to the police station people kept looking at us and when we got to Great Barr Bridge an old lady coming in the opposite direction recognised us. It was the woman from Garrison Street who'd shouted at us earlier that afternoon. She stopped the copper and told him what she saw us doing. The copper turned to Johnny and I and asked if this was true, was we trying to break into people's houses?

We got to Digbeth Police Station and went through some swinging doors. I remember that the copper pushed the doors so hard they came back very quickly and nearly knocked Johnny in the face. Johnny told the copper we was very hungry as we'd had no dinner. We was simply told that it was our fault and that we should have stayed at school for dinner. Time was getting on, the copper put us in a dimly lit room. Straightaway I tried the door, it wasn't locked so I went to walk out the door. As I did I looked up to see a giant of copper with ginger hair and a deep voice 'Where do you think you are going?' he said. 'Going home sir,' I remember saying, 'I haven't done anything wrong.' 'You are staying till your parents come for you.' I told the copper I was hungry and said he that I should go back into the room and he'd find me something to eat. I did as I was told and went back into the room, but then I went back out again. The copper was still standing there. 'Now what do you want?' 'I want to go to the toilet sir', I said. He got me by the neck and as he did my shoe came off. The copper told me to pick it up. As I bent to pick it up he saw the hole in the bottom of the shoe and he asked 'Where's your father?' 'I haven't got one sir, only me and my Mom,' I replied. 'Okay, there's the toilet hurry up then.'

When I went in it really stunk and I was glad to get out of there and back to Johnny. I told him not to go have a wee if he could help it, the toilet stunk. After a while Johnny's Mom and Dad arrived, his Dad was really telling Johnny off and the big copper came in asked Johnny's parents to come outside for bit. I popped my head out to see was happening, but the copper shouted back in a loud voice, 'Get back into that room!' Then, I heard my own Mom's voice, and next thing the door open and the copper brought seven chairs in to go round the table in the middle of the room. After while everyone came into the room including the headmistress. I thought to myself, 'What's she doing here?' then the copper came in and closed the door behind him. He started to talk to us in a low voice. He got up came round to where we was sitting, he sat on the edge of the table just looking at us. I started to get frightened and I knew Johnny was too. The copper got up and, still looking at us, he walked to the side of the table.   Suddenly he punched the table-top really hard making Johnny and I jump. The copper sat down on the other side of the table from us and started to talk to us in a quiet voice telling us what we should do and what not to do. Every now again he punched the table-top. Next the   headmistress talked to Johnny and I, we just tried not to laugh. She asked me why I was laughing and I said that she was talking differently. The headmistress asked what happened to letter she gave me for my mother. I replied that I had thrown it in the cut. When I said this the copper punched the table-top making Johnny and I jump again, then he gave us right telling off. I remember looking over at my mom, she stood up and said that she'd make sure I got to school on time. She pointed her finger at the headmistress and said she needed to make sure I stayed at school and didn't wander off. I shouted to my Mom 'I'm hungry', but she shouted back that I was going straight to bed when we got home, without anything to eat. The copper said we could all go home and that he didn't want to see Johnny and I here again. Just as we was leaving the copper grabbed us both by the arm and took us to the cells. He told us that if we came to the station again we'd be locked up in there.

I was glad to get out of there, although we had to walk all the way home listening to Johnny's Dad telling him off. He slapped Johnny really hard round the head making him cry. Then my Mom gave me slap over the head. When we got home Mom, as she said she would, sent me to go straight to bed. She eventually did give me something to eat, a piece dried crusty bread. It was hard but I was hungry so I had to eat it. The next morning Mom came into my bedroom and shouted at me to get up, get washed and get ready for school. I had two pieces of toast and a cup of milk (made with half milk and half hot water). Once I was ready Mom took me to school. Johnny's Mom was standing outside the school gates, so he was already there. I walked into the playground and Johnny came up to me to say that his Dad told him to keep away from me. Johnny said he wasn't going to though, but we did keep out of trouble. I went to round to Granny Pegs after school and stayed there till Mom came to fetch me.

    I think Johnny and I kept out of trouble for about two weeks till a new kid came to our class. His name was Terry Williams he sat behind me and next to a girl call Ann. She became our mate after a while, when he got to know Johnny and I he started to play up and would pull Nancy's hair in class. Come play time Johnny, Terry, and I all played together. Then, a few weeks later, Tom, Dick, and Harry came to the gates trying to get us to leave school. One day when they came, Terry was at the gates on his own, Johnny and I we was late going into the playground. As we was going towards the gates we saw Terry leaving with Tom, Dick, and Harry. Johnny and I we ran after Terry to try and stop him going with them, but as we walked passed the main entrance of the school our teacher came out asking us where we all going. Tom, Dick, and Harry all ran off while our teacher took Johnny, Terry, and I to the headmistress' office. Thankfully, she believed what we told her and then she told us go back to our classroom.

    When it was time to go home, Terry asked Johnny and I back to his house, he lived in the Palmer Street flats. Johnny said no, but I went back with Terry. I remember Terry's Mom was a nice lady and that she gave me something to eat. I can't remember what it was but I can remember asking her for more (she gave me just little bit more.) When I was leaving I said, 'Thank for the food Mrs Williams,' and then I ran all the way to Granny Pegs. I knew I was late when I got to Granny Peg's as Mom was already there. She asked me where I'd been and, at first, she didn't believe me when I told her I was at Terry's. Granny Peg told Mom to 'Leave the lad alone,' but still mom wouldn't believe me. I had to take her down to Terry's house; we had to walk all the way down St Andrews Street then onto St Andrews Road, cross the horse road into Watery Lane then into Little Barr Street. Terry's house was on the corner of Little Barr Street and Palmer Street. When we got there, Mom still wouldn't believe me till I knocked on the door and Mrs Williams came out. Terry's Mom asked us in and they spoke for a while. Terry and I, we never spoke about what went on earlier in the day. Mom never said she believed me till we got back to Granny Pegs. When we did then Granny Peg had right go at Mom for not believing me to begin with. 'I told you the lad wasn't lying,' I remember her saying. Later, when Mom and I got home, Mom said 'You must go to straight to Granny Pegs after school, do I make myself clear?'

Johnny and I both had to stay in before and after school for about three weeks. Tom, Dick, and Harry kept coming to the school gates trying to get Terry to run off with them. On this one accession they showed Terry a bag full of pennies, one of the lads said 'Come with us, we will get you a bag of pennies.' Our teacher came over to see what was happening and again Tom, Dick, and Harry ran off. Afterwards the school gates was closed.

A few days later Terry asked Johnny and I to go back to his house again, but we both said no. I said I'd ask Mom if I could go the day after. When school finished, I went to Granny Pegs, Mom was already so I asked her straightaway if I could go to Terry's after school the next day. I told her I'd said to Terry that I knew I had to ask her first. Mom was doing cleaning not far where Terry lived, so she said it was okay and that she'd fetch me. The next morning Johnny's Mom came to our house to see if my Mom could take Johnny to school. Mom said it was fine so she walked us both to the school gates. Terry was waiting there for us and my Mom shouted to him to 'Come over!' She asked if it was right that I could go back to his house after school. Terry replied 'Yes Mrs Round.' My Mom said that I was to stay there till she came to fetch me.

Tom, Dick, and Harry was hanging around the school gates all day long, when we was leaving school at four o'clock they came over to us asked us to go with them. Johnny said no, that he had to go straight home and he left. The three lads, Terry, and I started to walk down Garrison lane towards Lawley Street. Terry's Mom was on the other side of the horse road and pointed her out and said that he'd have to go. Tom, Dick, and Harry carried on walking up Lawley Street and Terry and I went back to his house. I asked Terry's Mom if I could I stay here till my Mom fetched me and she said it was okay. I remember there was a lovely smell when we went in to Terry's house. It was the same food from the last time when I was there. After dinner, Terry and I played out in the yard then my Mom came to fetch me. Mrs Williams and Mom talk for bit and then Mom said we had to go. Before we left she thanked Mrs Williams and then Terry walked with us to the end of Great Barr Street. We crossed the horse road onto St Andrews Road and I turned round wave to Terry. He waved back and shouted that he'd see me at school on Monday.

Come Monday morning Mom came into my bedroom throwing old coats off me, it was all I had to keep me warm. I went into the kitchen, had a wash in cold water and then Mom gave me a piece of toast and cup of hot milk. As we was going out the door Mom looked at me and told me to get back into the kitchen. She took my clothes off me and then got a smelly, old rag and washed me. 'You got a tied mark round your neck Peter,' she said. I remember horrible smell of the rag as Mom wiped me with it.

Johnny and his Mom was waiting for us, as we all walked up to the school gates Johnny whispered to me 'You stink!' Johnny and I went running into the playground and Ann came up to us. 'You stink!' she said. Then the morning bell went and we got in line, I had to go to the back because I stunk. When we got in class Nancy said 'You're not going to sit by me you stink!' Our teacher heard and she told me to go stand by the door, then she started to call our names out. The teacher called 'Terry Williams?', but there was no answer. She asked if anyone knew where Terry was, but we all replied 'No Miss.' When she had finished calling out our names, our teacher told me to come with her. I followed her to a room, I think it was the staff toilets. She told me to strip off all my clothes, 'You're going to have a proper wash', she told me. Shortly after, the headmistress came into toilets and asked what was going on. 'This naughty boy smells horrible,' my teacher said. They both told me to take my trousers off so they could wash me all down, the headmistress even washed my hair with some green soap. Then she started to wipe me down, but I shouted at her that I could do it myself. She slapped me across my head, 'You will do has you are told. You look nice and clean boy, now go back to your class,' the headmistress said.

When I got back to the classroom I sat down Nancy and she leant over to smell. Then, she kissed me on the cheek! After that Nancy and I helped one another out with our reading and sums. Come break time we went to have our makeshift dinner, this time we had rice pudding. Afterwards. Johnny and I went to sit by the gates, there wasn't any sign of Tom, Dick, and Harry. The afternoon bell and went we back into class, but there was still no sign of Terry. The headmistress came to see Johnny and I was in class on the afternoon and I can remember we did lot of reading.

Come four o'clock we were going out the front entrance and the headmistress called me over and gave me some soap to take home. I went to Granny Pegs and waited there for Mom to come fetch me. I told Granny Peg what the teacher did to me and what the headmistress gave me at the end of the day. Granny Peg done her nut! She made me strip down saying that I smelt. When Mom came in Granny Peg never gave her time to sit down; 'Why did you send the lad to school dirty?! The teacher said he smelt, they stripped him down and washed him! The school gave him some soap what's that telling you?' When Granny Peg would shout she would do a gig making me laugh. I remember having to put my hand to my mouth so couldn't see me laughing. After Gran had her say Mom got me by the arm and we left. When we got home Mom had a go at me. She gave me something to eat and told me when I'd finished I was to have a proper wash. Again I had to wash in cold water with Mom watching me. She went to give me some rag to wipe myself with, but when she smelt it she went on to the veranda and shoved the smelly rag down into the shoot. When she came back in she gave me a proper towel to wipe   myself dry.

      The next day Johnny came calling for me, he was on his own and as he was so early I wasn't ready. Mom called him in to wait for me and asked him where his Mom was. Johnny replied that she had to go to work early. I remember I got myself ready and then Mom gave me a piece of toast, but nothing to drink.

      Once we got outside Johnny and I started to run, Mom lifted the window up and she shout to us to wait there until she came down. When we got to the school gates Johnny and I ran into the playground, Mom went once the bell rang and we got into line and marched into our classroom. The teacher called our names out and there was still no Terry. Again she asked if anyone had seen him, but we all replied no. In the afternoon two coppers came into the classroom with the headmistress, they asked the class if any one of us seen Terry Williams. The class went quiet, no-one replied, after while the coppers went to leave. They told us if any of us remembered anything we needed to let our teacher or the headmistress know. Come four o'clock Johnny and I ran out main entrance and there were lots of coppers about. We both looked at each other then we ran all they home, Johnny carried on up Garrison Lane and I went up the gully to Granny Pegs. I sat down inside and Granny asked why I was so quiet and if there was anything wrong. When Mom came in first thing Gran said was that there was something wrong with Peter. Mom said that something was going on down the bottom of Garrison Lane, that there was loads of coppers running around. Gran said asked if they had stopped her, but Mom said they hadn't. Then she turned to me and said we were going home.

Once we got home I had what you call tea and sat by the window watching the kids playing outside. I looked over at Mom; 'No, you're not going out,' she said. After a bit I went to bed. Mom got me up the next day and said that she was going to trust me to have a proper wash. Johnny came calling for me and I was ready for him this time. Before we left Mom checked me to see if I had washed myself properly and then off we went. Mom was walking behind us as we got near to the school where there were still load of coppers about. The headmistress was waiting by the school gates and told us all to go straight to our classrooms. When everybody was in the class the two coppers from the day before came in started to ask the same questions; 'Have you seen Terry Williams?' The class was quiet then suddenly Arthur White stood up said to the copper, 'I saw him Sir going up Lawley Street with three kids and two blokes on Saturday afternoon. He waved to me I waved back, I was with my Mom.' The copper asked Arthur White if he knew the kids but he said no. Then he said 'Peter Round does though.' Before I could say anything Arthur carried on and said that the lads had been hanging around the school gates every day. The copper asked Arthur why he hadn't said anything yesterday, but Arthur replied that he hasn't been in school. The copper look at me and asked who the lads were, I replied that I didn't know.

The copper said that Terry been missing since Saturday and asked again if I was sure I didn't know who the lads were. The bell went for break time and we went for our dinner. Afterwards the headmistress came to me asked me to go to her office. The two coppers were in there and they kept asking me questions about the lads who were always hanging round at the school gates. I kept saying, 'Honest sir I don't know who they are or where they live.' I said that Terry was speaking to them all the time though. Finally, the two coppers went out of the office and then the headmistress came in and *she* started to ask me questions. When she was done she left the room. I waited for a bit then I ran out school.

The coppers were still about and I ran all the way to Granny Pegs, I didn't stop till I got there. Granny Peg took one look at me and asked if I was okay. I told her that the coppers kept asking me questions about Terry Williams at school. She asked me 'Who the bloody hell is Terry Williams?' and I explained that he was the kid who was missing. Granny Peg asked why I'd run out of school, did I now something? I told her I didn't know anything, she said it was good enough for her to know I was telling the truth

Later, when we got home Mom said I was bloody lying. I replied that Granny Peg believed me, but Mom said it didn't matter what she had said. Mom made me makeshift tea and while I was eating it she told me she'd find out what had been going on. After tea, when I was getting some coal for the fire, there was loud knock on the door. I opened it and standing there was the big ginger copper from Digbeth Police Station. He frightened me with the loud knock on the door, but he kindly said hello and asked if my Mom was home. I was about to say yes when mom came to the door, she asked what I'd he done now. The copper replied that I'd done nothing as yet and asked if he could come in. When he got inside the copper said he'd brought me some shoes, two pairs! When I managed to find cardboard I had to keep putting it in the shoes Mom got me because I got holes in them. I tried the new shoes on and one fitted okay, but the other pair was bit tight. Mom said I could have that pair for best. The copper sat down, there was only two chairs in our house, Mom sat on the other and I was left to stand in front of the copper. He started to ask me questions about Terry Williams, was he my mate? I said no, but Mom shouted that I was a bloody liar, that I'd been at his house last Friday. 'Come on Peter, tell me the truth, if you don't I will take you to the cells,' the copper said. I told him that these three kids kept coming to the school gates every day asking us to go with them, I said that they were older kids. The copper asked me their names, but I replied that I honestly didn't know. Then, he asked if I knew where they lived. Again I said I didn't. He kept asking me different questions and all the time I kept saying no. Then I told him what the kids showed Terry, the bag full of pennies. The copper asked if I knew where the pennies were from and again I said I didn't.

After the copper had gone Mom said that she hoped I was telling the truth, then I was sent to bed. I went to school next day on my own, Johnny was already there. I told him that the copper was at my house the night before and that he was asking me questions about Terry. Johnny wondered if the coppers would go to his house, but I said I didn't know. 'If they come my dad will kill me,' Johnny said. The morning bell went and as we going into the classroom the headmistress shouted to Jonny and I to go to her office. When we got there Terry's Mom and Dad were inside, they started to ask us the same questions as the coppers. I told Mrs Williams the copper came to my house the night before and Terry's dad asked me if I knew where the kids lived. I replied that I thought it was somewhere around Saltley, but I still never told them Johnny knew them. Mr Williams was about to ask Johnny some questions, but he asked the headmistress if he could go to the toilet. I went with him and when we came out of the toilet the headmistress was waiting for us to come out, making sure that we didn't run off.

Terry had been missing for about three weeks and come one playtime Johnny and I went to stand by the gates. I told Johnny what I said to the copper about the full off pennies, I think Johnny was getting worried about the coppers coming to his house. Come dinner time Johnny suggested we skip school go find Terry. As we was going out the main entrance Mr Williams coming in with a copper. The copper asked where we thought we was going, Johnny said that we was going to the park and then to look for Terry. 'No you're not, back into school,' the copper said. Then he asked us if Arthur White was in school, 'Yes' we told him.

Come four o'clock Johnny and I ran out of school and found Mr Williams waiting on the other side of the horse road, he shouted at us to come over to him. He asked us to go with him to go look for Terry, I said no that I had to go to my Granny Peg's after school, Johnny had already run off. I went straight to my Granny Pegs'. A little later Mom came and asked if they had found Terry, I replied that they hadn't yet. When we got home I told Mom that Mr Williams wanted me and Johnny and I to go with him to look for Terry. Later on when we got home Mom asked me to clean out the fireplace. I swept the ashes up and got the fire ready, when I got up to get some coal Mom shouted at me to 'Close the living room door!' I don't know what made me look through the crack of the living room door, but I saw mom bending down by the cupboard where the gas and electric meters were kept. She was putting the money in and then taking it out. As she was getting up again she shouted to me and asked if I'd got the coal yet. I shouted back that 'Yes, I was coming' and she replied that it had taken me long enough. It was the next day when I took a closer look at the meters when I realised what Mom was doing. She'd broken into them.

After school the next day, when I'd got home from Granny Pegs and before I went to bed, Mom sat me down. She asked me if I knew anything about Terry. I remember saying, 'Mom you got to believe me, all I know is that Terry ran off from school, you can ask Johnny.' I can remember on the blackboard in big letters it was Wednesday 16th or possibly 18th October 1945. As the class sat down our teacher started to call our names out, then the classroom door opened and in came Terry and his Mom. Our teacher look at Terry and asked me to go to his desk. When he sat down I turned around to look at Terry and, even at my age, I knew something was wrong, At playtime and dinner time Terry never spoke to Johnny and I, on the afternoon playtime Nancy and Ann went up to speak to him and he punched Nancy in the face. Johnny and I ran over to get him, but then the bell rang and Nancy ran to our teacher and told her what had happened. Terry had to go see the headmistress. We never saw Terry till the next day, when I got to Granny Pegs I told her   Terry was back at school and all she said was 'Good.' When Mom came in from work I told her about Terry and then I told her what happened to Nancy. Mom never said anything till we got home; first thing she said was that I had to clean out the fire, which I did. We had a makeshift dinner which was mashed potatoes and dry bread, only then did she started to talk about Terry. I asked Mom what had happened to him, all she said was 'Long as he's okay.' It had started to get really cold mom, so come bedtime Mom brought another coat in to me. I had got four coats, which I had on my bed I think they were army coats, where she got them from I don't know.

   The next day at school Terry's Mom came into the classroom and told Terry to say sorry to Nancy. When he said sorry Nancy said that she hated him and that she tell him what happened. Terry replied in a loud voice 'F***k off!' Terry's Mom walked across the classroom and she slapped him across the face. 'You better say sorry to Nancy again,' she demanded. Terry said sorry in a quiet voice and he sat back down. The morning went on and then we had our morning break. Before we knew it the dinner time bell went and as we all got up to go out Terry fell to the floor. Our teacher rushed over to him and then she shouted for someone to go and fetch the headmistress. When she arrived the headmistress told us all to go out the classroom and go get our dinner. We didn't see Terry again for the rest of the day and the next day, Terry never came to school.

   On Saturday I went round to Granny Pegs, when I did I always got something nice to eat. She asked me if I could do errand for her so off I went to get her some snuff. Granny Peg told me where to go on the way down Garrison Lane. I saw an ambulance rushing down the lane, it was first time I heard an ambulance ring its bell. As the ambulance passed me two old ladies came out of the paper shop I overheard one of them say 'I wonder if it's for that poor lad from Palmer Street,' then she said 'Come on Daisy let's go have half pint at the sailor.' I went into the shop to get Granny's snuff and when I came out onto Garrison Lane I looked up to Gordon Street. I saw Tom, Dick, and Harry coming along Gordon Street. I didn't hesitate and I ran straight up Barrwell Road and turned left into Dartmouth Street. As I ran cross the horse road into Sarah Street I never saw the car come round the bend - I nearly got run over! How the car never hit me I don't know. I ran up St Andrews Street to Granny Pegs and went round the back way. I stopped at there a little longer after I gave Granny her snuff. She gave me something to eat, when she did she look at me said 'What trouble are you in now?' 'I'm in no trouble Gran,' I replied. She told me she believed me and then sent me home.

Tom, Dick, Harry were waiting for me by gully into East Holme, I never saw them at first otherwise I would have run. One of them said that I was coming with them, I replied that I couldn't, that my Mom was waiting for me. They got hold of me and we walked round the back way of East Holme. When we got round the other side we started to run, because they were holding me I had to run with them. We got to Tilton Road and turned onto it, then we got to the tip and went through the open across the top and onto Adderley Road. I think we went about halfway down the road and then up an entry way into a backyard. In the house I was made to inside sit by the door, there were two men standing around in the yard and I said to one of them 'I want to go home.' I was told that I wasn't going yet, that I was going to climb through a window. I asked to go home again, but then one of the blokes got hold of me. 'You're going to do as your told!' he shouted. He lifted me up and slapped my face hard, then he put me down on the chair by the door again. I wanted to cry but I held back. The time was getting on I knew my Mom would be home by now. The three lads and the two blokes all went away from the yard, leaving me sitting on my own. I don't know where they went, but they had left the door open. I sat there for a bit and then I got up went outside where I saw nobody about. Then I ran down the entry, I ran and ran. Suddenly I looked around and saw Tom, Dick, and Harry running after me. I ran fast as I could go ran across Adderley Street and onto the tip. It was very dark and I couldn't see where I was going. I just kept on running then all of a sudden I slipped and went down the bank. I scratched both my legs and I could feel them bleeding. I lay there for a while and felt something crawling over me, but I was too scared to move. I could hear Tom, Dick, and Harry shouting my name nearby. I tried to get up but I slipped down again scratching my legs even more. When I finally got to the top I heard somebody but I couldn't see anyone. Then I heard them shouting my name again. I was really getting scared and frightened, I started to cry. The shouting stopped and I started to walk, but I was going the wrong way and I found myself by the opening of Tilton Road. Going through an opening I ripped my trousers. I started to walk down Tilton Road and this bloke came along. He stopped me and asked me where I'd been out this late. 'Some big kids have been chasing me over the tip,' I told him. He asked me where I lived and I told him I lived in EastHolme, he kindly said he would see me home safe.

  As we were walking along Tilton Road I started to hang back, so he asked 'What's up lad?' 'I can't walk,' I replied, my legs were hurting too much. The bloke got hold of me and lifted me up into arms, he carried me all the way home. As we got closer to EastHolme I saw Tom, Dick, and Harry on the corner of Venetia Road. The bloke asked if they were the big kids I'd mentioned, I was about to say it was but they suddenly turned and ran up away. Mom and Tommy came running out our block, Mom started shouting at me, 'I have been worried sick where have you been?' The bloke was still carrying me, he carried me up the stairs and when we got inside he put me on a chair. I could see that Mom had
started to cry. Mom and Tommy thanked the bloke; I found out sometime later who the bloke was, his name was Sheldon. Tommy started to have go at me and then I started to cry. Mom saw my legs and asked where I'd been to get in a state like that. 'These kids were chasing me,' I told her. Tommy asked me who the kids were, but I said that I didn't know. I explained that when I left Granny Peg's these three kids was waiting for me, they

took me to somewhere on the other side of the tip, to a house with two blokes waiting. I said that one of them had wanted me to climb through a window, because I was small I thought. Tommy asked what window, but I said again that I didn't know. He said it was okay and that he'd find the house the next day. He left and we didn't see him for few days.

Come Sunday morning Mom took a look at me and saw that my legs were scratched and my trousers were ripped. 'I'll go up to Oakley's to see if they are open, maybe they have a pair of trousers for you for school tomorrow,' Mom said. I saw her look into her purse. 'I'll have to see if I can get you a pair of trousers for 1/6pence, that's all I got in my purse.' Mom was going down the stairs outside when Mrs Bloomer came out asked her if I'd been found and if I was alright. Mom replied that I'd been bloody somewhere but that I wasn't saying where exactly. Mom asked Mrs Bloomer to keep and eye on me so that I didn't run off while she was out. Mrs Bloomer shouted up to me 'Peter come on down to my house'. I went to her and she sat me down, straightaway she asked me 'Now what have you been up to my lad.' I could see Mr Bloomer sitting there smoking his pipe, he was winking at me smiling at me. Mrs Bloomer look at my legs and asked what I'd been doing. I explained that I'd fell down the bank over at the tip. Then she went into the kitchen and bought this bottle out.

She tipped something out of the bottle onto my leg, I shouted out loud, it really stung! Mrs Bloomer put the liquid on both of my legs, it was burning me and Mr Bloomer was just laughing at me Mom came back a little while later moaning to Mrs Bloomer that she had pay Mrs Oakley a half crown for my trousers. She thanked Mrs Bloomer for looking after me and as we were going up the stairs Mom was still moaning that she owed Mrs Oakley one shilling. She kept on once we got inside saying that I'd been in some sort of trouble. I told her that I really hadn't, but she just said that if the police came knocking on the door she'd tell them to lock me up.

Come Sunday afternoon I was looking out the window and I could see Tom, Dick, and Harry walking down Garrison Lane with two blokes. When they got to the bottom of the Holme one of the kids came up to our block and into the garden, he shouted my name. I lifted the window up and I was about to say something when my mom lifted the other window up and shouted to the lad 'No Peter can't come out now, piss off go down your own end!' Then the other two lads came over, 'Go on Mrs Round let Peter come out!' they asked. Mom told them no and to piss off again. Then Mr and Mrs Bloomer came out of our block. Mr Bloomer said, 'You heard what Mrs Round said, now *I'm* telling you to piss off!' Then one of the lads shouted that they'd see me tomorrow at school. Mom said that she'd never seen them at my school and asked if they went there, I simply nodded my head.

I tried the trousers Mom bought me, but they were tight and I just about got them on. Mom made a makeshift dinner again and I had to go to bed early. She got me up early the next morning and told me to go get wash. I had to wash in cold water again and Mom came into the kitchen to check if I was doing it properly, then she gave me a dry of piece toast and a cup of hot water with drop milk in. She took me down to Mrs Bloomer to ask her if she would take me to school, I remember her saying that she didn't trust me not to skip school. Mrs Bloomer agreed to take me. We started to walk down Garrison Lane and then we crossed the horse road at the other side of the canal bridge. I jumped up on the canal bridge and looked for the barges, there was one just coming under the bridge. I went to shout down to it, but Mrs Bloomer dragged me of the bridge. As she grabbed me I ripped my new trousers – Mom wouldn't be very happy. I got to school gates and Mrs Bloomer told me that I was to go straight to Granny Pegs' when I finished. She was pointing her finger at me to make sure I understood what she was saying. I went into the playground where some of the girls in my class started shouting 'We can see your bum!' The bell rang and Nancy went up to our teacher. 'Peter Round is showing his bum Miss!' she told her. Our teacher came over to tell me to go see the head cook and ask her to sew my trousers. Off I went to the kitchen, I think the head cook name's was Mrs Duffy and I think she lived in Barwell Road. When she looked at my ripped trousers she started to laugh at me, 'You're showing your nice bum,' I remember she said. I was told to take my trousers off, but I said no at first. Mrs Duffy told me not to be shy. I went to run out of the kitchen, but the headmistress coming through the door. When she saw me she ask me what I was doing in the kitchen. I explained that my teacher, Miss Caroline sent me to ask the cook to sew my trousers up. The headmistress saw the rip and then said in a loud voice that I had to get them off and that Mrs Duffy was to sew them up quickly as she could. After they'd been sewed, the trousers were even tighter than before.

Afterwards I went back to my class. Break time came and we were told to sit down not to go out. All we did sit was there whilst our teacher read to us. Come dinner time and again we were told not to go out. We had to wait for the headmistress to come and speak with us. After a short wait she came in and closed the door behind her. She looked at all of us and then she came into the middle of the room. 'Children I have some very bad news to tell you. Your friend, Terry Williams has died on Sunday morning.' At first the class went all quiet, Nancy and Rose started to cry I can remember putting my arm round Nancy. She took one look at me and then she pushed me away, told me it was my fault Terry had died. I went to get up to run out of the room but the headmistress and our teacher grabbed hold of me. My trousers ripped again the class started to laugh, our teacher told them all to keep quiet. I started to shout that it wasn't my fault, that it was them three kids and that they were outside now. The headmistress and our teacher they took me outside straightaway. I could see Tom, Dick, and Harry over in the park. I pointed to them out and they shouted over to me, 'Come over Peter!' The headmistress grabbed hold of my arm so I wouldn't run off. There were two coppers coming down Garrison

Lane and when they got by Gordon Street, our teacher and the headmistress ran into the middle of the horse road dragging me with them. They both started to shout to the coppers to come over quickly. When Tom, Dick, and Harry saw what was happening, especially the coppers coming down the road, they turned and ran. When the coppers got over to us we all went back into the school. The headmistress started to talk to the coppers, but I couldn't hear what she was saying. I had to sit outside her office with my teacher so I wouldn't run off. A little later the coppers came up to me and told me to go into the office. I went to run again, but one of the coppers said 'Oh no you don't,' and they pushed me into the room. Then they started to ask me questions about Tom, Dick, and Harry. They wanted to know who they were, they said that they knew my name; 'Come on Peter tell us who they are.' The office door opened and Nancy and Rose came in, both of them had their fingers pointed at me. 'He killed Terry and his friends come to the school for him and Johnny every day,' they said in loud voices. One of the coppers asked me where I lived and I told him EastHolme. Then the copper asked the headmistress who the boy was, she replied Terry Williams and that he had died Sunday morning, that he was the boy who went missing three weeks ago. The copper said that Terry's photo was on the board in Coventry Road Police Station where he was based. The copper asked the headmistress who these lads were who kept coming to the school, then Nancy suddenly shouted that they were the ones who took Terry away.

   The copper said to me that I'd have to go with them to Coventry Road Police Station with my Mom, but straightaway I said I wasn't going with them. 'Where's your Mom?' they asked next, but I wouldn't tell them. I said I hadn't done anything wrong and that I didn't know who the lads were. Nancy shouted that I was a bloody liar and that I did know who they were, that they were out there today. Like Mrs Bloomer had done earlier that day, the copper pointed his finger at me and said that I was to come down to the station tonight with my Mom at 6 o'clock. He warned that if I wasn't there he'd come to fetch me. Shortly afterwards the dinner time bell went again and I got up to go out of the office. The copper stopped me for a second, but then he told me I could go. I went to get my make shift dinner and all the kids were all laughing at me because I ripped my trousers even more. Just then the headmistress came into the hall and she shouted to us all to be quiet. Then she told us that when we had eaten our dinner we could all go home. Then she shouted over to me that I had to go to her office again before I went home. When she had gone I left my dinner on the table and quickly ran through the kitchen into the playground and out the gates. I ran all the way up to Granny Pegs and saw that the door was open and that she was she was sitting by the radio. 'What are you doing? You should still be at school.' I told her that the headmistress said that we could all go home after we'd had dinner. I went to turn around and Gran noticed my ripped trousers. 'You haven't been to school! If you had, you wouldn't have ripped trousers,' she said. I explained that of course I'd been to school, I said that the trousers were too tight for me and that when I bent over they'd ripped. I told her that the dinner lady had sewn them up, but that that they'd only ripped again. Gran asked where Mom had got the trousers from and when told her she said that we'd go up to Oakley's straightaway and see what we could get for me.

      Oakley's second hand shop was on the corner of Garrison Lane and Camp Street. When we went into the shop Mrs Oakley, who knew Granny Pegg, asked what she wanted. Gran explained the problem with my trousers and that my Mom had only bought them yesterday. Mrs Oakley said that she remembered seeing her and that my Mom still owed her a shilling. In the end Gran bought me two pairs trousers and a pullover. As Gran was paying Mrs Oakley looked at my shoes and said that I could do with a new pair of those too. Mrs Oakley sorted me out with a new pair and then Gran spotted some shirts. She picked me out two of these too and then asked how much it all came to. Mrs Oakley said it was eight shillings altogether. I remember very well what Gran said as she handed over the money;

'Here's six shillings you robbing b**stard!' As Gran and I turned away from the counter Mrs Oakley turned to go to the back of the shop and she shouted back to us 'Piss off and don't come in my shop again!' Gran and I were walking towards the door when she spotted another pair of trousers; she nicked them as she went past.

When we got out of the shop Gran told me to wait where I was and then she went back into the shop. I heard her shouting to Mrs Oakley and asking if she had a pitch snuff. Through the open door I could see Mrs Oakley appear at the front of the shop and give Gran her pitch snuff, then they just stood there chatting away whilst it started to rain. 'Come on you little B let's get you home,' Gran said as she came out of the shop. As we were walking away Mrs Oakley shouted to Gran that she owed her a half pint. I never said anything to Gran about my shoes because I had already got good pair shoes from the copper.

We got back to Granny Pegg's house I tried the trousers on that she'd nicked, but they were very tight and I couldn't pull them up properly. When I was trying the trousers on Gran pulled something out of her bag; it was a snake belt. I never saw her put the belt into her bag she must have pinched that as well. I had only had string for a belt so I was glad of the new one. Shortly afterwards Gran said that as Mom would be home soon I should get back too. As I was going out the back door she shouted to me, Have you played the wag?' I told her that I honestly hadn't and Gran said it was okay, but that she was coming to my school the next day to see if I was telling her lies.

I ran home and Mom was already there, she'd finished work early. I showed her all the things that Gran had bought me. She shouted at me and asked how much it all came to. I told her I thought Gran had paid six shillings. 'Six shillings?!' Mom had said, she told me that she couldn't afford that much money. Mom said that she'd have to pay Gran a shilling a week and that she'd go round and see her later. Later, while she was gone I had to clean out the fire so it was ready for when she got back.

I know Mom and Gran hardly got on at all. Granny Pegg thought the world of me and now and again Mom and Gran would go down to the Acorn pub together to have a half pint. When Mom got back from Gran's she didn't speak at first, instead she got the fire started. I was looking at her and then asked what Gran had said to her. She replied 'Never you mind what she said.' Mom was about to carry on but there was suddenly a knock on the door. Mom told me to go and answer it and then asked who it was when I opened the door. I shouted to her that it was the bloody coppers. They pushed passed me and went into Mom. When they said that they'd come to talk to me Mom asked what I'd been up to now, then she came over and went to hit me. Before she got the chance one of the coppers told her to hang one and that I wasn't in any trouble yet, that they just wanted to ask me about the three lads who kept coming round the school. Mom shouted 'What three lads?' The copper asked me if I knew why the lads kept asking me to go with them, but I replied that I didn't. I told them that the lads lived down Adderley Road somewhere and the copper asked me if we they took me there whether I could point out where they lived. I said that I'd never been there, but then the copper asked how I knew where they lived if I'd never been. I just stood there said nothing, when the copper asked me again I ran into my bedroom, closed the door behind me and pulled the window down. I went to climb out the window but the copper got hold of me and asked where I thought I was going. 'Piss off leave me alone!' I shouted. He grabbed hold of me took me back into the living room. 'We'll take him up the station where we can ask some more questions' the coppers told my Mom. Just then my big brother Tommy came into the house and said 'What the f**k is going on here?' Mom told him that the coppers were taking me to the station for questioning about three lads. Tommy came over and picked me up by the scruff of my collar, 'You tell those bloody coppers the truth!' he shouted at me. 'I don't know, honest I don't know,' I told him. Tommy paused a moment and then turned to the coppers, 'He's telling you the truth now leave the kid alone' he told them. 'All we want is to know where those three lads live and why they keep coming to the school every day,' the coppers said. Tommy looked at me again and said that he knew when his little brother was lying. Then he picked me up and asked me why the lads kept coming to my school. I told Tommy that I honestly didn't know. He put me down he looked at the coppers, they said, 'Okay,' and then they left. When they had gone Tommy told me 'You'd better be telling the truth. otherwise you'll feel the back of my hand.'

A little later, as Tommy was leaving Mom asked him if he was coming back. Tommy replied 'No.' Mom made me some horrible mash potato on toast, but I had to eat it because I was hungry. Mom told me to go straight to bed when I'd finished. As I was going into my room Mom said, 'I hope you are telling me the truth, god help you if you're not.' I just went to bed.

The next day Mom said that Mrs Bloomer was going to take me to school again so I'd better behave myself. I got ready (Mom shouted that I better wash myself properly) and then had some toast for breakfast. Off to school I went with Mrs Bloomer, when we got to the rail bridge she pulled me round to face her. 'Now listen here you little b******d.' I looked at her started to laugh. She said, 'I'm not laughing, you better go straight to school, I'm going to trust you, I will be down later to see if you are playing the wag and god help you if you. I will take Mr Bloomer's belt to you.' As she was saying that she had a smile on her face. When we got to school I went into the playground and we were all told to go straight into the class. Inside our teacher told us to sit down and be quiet then she called our names out. Then we did nothing all morning, all our teacher did was read aloud to us. A little later then the door opened and in came the headmistress and told us all to go home. Johnny and I went over to the park with Arthur White and Brian Cox. We were playing about when Arthur shouted 'Here comes them kids again!' Johnny and I ran off straightaway and left the other two in the park. Johnny could run faster than me; he left me behind and I had to find somewhere to hide. I got to St Andrews Church and I could see that the church doors was open, so I ran up the steps and went inside.

Nobody was about but as I got down between the pews I heard the church door close. I stood up again and went to see if door was closed shut. I tried to open it but the door was locked; I was locked in. I tried to find another way out but all the doors were locked even at the back of the church. I banged on the door to see if anybody could hear me, but didn't hear anything back. I went looking round the church and came across a side room. I went in and saw two dry pieces of bread on a table. I sat down and ate them because I getting hungry and time was getting on. When I'd finished I went looking around again, but I still couldn't find a way out. I decided to go back into the room and sat on a chair. I must have fallen to sleep because a while later the vicar who woke me up. He asked me what I was doing in the church and how did I get in. I told him three kids were chasing me and that I saw that the church door was open so I ran in to hide. He asked why they were chasing me and I told the vicar that they wanted me to go with them to climb through windows. Then the vicar asked where I lived and I told him the flats in EastHolme. He said that I must have been playing truant, but I promised that I wasn't and that we was told we could go home. The vicar wondered if my Mom knew where I was, I told him that I just wanted to go home. Then another bloke suddenly came into the room and asked what was going on. The vicar explained to him and said it was time for me to go.

I think it was the vicar who took me home, as we were going into WestHolme and passed Granny Pegg's, she saw me through her window. She came out of her block shouting, 'Where have you been? Your mother's been worried about you!' The vicar told her that he'd found me in the church. Gran looked him and said 'Who the bloody are you?' 'I'm the vicar from St Andrews church,' he said, 'he was hiding from three lads who were chasing him.' Gran asked if I'd been to school, I told her yes but that we'd been sent home, but that I didn't know why. Gran asked if I'd been playing truant but when I said I really hadn't she told the vicar that she'd take me home. 'I would like to know if the lad is in any trouble, I want to help him,' said the vicar. Gran looked at the vicar and said 'Not on your Nellie! I'm the one who will help the lad I'm his Gran.' I looked up at her, she was making me laugh. 'Come on you little B let's get you home.'

We walked through the gully into EastHolme and I asked Gran why the vicar wanted to help me. Gran told me 'Never you mind, let's get you home.' Then, I heard a lady shouting to 'You found him then?!' I think it was Mrs Exall, she was standing in the block. I looked up and saw Mom hanging out the window, 'Get up here now!' she shouted down to me. I ran into the block and started to go up the stairs when Mrs Bloomer came out. She asked where I'd been and I told her that I was in church. 'Church? Never in a month of Sundays! Go on get up the stairs, your Mother's waiting.'

The door was open when I got up there, so I went in and then through to the living room. Mom was standing there and she gave me such slap across one side of my face then again on the other side. It was dark and I was hungry so I asked Mom for something to eat. 'No there's nothing in the house, go to bed,' Mom replied. Although I was really hungry, I went to bed. I was going to wait until Mom went to bed and then sneak into the kitchen for some food, but I must have fallen asleep. I woke up feeling very hungry. I listened by my Mom's bedroom door to see if she was awake. When I didn't hear anything inside I went into the kitchen to see if there was any food there. I look into the pantry, but it was empty. I quietly got dressed and then went to knock on Mrs Fleetwood's door, but she didn't answer. Next I went down to Mrs Bloomers' and when I knocked Mr Bloomer answered. When he opened the door and saw me standing there he asked me 'Peter, what do you want?' I told him that I was hungry and that there was no food at home. Mr Bloomer told me to go back to bed and that he'd look after me in the morning. When he shut the door I didn't go back to bed, instead I went round to

Granny Pegs. As I got near I could see there was a light on and when I knocked on her door Granny Pegg shouted 'Who's there?' I shouted back that it was me and that Mom had sent me to bed without food and that I was really hungry. Gran opened the door and as she let me in, Mr Peg (Gran's son) came out of his bedroom. 'What the bloody hell going on here, what's all the noise about?' Gran explained what was going on and that I wasn't in any trouble. I said that I was just really hungry, but then Mr Pegg said I should be eating my dinner at school. I replied that they had sent us home from school the last two days. Mr Pegg told Gran that she should go down the school and see what was going on.

Granny Pegg gave me two slices of dry toast and some hot milk, with no water in it. I drank the milk up quickly and then Gran told me to get myself back home. She said that she'd have a word with Mom to find out what was going on. Then she asked me that if I wasn't having my school dinners, what was I eating? I told her nothing much but that last week they had sent us home after our dinner. When I left Gran stood on the doorstep and watched me go. Whilst I walked I ate what was left of the dry toast. When I got to our block I took my shoes off, the stairs was very cold. When I got to our door I saw that it was closed, I was sure I'd left it open. I sat on the stairs in front of Mrs Fleetwood's door wondering whether I should knock and wake Mom up. After a while I got up again and went to knock our door, but I found that it was open and on the latch. I crept inside and went straight to my bedroom, Mom was standing there waiting for me. She slapped my face and she started to cry. 'I don't know what's been going on with you, I will have you put away! Go on get to bed, I'll sort you out in the morning.'

The next morning Mom never asked me where I'd been the night before. She came into my room, she stood there but she never spoke, she just looked at me. 'Mom,' I asked, 'are you going to have me put away? If you are I'll run away now and you'll never see me again.' My Mom came over to me and she slapped my face, 'Never talk like that again' she said. Then she asked where I'd been and I told her that because I was hungry I'd gone over to Granny Pegg's. Mom told me never to tell Granny Pegg anything, that she didn't want her knowing what was going on. 'But Mom,' I said 'she can help.' 'I don't want her help, I'll never hear the last of it,' Mum replied. 'Go and get ready for school, do you hear me you go straight school.'

  Once we got into school our teacher called our names to see if we were all there; then she said we could go home. We all got up and ran across to the park to play. Tom, Dick, and Harry came along when they say us there. The lads said they were going and asked us if we wanted to go with them. We all said no, but then Tom came over to Johnny and I. 'You want to come with us don't you?' he said. I looked at Johnny and we both shook our heads and said no again. Harry said to me, 'You want to come with us don't you Peter?' Johnny started to walk away and I went followed him, but Harry pulled me back and pointed his finger at me. 'You're coming with us tomorrow, we will be waiting for you when you come out of school.' I saw Mr Williams cutting through the park and then I saw Nancy running towards him. Tom, Dick, and Harry saw this too and they ran away as fast as they could. When Nancy got to Mr Williams she pointed her finger in the direction of the three lads. 'That's them three lads Mr Williams,' she told him. He started to run after Tom, Dick, and Harry but he must have tripped, he fell cut and his chin. By the time Mr Williams got up the three lads had gone had gone. He came over to me and asked who the lads were, but I told him that I really didn't know. Nancy shouted that I was a bloody liar, that I did know them. 'Come on Peter tell me who they are you,' Mr Williams said 'you won't get in any trouble.' I said again that I was being honest and Johnny said that I was telling the truth. Then Nancy told Mr Williams that Tom, Dick, and Harry were coming back for me the next day. I nodded my head that this was right and Mr Williams told us all to get home. As we left I could see that his chin was still bleeding.

  Johnny and I started to walk up Garrison Lane when we looked back and saw Mr Williams going into the school. We both went straight to Granny Pegg's and when we walked through the back door, she was sitting by the radio. The first thing she said 'Are you two playing the wag?' We both said no and that the school had sent us home again. 'What about your dinner?' she asked, when we shook our heads Gran said she'd find us something to eat. As she got up Gran asked what Mom had said about the night before. I told her that I got a slap in the face and that Mom said she'd have me put away. Gran sighed and said, 'We will see about that, wait till she comes here and I will have it out with her.'

Gran made Johnny and I some toast and although she burnt the bread on the gas burner, but we had to eat it she stood there watching us. We also had some mash potato, which was lumpy. Granny Pegg was starting to get angry; 'Going to have you put away is she? I'll come to your school in the morning to see what's going on with your mother, you are not going to be put away, I'll see about that.' Johnny and I played outside close to Gran's house so she could keep eye on us. We were walking up to the air raid shelter when Johnny said 'If I get into any more trouble my mom is going to have me put away as well.' As we got near to the shelter this kid came running out, he looked at us and told us to piss off quick. Then two blokes came running out after the kid, I recognised one of the blokes, he was the one with Tom, Dick, and Harry. We ran to hide in the big garden, but one bloke stood there waiting for the other one to come back. When they met up they both went into the shelter and came out pushing a pram with some bags on it, they looked very heavy. As they walked and pushed they covered the bags up, the whole time they were looking around. When they'd gone Johnny and I went into the shelter to see what was going on. We had good look around but it was very dark, though we could smell something. Johnny must have touched something in the dark because he was so scared he ran off and left me there. In the dark on my own I started to get scared too, so I also ran off. I saw Johnny running in the direction of his house so I ran to straight back mine. When I got there I saw that the key wasn't behind the door, so I ran out the block and round the back to climb up the drain pipe. Mrs Price shouted up to me 'What's going on Peter? I saw you running down the Holme, who are you running away from?' I told her that Mom had locked me out and that nothing else was going on. I eventually got on the veranda but both the toilet and the kitchen window were locked. I'd have to wait there until Mom got home. I was sitting on the veranda getting cold when Mrs Price came out again and looked up to me. She asked me if I was okay, when I said I was cold and hungry she told me to come down and that she'd find me something to eat. I had to climb up on to the ringer and I nearly fell but thankfully I managed to grab hold of the drainpipe, but I couldn't move for a while. I got down in the end and went into Mrs Price house. She gave me something to eat, it looked like piece of cake and although it was nice it was only a small piece. 'That was nice Mrs Price, thank you, but can I have bit more?' I asked. 'No you bloody can't,' Mrs Price was standing by the window looking out for my mom. 'Here comes your mother, I will be keeping my eye on you.' Then I turned around and said, 'You've only got one eye Mrs Price.' 'Go on don't be cheeky you bugger,' she replied.

    I got home and Mom looked at me and asked where I'd been. When I told her Mrs Price's house Mom said, 'She let you in her house? You must be in her good books, what did you do for her?' I told her nothing, just that Mrs Price had seen me locked out on the veranda and that she'd given me something to eat because I was so hungry. 'You are always bloody hungry, go get the fire started.' Later that evening I watched Mom put the money in the gas and electric meters and then she took the money back out of the boxes about three times, she twisted the handle then she took the money back of the box. After I'd got the fire started I told Mom that I was hungry. She told me to run over to Able's to see if there had any bread left, 'it's the only thing not on ration' she said. I ran over the shop but the front door was closed, so I went round to the back and knocked on the door. Mrs Able shouted 'Who is it, what do you want?' I shouted back that Mom had sent me over to see if there any bread left. She came out with half loaf and said that I had to tell my Mom that she owed sixpence. As I went home again I nearly dropped the bread because I wasn't looking where I was going. I ran up the stairs and as I went in I left the front door behind me. Mom did her nut, 'Don't you know how to shut the bloody door!' she shouted. I said I was sorry and told her that Mrs Able said she owed a shilling and should I run back over with it. 'No you Nellie,' she replied.

    I seemed to live on toast. Mom had a tin of meat and although I didn't know where she got it from and it was dry, it was good on toast. Looking through the window I saw the two blokes from earlier walking up EastHolme. They looked up and saw me watching them, one of them pointed up to me. The one I recognised from hanging around with Tom, Dick, and Harry waved up to me to come down. I shook my head to say no. Then Mom came to the window and asked what was going on. I told her nothing just that there were two blokes walking up the Holme. I watched as the the two blokes carried on walking and then went through the archway round to the big garden. I had lost sight of them so I came away from the window. 'Who are those two blokes ? Mom asked, 'you better keep away from them do you hear me?'

    The caretaker came round to put the gas lights on in the Holme, there were two gas lamps on between block 6 and 7 and the other one at the top of the Holme outside block 4. Mom told me to draw the curtains and then get to bed. The room was so cold like always, so I jumped into bed and put the heavy coats over myself to keep warm. I woke up in a daze when I heard voices then my bedroom door shut quietly. I think it was my brother Tommy speaking very quietly to my Mom. I went to the door to try to hear what they were talking about and I heard my name mentioned. Shortly afterwards I got back into bed. In the morning Mom came into the room, she told me to wake up and to go get washed. I went to the kitchen, the water was freezing so I had a quick wash. Mom came in and she looked at me, 'You haven't washed behind your ears and your neck, go and wash yourself properly,' she told me. She got me some toast ready and cup of hot water with a drop of milk in. 'I'm off to work now, you better go straight to school my lad, god help you if you don't go to school,' she said. 'Tommy may come to pick you up from school at 4 o'clock.' I asked her why and Mom replied that he was going to give me a bag to bring home; 'Never mind what's in the bag, just make sure you bring it home,' she said.

I was coming down the stairs when Mrs Bloomer came out of her house, 'Where are you going you little B?' 'Off to school Mrs Bloomer,' I replied. She told me that she'd be watching me to make sure that I was going there. Going out the block I got hold of the block door and I slammed it very hard, then I ran all way to school. I was told to go straight to the classroom where our teacher told us to sit down and be quiet. After a while the headmistress came in and gave us all a letter to give to our parents. Then Nancy stood up and said, 'My mother said we got to have our dinner before we go home.' The headmistress replied that there would be no dinners till the next week, that we should all go straight home and give the letters to our parents. Johnny and I rushed out of the classroom and nearly knocked over the headmistress, she shouted at us to come back but we just kept on running to the park. When we got there Tom, Dick, and Harry were waiting for us. We went with them and as we were going down to Watery Lane, my brother Tommy was on the other side of the road by Lawley Street. He saw me and he shout to me to come over. One of the lads said, 'He's a bloody copper!' and they all ran off. I started to laugh and then Johnny and I went over to Tommy. He asked if they were the lads who kept coming to the school wanting us to go with them. Before I could tell Tommy 'No' Johnny said 'Yes, they are.' Tommy said 'I think I know who they are.' Tommy gave me the bag that Mom had mentioned, then he told me to take it home before we ran back to school. I asked 'What's in the bag Tommy?' but like Mom he replied 'Never you mind.' It was a bit heavy and I couldn't see inside the bag because it was covered. 'Go on hurry up or you'lll be late,' Tommy said to us. As we started to walk away the bag was getting heavy, so Johnny and I took one handle each. We went into my block and Mrs Bloomer and Mrs Price came out their houses and started talking to us. The first thing Mrs Bloomer said to Johnny and I was 'Where have you two been? What have you been nicking, let's have look in that bag?' I told her I couldn't show her as my brother Tommy had given it to me. 'Is that right?' she asked. Both Mrs Bloomer and Mrs Price followed Johnny and I up the stairs. Then Mrs Fleetwood came out to see what was going on. When we reached my door I put my hand through the letterbox to grab the piece of string that our key was attached to. Mrs Bloomer was still trying to look in the bag. I went inside and they all follow Johnny and I into the kitchen. They stood by the kitchen door and I asked Johnny to help me to put the bag into the pantry. The we sat on the kitchen floor with our backs to the pantry door. Mrs Bloomer said, 'Come on you two, you've got to go back to school.' Johnny said that we didn't have to because the teacher had sent us home. 'I don't believe you, come on you two tell us what's going on.' Johnny that we couldn't because we didn't know anything and that Tommy really had given us the bag. They all went out and Johnny closed the kitchen door behind them. He went to the window and said, 'Peter look who's in the Holme.' It was Tom, Dick, and Harry. Johnny lifted the window up and shouted to them, they shouted back 'Can we come up?' I went to the other window, lifted it up and shouted back that my mom would be home soon. As I was saying that Tommy was coming up the Holme. I didn't see him at first, but when Tom, Dick, and Harry saw Tommy they all ran up the Holme. Tommy went to chase them, but they were too fast. Then he came into the block and Mrs Price came out and said, 'Tommy, your Peter has been nicking with his mate, I think his name is Johnny, he came home with a heavy bag.' 'If he has been nicking I will take him to the cop shop myself, it's none of your business. I'll take care of him.'

Tommy came into the house and asked where the bag was, I told him Johnny and I had put it in the pantry. Tommy went into the kitchen and got the bag out of the pantry. I stood there looking to see what was in it. Tommy took everything out the bag; 'Where did you get all that food from Tommy?' 'You keep your mouth shut, that goes for you too Johnny, you don't tell your mom and dad.' He was pointing his finger at Johnny. 'I won't Tommy,' Johnny said. 'You better not or all of us will be put away,' Tommy said. Just then Mrs Bloomer came in and asked what I'd been up to now and whether I'd been playing the wag again. Tommy said I hadn't and that I'd been sent home from school again. He said he'd been into the school to find out what's been happening but that they wouldn't tell him what was going on. 'I'm going to tell his Mom to pull him out that school, he not learning anything Mrs Bloomer.' She said that I knew how to play up and give answers back. 'I'm going now Peter I will see you on Saturday, you better behave yourself,' Tommy said. Mrs Bloomer told Tommy that she'd look after me until Mom got home. Tommy told her to keep an eye on me, that some kids were hanging around and that he didn't trust them, that they ran off when they saw him. The Tommy told Johnny he should go home and not to forget what he'd said. 'What was that?' Mrs Bloomer said. 'I told him to behave himself, isn't that right Johnny?' Tommy said. Johnny told him yes. We all went down to Mrs Bloomer's house and Johnny went home. Tommy came inside and told me again that he'd see me on Saturday. He gave me the key to our front and then left. Shortly afterwards Mrs Bloomer went out of the room and I sneaked out the back door and ran towards what we called the 'secret wall.' I climbed halfway down from the railings, jumped and fell and scratched my knee and hurt my ankle. I couldn't walk for bit so I had to sit on the cold floor. I heard Mrs Bloomer shouting to someone up on her veranda, 'Have you seen that bloody Peter Round?' The person replied that they thought they'd seen me running towards WestHolme. I stayed where I was and after a while this bloke came through archway from

NorthHolme, when he saw me he asked what I was doing sitting on the cold floor. I said that some kids was chasing me and that I'd hurt my ankle. The bloke pulled me up, but I couldn't put my foot to the ground so he lifted me up and asked me where I lived. I told him I wanted to go to my Granny Pegg's and I gave him directions to get there. When we got there he took us round the back and he knocked on the door. I heard Granny Pegg moaning and asking who it was. She opened the door and looked at me in the bloke's arms. 'What the hell is going on here, what have you been up to now, what's that bloke carrying you for?' The bloke told Gran that as far as he knew some kids had been chasing me and that I'd hurt my ankle and couldn't put any weight on my foot. 'It's all excuses with this lad, always kids chasing him I bet he been playing the wag from school again. Was another lad with him?' Gran asked the bloke. 'No he was on his own,' the bloke replied still holding me. Gran stood back from the door and told the bloke to put me on the chair by the window. As she was closing the door Gran asked 'Why are those bloody coppers going into the air raid shelter?' The next thing the bloke ran straight out the door. Gran said he'd obviously been up to no good. She went to close the door and when she came back in she banged her fist on the table. 'I know where I've seen that bloody bloke,' she said. I asked her where but she told me 'Never you mind you just keep away from him and his family do you hear me?'

Gran bathed my knee with something that really stung and then she took a good look at my ankle and said that it was still quite swollen. She ripped some rags up and put them in cold water, then she used them to wrap up my ankle. Gran told me that the cold rags would do my ankle good. Then she saw my socks and noticed that they holes in them look at the back of the heels. 'Your shoes must be rubbing your skin off, have they been hurting you?' I replied that they had. Then she got some stuff to rub into my heels and told me to get my mom to buy me some socks down the rag market. 'You look like a lost kid,' Gran said then, 'you want a good wash, take your other shoe off. God blind me you got holes in your toes as well, no wonder your feet are always hurting you. What am I going to do with you?'

Once she'd sorted me out Gran told me to get home and to remember to tell Mom about my socks. I went limping home and when I arrived Mrs Bloomer came out of the block. 'Okay you little B, where have you been your mother has been looking for you. Have you got your key because she's been locked out.' I told Mrs Bloomer that I'd been round at Granny Pegg's. She took a look at my ankle and said that it looked very swollen. 'What have you done, can you put your foot on the floor?' I told her I'd fell off the secret wall hiding from some kids, she said I was liar and told me to get up the stairs. I had to hold on to the rail and hop up the stairs one at a time. All the while Mrs Bloomer stood at the bottom of the stairs watching me, she shouted 'Go on then get upstairs you little B, I will be up there in minute.'

As I got to our door Mom came into the block. Mrs Bloomer's door was open and I heard Mom shout to her and ask if I'd come home yet. Mrs Bloomer told her that I was already in the house. When Mom came through the door she asked what I'd been up to and if I'd been in school. I was sitting by the window, 'Yes Mum, but they sent us home again. Look Mom there's lot of bloody coppers running up the Holme.' Mom told me to come away from the window and then she had a look herself. She saw Mrs Price running down the Holme, so Mom lifted the window up and shouted down to her, 'What's going on?' Mrs Price replied that they had found a body in the air raid shelter. Straightaway Mom looked over at me, 'Do you know about the dead body, I been told you were hanging around there.' 'No Mom,' I promised, 'you told me not to go anywhere near the shelter and I haven't that's the truth mom.' Then I asked her 'What did Tommy bring us? Mrs Bloomer wanted to know, but I didn't say anything.' Mom told me to tell no one where the food in the bag came from. I said that Johnny knew as he helped me to carry the bag up from the school, but that Tommy told him not to say anything. 'He better not,' Mom said 'we'll all go to jail with what your brother Tommy got.' 'Why Mom has he nicked the food?' I asked. 'He never nicked it, so you mind keep your mouth shut!' Mom told me.

    Before we had tea I asked Mom why I hadn't had my school dinner, that I thought she paid for it though Granny Pegg said I should get them for free. Then I told her that Granny Pegg said she should take me to the rag market because I had holes in my socks. I showed them to her but she said she'd fix them as she didn't have money to get me new ones. Afterwards Mom did our tea, the mash potato was lumpy but the tinned meat wasn't too bad (if my memory serves me right the meat was spam), the powdered milk was made with hot water and I could taste the powder. After my dinner Mom said that I had to get myself to bed. I hopped into my room and as I went she told me I couldn't go into school the next day because of my ankle. 'You never told me it was bad,' Mom said, 'you are going to school tomorrow even if I've got to push you in Mrs Price's pram.' I tried to show her how swollen it was, but she said I was going to school the next day and that was that. It was really cold in my bedroom so I covered my feet up in one of the overcoats and made sure the other three was well over me. I went to bed with my clothes on like I did very night.

    The next morning mom shouted at me to me to get up, but I really didn't want to. Mom came into the bedroom and stood looking at me till I got out of bed. She told me to get up and wash, but I said that my ankle was still really   hurting me. She looked at me and then said. 'Okay I will ask Mrs Bloomer to keep eye on you before you get to school.' She still never asked me how I'd come to hurt my ankle. 'I'm off now, you better behave yourself,' she said, 'you better get to school and don't you try to pull the wool over my eyes.' I didn't know what she meant but 'pull the wool over her eyes'.I couldn't put my foot to the ground and so I was still limping a bit. I never went to school, instead I went to the pantry and got out the powdered milk and made myself a drink; only with milk this time. I put the powdered milk into the kettle and I kept stirring till all the lumps had gone, I must have put in four big spoons in. I started to drink the milk and it tasted really good. Somebody was banging on the door so I went to answer it and this big bloke pushed his way. He knocked my cup of milk out of my hand and it smashed on to the floor, milk went all over the place. I told him to get out of my house and piss off, but he told me that I couldn't tell him what to do and that he was there to turn our gas off. I ran out of open front door and went to Mrs Fleetwood's. 'What's up Peter?' she asked when I knocked her door. I told her about the bloke that had pushed into my house, so she came up with me to speak with him. 'What are you doing?' she asked him. 'Are you Mrs Round? No?' The bloke looked at me and said, 'Your mother in some trouble my lad.' I ran to the door and I wouldn't let him out, but he pushed passed me and I fell to the floor. I can remember what the bloke looked like, he had a black moustache and a scar on his right hand, he had a big nose, and his uniform was dark navy blue with flat cap that had a badge with 'Gas' written on it. He left his big overcoat in the house and I went to nick it, but he came back and took it from me. It could have been another coat for my bed. Just as the gas bloke left, another one came through the door. 'Who are you?' Mrs Fleetwood asked. He said he was here to cut off the electricity. He had the same uniform as the gas man. Mrs Fleetwood asked what was going on, he explained that over the last few weeks he had tried to empty the meters. He said that he let himself in with the key behind the door, but that both meters were always empty. He'd left my Mom a note telling her to get in touch with the office but hadn't had her reply. 'We got in touch with the gas, I see they cut that off,' he said. Mrs Fleetwood asked 'How much does Mrs Round owe?' The bloke said it could be five pounds or more but that he wasn't sure about the gas. 'When she pays we will put the electric back on, but there will be a connection charge as well, she'll have to pay in full before she connected,' he explained.

    After he left Mrs Fleetwood told me not to worry and that my Mom would be fine. 'She'll find a way to get the gas and electric back on. You better clean this mess up before your she gets home though.' My ankle still hurt and I couldn't really walk on it, but I thought I'd better go look for Mom. I was limping up to Maxstoke Street when I bumped into Tom, Dick, and Harry. They asked me where I was going and I said I was going to look for my Mom. 'Come with us, we are we're going to get some bread down Montague Street. Come on we will get you some bread,' they told me. Off I went with them and as we was walking down Garrison Lane one of them put his arm around my shoulder, 'We will look after you,' he whispered. We got to Montague Street and walked up to the entrance of the bakery, I remember it was like a yard with a small shed that was the bakery itself. The bakery was called 'Wilson's Bakery', they was the first to bring out 'mother's pride' and (I think) sliced bread. We all went in there and saw the bread was on racking inside. We went to help ourselves and suddenly the three lads ran off and left me standing there. The this bloke came out of nowhere and he grabbed hold of me. He'd seen the other three lads running down the lane and he shouted to another bloke to come out. 'Watch this kid and I'll try to catch them other three lads,' he told him. The bloke looked at me, 'You're Dolly Round's son, I've seen you going into the Pegg's house. I live in WestHolme facing the Pegg's. I'll will see if I can help you lad, the other bloke is the gaffer.' The other bloke came back without Tom, Dick, and Harry and he looked at me, 'I'm going to call the police,' he said. The bloke that had stayed with me said, 'I know who this kid, his name is Peter Round, I think his Mom works round at the Doctors.' The gaffer thought about it and then said he'd let me off, but if he saw me round there again he'd tell the police. Then he asked me if I knew who the kids were. I replied that I didn't know them but that they lived down Saltley and that I could show him where they lived.

'You can go, but I'll be talking to your mother now I know where you live,' the gaffer said. I went to walk away, but then the bloke said that I hadn't said thank you. I thanked him and then asked if I could keep the bread. He told me I couldn't and as I walked of out the door I thanked him again, this time for not calling the police. As I began walking out the yard the gaffer called me back again and said 'Here you can have the bread, but don't let me catch you round here again.'

Off I went limping with the two loaves and the bloke from the bakery who recognised caught up with me. He told me that I owed him a favour and that he wouldn't let me forget it. I just carried on walking and eventually he wandered off. I went pass the school and the headmistress came out. 'You haven't been to school have you?' she asked me. 'Yes miss, I mean no miss. . .' I replied. Make up your mind, is it yes or no?' I told her no and that I had a bad ankle. She said that I seemed to be walking alright and that I'd better be in school on Monday. Then she asked where I'd got the bread and when I said that they were from the bakery she asked if I was telling the truth. 'Yes miss, the bloke gave me two loaves, he lives in the flats near me,' I said. I started to walk away but the headmistress called me back and told me to follow her to her office. When we got there she started to tell me off and asked why I was missing school. I tried to explain to her that I'd done nothing wrong, that she has sent us home from school every day and I had no dinners even though my Mom had paid for them. 'Don't answer me back,' she shouted, 'I'm going to report you for your behaviour, bring your mother to my office on Monday morning.' When I was allowed to leave I came out of the office and I look around, the school was empty.

A little later I was walking up Garrison Lane when my ankle started to hurt again, I couldn't put my foot on the floor and I began to limp. Just then the rag and bone man came along and asked me what was up. I told him about my ankle and then he asked where I'd got the bread from. When I told him it was from the bakery around the corner he asked where I lived. 'Just in the flats,' I said. 'Get on the barrow and I'll push you up there.' I sat over the wheel and held onto the bread. He kept asking me about the bread and when we got to the shops I jumped off, he grabbed hold of me. A tram came up and stopped nearby, the rag and bone man was still holding me. I saw my Mom get off the tram and she shouted over at the man to let go of me. 'Why are you holding my son?' she asked when she go over to us. 'He's nicked bread off me,' the man told her. I said that this wasn't true, that I could take her to where I got the bread from. Mom must have believed me because she told the man to piss off. As he let go of me we saw that there were two coppers coming down the lane and the rag and bone man ran up to them. He told the coppers that I'd nicked bread off him, so they came over to my Mom and me. The coppers asked where I'd got the bread from and I told them about the bakery and said that I could take them there.

They agreed that I could show me so we all set off, I rode in the back of the rag and bone man's barrow. We got to Lawley Street the man tipped his cart up in the air. I went tumbling out of the barrow into the middle of the horse road. The man quickly ran off. I couldn't move my ankle, it was really hurting, so one of the coppers picked me up and put me back onto the cart. Both of the coppers started to push me back up Garrison Lane towards home. Mom said to the coppers 'Peter said the bakery was on Montague Street, it's that way.' The copper looked at Mom and simply said 'The kid's telling the truth.' The coppers took it in turns pushing me up Garrison Lane and when we got to our block one of the coppers carried me all the way up the stairs. The other copper asked Mom where he should put the rag and bone man's cart. She told him to put it in the garden round the side and that it would be okay in there.

Once we were in the house and the coppers had gone Mom told me to start telling her the truth, When I promised her that I was already telling the truth she said, 'I hope you are telling me the truth otherwise them coppers will find out and they'll put you away.' I paused for a moment and then told her about the two men that had come round earlier and that that they'd cut off the gas and electricity. She went over to the cupboard with the meters in and said, 'They've bloody cut us off?! We don't have much coal, it won't last the night.' Shortly afterwards she started to light the fire, it quickly got dark that night as we had no candles. A little later Tommy arrived and asked what was going on, why we was sitting in the dark. Mom simply said that she didn't have any money. So Tommy offered to use the change he had to go get us some coal. When he came back with some coal he said, 'Come on nip help me with this.' I told him I couldn't because my ankle hurt.

It looked like there was just enough coal to last for one day. After Tommy had left Mom told me to go straight to bed. The bedroom was really cold so I waited till Mom went to bed and I came back out and slept on the floor by the fire. I could feel a draft coming from the kitchen and living room doors, but I got two coats put one under each door and then I lay down. I could still feel a draft coming from my bedroom so I got up again and put another coat by that door. Once I lay back down and got settled it started to get really warm, although the fire kept going out throughout the night. When Mom got up she came out of her room and she saw me lying there on the floor. She did her nut, but I tried to tell her I did it because I was cold. It was Saturday morning and so Mom told me to go over to Able's and see if they had any candles, 'Ask her to put it on my slate till next week,' she told me. Before I left I asked if I could have something to eat as I was hungry. She cut me a slice of dry crust from the bread that I'd brought home the day before. Once I'd finished she told to 'Now go over to Able's and get me them candles.' Off I went hopping on one leg, my ankle was still hurting. When I got to the bottom of the stairs (hopping down one at a time) I saw that Tommy was with the coalman. I heard him ask how much the coal was and I think the coalman said three shilling and sixpence. Tommy gave him 10 shillings for four bags and then the coalman said something in reply. I couldn't quite catch what he said but then an argument broke out. I was standing at the bottom of the Holme when Tommy called me back and told me to make sure the man took four bags of coal up to our house. I had to go back up the stairs and stand by the door. When Mom saw I was back she asked me why I hadn't gone over to Able's, so I explained about Tommy and the coal. I don't know how the coalman put four bags in the cupboard, but I managed to put the coal boards up, then I went over to Able's to get the candles.

Mrs Able had moaned for a bit but she put the candles on the slate as Mom had asked. As I was going out the shop door she said, 'Tell your mother that she owes me one shilling and sixpence.' I replied that you could get candles for a penny a go. 'Go on you cheeky devil,' she said, 'wait till I see your Mother, you are too big for your boots.' I left Able's and as I was crossing the horse road I saw a bunch of coppers going into top Holme (SouthHolme). I told Mom about the coppers when I got home. 'I'll pop down to Mrs Price to see what's up,' she said. I can remember before she went Mom was saying 'I'm going to make you a lovely meat and potato pie for tonight's dinner.' I told her she could make it now because I was hungry! She said that she was fed up with me being hungry all the time and asked if they didn't feed me dinners at school. 'Mom I haven't had school dinners for a long time, they've been sending us home every day.' She said she was going to find out if I was telling the truth on Monday.

Mom went down to Mrs Price to find out what she knew about the coppers, but Mrs Bloomer was already standing outside. Then Mrs Fleetwood also followed Mom down so I saw on the stairs trying to listen. Just as I sat down I heard two coppers come into the block. 'What do you two want? Mrs Bloomer asked them. 'If you're looking for anybody he's not here, only women live in this block,' Mom told them, 'if you want to search you can search me first.' I heard one of the coppers say 'How do you know we are looking for anybody?' I moved to the top off the stairs on the landing and heard Mom ask 'What the hell do you want then?' 'We want to ask few questions,' a copper said, 'don't try to be funny or I'll take you all down to the station.' The copper started to ask some questions and suddenly the vicar came into the block and asked one of the coppers if they were there because the coalman got robbed. 'He was robbed in Maxstoke Street,' the vicar explained. 'We know nothing about that,' Mom said to the copper, but replied that they weren't there for that. 'We are here to see if anyone had noticed anyone who don't live in the flats hanging around. Do you know anything about the body found in the air raid shelter?' Then one of the coppers asked 'Which one of you is Mrs Round? Got son called Peter?' When Mom said that she was Mrs Round the coppers told her that they'd like to speak with me and that I'd been seen hanging round the shelter. Straightaway Mom shouted up to me to come down, but one of the coppers said they'd go up and talk to me in the house.

The two coppers followed Mom up to the house, I was sitting on the floor by the fire when they all came in. Mrs Bloomer had also followed the coppers up, but one of them told her she'd have to wait outside and then he closed the door on her. I was still sitting on the floor when one of the coppers said 'Hello Peter, I want to ask you a few questions. When did you last play by the shelter? 'My mom told me not to play there, she said it's too dangerous,' I replied. 'Now Peter we will start again, when did you last play there? We know you were there,' the copper said. I looked over at my Mom and she told me that I'd better tell the bloody truth. 'Okay yes I did go in the shelter but it was really dark in there so I ran out,' I told them. 'Did you see anybody before you went in?' Again I looked over at Mom and she told me to answer their question. 'Yes two men came out pushing a pram. I ran to the big garden to hide, but I think they saw me.' Then the coppers if I saw which way the men had gone and if I had anyone with me. 'I don't know which way they went and nobody was with me,' I replied. 'Come on Peter, it was your mate Johnny wasn't it?' one of the coppers said, 'when you and Johnny went in to the shelter what did you see? 'Nothing,' I replied, 'it was really dark, I think Johnny touched something then he ran out and I followed him. He went home straightaway and so did I.' The copper looked at my ankle and asked what I'd been doing to myself. Then Mom piped up and said that I kept saying that three kids were chasing me. The coppers asked if I knew who they were and if they went to my school. I told them that I didn't know the kids, but thought that they lived in Saltey. 'You must know why they keep chasing you?' the coppers asked. Mom spoke again, 'It those three kids who Terry Williams went off, wasn't it Peter?' 'Yes, Mom,' I replied. One of the coppers told me that he thought I knew more than I was letting on, but I said nothing. 'We'll will leave it for now Mrs Round, but we'll be in touch. You may have to bring Peter to the station, I'll see what the inspector says I'm not satisfied with what Peter is telling me.'

When the coppers had gone I was still sitting by the fire and Mom said, 'I hope you are telling the coppers the truth.' Shortly after the vicar knocked on the door, Mom answered it and asked him what he wanted. 'I'm here to see if I can help Peter in anyway,' he told her. Mrs Bloomer followed the vicar in and asked Mom if everything was okay. 'No,' Mom said, 'I think Peter is in some kind of trouble, though he keeps saying he is telling the truth.' The vicar told Mom, 'Mrs Round if Peter comes to the community centre on Tuesday evening, I will talk to him. He may open up to me if police can't get anything out of him.' Mom looked at the vicar, 'I can't see how you can help. He is going to be the death of me!' Then she started to cry. Mrs Round turned to the vicar and told him, 'You better go, leave Mrs Round to me. Come on Dorothy stop this nonsense let Tommy deal with Peter, he'll probably listen to him, won't you little B?'

By then my ankle had started to hurt again, but Mom told me to go and get some coal for the fire. I got up and Mom finally saw me limping in pain. When she asked how I'd hurt it I told her that I jumped off the secret wall. 'He was running away from me,' Mrs Bloomer said, 'serves you right you little B, that will teach you a lesson. You got to start to behaving yourself, look what you are doing to your poor mother. They will put you away if don't tell the truth my lad.' I said nothing, instead I went to fetch the coal. 'Come on Peter what have you got to say for yourself?' Mrs Bloomer asked. I looked at her as I was putting the coal into the fire and I just laughed. Mom went to hit me, but Mrs Bloomer told her that it wasn't going to help. 'Wait till Tommy comes or if the police come back. Just look at him he couldn't care less,' Mrs Bloomer said. I was still laughing a little as I turned to Mom, 'I'm telling you the truth,' I said to her again.

There was another knock on the door, it was the police again and they were looking for Tommy. Mom fell onto the chair, but the chair turned over and she fell to the floor. I just stood there at first, then I went to help her but the coppers pushed me out of the way. When they'd lifted her up into the chair mom asked, 'What's my son done?' 'Nothing Mrs Round,' the coppers told her, 'it's the coalman who wants to say thank you for getting him to the hospital, it could have been lot worse if it hadn't been for your son. We want to ask him few questions.' Mom replied, 'Tommy could be anywhere, he moves about lot.' They asked where he lived and where he worked, then they told Mom to ask Tommy to go down to Digbeth Police Station. He needed to ask for Sergeant James. As the coppers were leaving I heard them ask Mrs Bloomer if she knew where Tommy was and what he looked like. 'Here's here one minute, gone the next,' she told them, 'he is dashing young man, very good looking. I wouldn't mind giving my old man up for him!'

The night was drawing in and it started to get very cold mom told me to draw the curtains. She made me a cup of powdered milk and this time it wasn't too bad this time, but I could still taste the power. Mom also made me a sandwich with thick bread, she cut the bread like door step and I couldn't eat it'd all. We had enough coal to last us all week, but I got another bucket before I went to bed. My room was freezing again, so I waited until mom went to bed and then I crept out, shutting my bedroom door quietly behind me. I put two old mat's down, one by the living room door and the other one by the kitchen door, then I put an overcoat by my bedroom door to stop the drafts. I put some big lumps of coal on the fire so it would burn slowly throughout the night. I got down on the floor, covered myself with two overcoats and went straight to sleep.

The next thing I knew my brother Tommy was waking me up. For a minute I didn't know where I was, I went to say something but he put his hand over my mouth. 'Shut up and come with me,' he whispered. I went downstairs with him and saw that he had a pram with two big bags of coal and bag full of food in them. He was talking to me quietly, 'You got too help me with this lot,' he told me. My ankle was still hurting, but I managed to help Tommy with the bag of food, then came the bags of coal. 'I can't help you up with the coal, it's my ankle,' I said. He replied, 'Okay nip.' Tommy lifted the coal out of the pram by himself, I had to grab hold of the open end of the coal bag so it didn't fall out. Tommy got hold of the bottom of the bag and we started to go up the stairs one at a time. I was trying to hold the bag up, but when we got to the top some of the coal fell out and because Tommy was holding the bag up I nearly fell forward. I managed to hold onto the railing to stop myself. As we were taking the second bag of coal up we saw that Mrs Price had her door open a little way so that she could see what we were doing. Once we were done with the second bag Tommy said, 'I will leave you to tidy up, but be very quiet so you don't wake Mom up ok?' I told Tommy that the coppers had been looking for him and when he asked what about I said that it was about some coalman. 'Oh that, never you mind don't worry.' 'You got to go down to Digbeth Police Station,' I said. 'If they come back you know what to say nip,' Tommy replied. As he was going he turned back and said that there were some bandages in the bag for my ankle. I thanked him and as I waved goodbye I saw that Mrs Price was still peeking through her door. Tommy walked past and I heard him say to her, 'Had a good look?' Her door shut quickly after that.

On Sunday morning Mom came out of her bedroom and saw me lying on the floor. 'You been there all night?' she asked me. When I nodded yes she turned to go into the kitchen and she said, 'I thought heard noises, did you hear anything? What the heck, where all this food come from?' I told her that Tommy brought it in the night. Mom wondered where he'd got it all from

57

hoping he hadn't got himself in to any trouble. 'I don't want the police here again, I'm fed up with it.' She went back into her bedroom and started to cry. I began to tidy the house; I got the ashes up off the floors and I built the fire up so I could get the house nice warm. Then I went into Mom's room and I asked if she was okay, 'I've tidied the house up for you,' I told her. She came out and said that we'd have some dinner later on. 'Tommy's brought me some bandages for my ankle Mom.' 'I know he has done something wrong,' she replied, 'I'll bet my life on it. Go and get the bandages then.' When I brought them to her Mom looked at the bandages and wondered where Tommy had got them from, 'These haven't come from no shop,' she said. I could see that she was getting worried, I tell by her face. She put the bandages in cold water and then she bandaged my foot. She tied the bandage really tight and at first I couldn't put my foot to the floor. I went over and sat by the window, there wasn't anybody playing out and about in the Holme, but then I saw Tom, Dick, and Harry coming down the lane. Mom was cooking by the fire, so she didn't notice. I moved away from the window because I didn't want to see them, but it looked like they were just carrying on down the lane. Mom made some mash potato with powdered milk, then she got meat from a tin. She also mashed the meat up into the potato and it wasn't too bad so I ate it. After dinner Mom drew the curtains and I remembered something. 'Mom I forgot to tell you, you owe Mrs Able one and sixpence for the candles'. 'She'll be lucky if she gets the money this week, I got nothing till next week. Three pence for candle! You can get them up on the Coventry Road for less.' Then I asked if I could sleep out here again tonight as it was so cold in my room. 'Okay,' she replied, 'but don't burn too much coal, we've got to use very little in case we don't get any more for while.'

    On Monday morning Mom came out of her bedroom and told me to get ready for school, 'I'm coming in with you to get to the bottom of what's going on,' she said. When I told her that my ankle was still hurting and that I couldn't put my foot down on the floor,

Mom told me that I was going, even if she had to drag me there herself. I limped all the way down Garrison Lane got to the school and when we got there Mom looked at one of the teachers. She asked if the teacher was the headmistress and she said she wanted to speak to her. 'She's not here at the moment,' the teacher replied and then she looked down at me. 'You told your mother did you?' I nodded in reply and then the teacher said that we should go into the office. 'Tell me what trouble he's been in,' Mom asked once we got inside. 'He told me you have been sending him home every day is that right?' When the teacher told her that was right Mom asked 'what's been going on here, why he hasn't Peter been having his dinners?' Just then another teacher came into the office because Mom had started to shout. 'Miss can I go to the toilet? I asked. She said I could but that I had to hurry back. I went straight out of school and over to the park. When I got there I saw Tom, Dick, and Harry but I made believe that I never saw them and kept on walking towards Lawley Street. I heard them running after me. They caught up with me eventually and asked me where I was going. I replied that I was going to see if I could get some more bread and they said that they would come with me. We crossed the horse road off Lawley Street passing Young's paper shop on the corner with Great Barr Street. As we approached the shop they told me to wait outside while they went in. After a while they came out and they started running back up Lawley Street. This big bloke came out of the shop and he tried to run after them, as he did he turned around noticed me. He grabbed hold of me, 'You're coming with me mister!' he growled. 'I'm not with them!' I shouted back, 'I've run out of school, my mom is there. The bloke told me that I was lying, but when I said that he could take me back there he got me by the arm he shouted to somebody in back of the shop, 'I'm taking this lad back to school to see if is telling me the truth.'

When we got to school we went into the office and my Mom was just about to come looking for me. When she saw us she told the bloke to put me down and that I was her son. 'He was with three kids who pinched a tin box with some money in it from me,' the bloke told her. My Mom started to have go with the bloke asking if he'd seen me with the three kids. 'Peter look at me, was you with them three kids?' she asked me. I told her I wasn't, that I was going to get her some bread and that I was passing the shop when the kids came running out. While we was talking the headmistress came into the office and said 'If it's the same kids that have been hanging round the school, I have had complaints about them.' The bloke looked at me, 'You know who they are don't you?' When I replied that I didn't Mom looked down at me and said she believed me. As the bloke was turning away he turned around and pointed his finger at me. 'Don't you dare point your finger at my son he hasn't done anything wrong,' Mom said to him. 'I'm going to get the police in,' said the bloke. After the bloke left Mom said that we were going home. Walking up Garrison Lane I looked round and saw that the bloke from the shop was following us. As Mom and I got over the canal bridge Mom stopped and shouted to him, 'If you want to know where we live keep going up the lane, I'll call the police on you when we got home.' Turned out the police were already there when we approached home. They told my Mom that I had to go to Coventry Road Police Station tomorrow because the inspector wanted to speak with me. We were all standing outside our block when the bloke from the shop came over, he could see police was there and he started to talk to them. Before he could say too much mom stopped him and said 'He's trying to get my son into trouble saying he has pinched some tin box with some money in it.' The copper looked at me and asked if it was true. 'No sir,' I replied 'it was them three kids who I saw running out of the shop.' The copper asked where the tin box was now, but then my Mom replied 'If Peter had the tin box this big idiot would have took it off him by now.' The copper told me to be at the station at ten o'clock the next day, but Mom said that I couldn't because I had to go to school. 'Mrs Round make sure he's there and we will get in touch with the school when he arrives,' the copper replied. The bloke asked the coppers about his money again and the police told him that he'd have to wait until the inspector had spoken to him the next day.

Going up the stairs I told Mom that I didn't want to go to the station the next day, she simply replied that I had to. When she opened the door I turned around and ran down the stairs. They were damp and slippery and with my bad ankle I slipped down and hurt my bum. Mom was shouting at me to come back, but I just carried on to Granny Pegs. When I got there I told her what had happened and she told me to go and fetch my Mom. I went back home and she done her nut at me for going round to Granny Pegs. After she shouted at me for a while we went back to Granny's and then she started to have a go at mom. 'I'm coming with you tomorrow,' Granny said, 'my Peter never gets into any trouble, I shall tell that inspector off.' We went back home where Mom kept on and on. I went straight to my cold bedroom and got all the overcoats over me to get myself warm. Just as I was settling down Mom came in and pointed her finger at me, 'God help you if you're not telling the inspector the truth tomorrow.' I didn't reply, I just turned over not listening to her.

The next day as I stood in the freezing kitchen washing in cold water and I told me that I didn't want to go to the cop shop. 'You're going, now come on we are going to the police station right now.' My ankle was still hurting and halfway down the stairs I slipped and fell. I grabbed hold of the railings but the stairs were still damp and slippery, so I slipped fell and hurt my side and my bum again. I sat on the on the bottom step and I could feel the damp coming through my trousers. 'Mom we can't go to the cop shop now I've hurt myself.' She grabbed hold my collar and she lifted me up. 'Get up we're going and that's that,' Mom told me. As we were going out the block I told Mom that we had to wait for Granny Pegg, but she said that she could follow us there. When we got to station Granny Pegg was already there waiting for us. We were told to sit down by the copper behind the desk, but after a while I got up and told Mom that I was hungry. Granny turned around to

Mom and asked 'Haven't you given the poor lad anything to eat?' Mom didn't say anything she just looked at her. Gran looked at the police sergeant behind the desk and shouted to him, 'Have you got anything to eat for my poor grandson?' The sergeant replied that they were there to feed people, but Gran asked about the people in the cells, she said that she'd heard them shouting as she came in and that the coppers must feed them. The sergeant replied that they were only drunks who were up in front of the beak later on waiting for the meat wagon to come to fetch them. I asked Gran what the meat wagon was, she simply replied 'I hope you never go in one.' Gran got up and went over to the desk. 'Look here you big lump, go find some bread for my grandson,' she said to the sergeant. He sighed and then told another nearby copper to go and get the lad some food.

The copper came back shortly after with some dry bread and some meat to put on it. The bread was bit stale and the meat was soggy, but I ate it because I was so hungry. It felt like we'd waited for ages when Gran asked 'When is the bloody inspector coming? He should have been here at ten o'clock, look at the time. If he's not in the next ten minutes we're off.' Mom was just sitting there not saying anything, though Gran kept looking over at her. In the meantime while we were waiting for the inspector to arrive, the meat wagon arrive for the drunks. We could we hear them swearing and fighting. The inspector finally arrived, the time was getting towards twelve o'clock. Gran had a go at him when he walked in and said, 'What time do you call this?' You told my grandson to be here at ten o'clock, he has missed school and his dinner because of you.' The inspector told me to follow him, that Mom and Gran should wait where they were because he wanted to speak to me on his own. Gran piped up 'Not on your Nellie, we are coming in with Peter whether you like it or not.' We all went into a small room where I had to sit next to the Inspector while Mom and Gran had to stand up. The inspector kept looking at me without saying anything. He was writing something down when Gran asked 'Are you going to talk to the lad or we are going home?' 'Mrs Round can you keep quiet or leave the room,' the inspector replied. Gran said, 'I'm not Mrs Round, I'm his Gran, that's Mrs Peg to you. You have kept us waiting for two hours and you still haven't spoken to the lad, he's getting hungry and he's missed his school dinner; now start talking". The inspector paused for a moment and then looked at me. 'Peter who are these three lads who keep coming to your school? Tell me the truth.' I replied that I was telling the truth, that I didn't know the lads but that I did know where they lived. 'You said they wanted you to climb through a window, do you know where this window was? And are they the same lads who Terry Williams went with?' the inspector asked next. I told him that 'yes, they were the same lads,' but that I didn't know where the window was. I went on and said that I didn't know the two men that were sometimes with Tom, Dick, and Harry either. I explained to the inspector that the men weren't with the lads when they stole the money from Young's. 'What about the man who came out of the air raid shelter,' the inspector asked, 'do you know him?' I replied that I didn't but that I thought he lived down Saltley way, where the three lads lived. The inspector paused again and then said, 'Right Peter can you show me where they live then?'

We had to wait a long time for the car to come and by the time it arrived Gran was getting really fed up. When the inspector came to collect us Gran said that she was coming too, but the inspector said, 'no' and that she was staying where she was. Then Mom spoke and said, 'I'm coming with my son, he's not going in car on his own.' I looked up at her and said I was hungry and that I felt really sick. Shortly after we finally got into the car, I sat in the front with another copper who was driving while Mom and the inspector got in the back. When we got to Adderley Street, with my directing the driver, I showed the inspector where I thought the three lads lived. As I was pointing out of the car window I spotted one of the lads and told the inspector. 'Mrs Round, Peter isn't telling me the truth.' Mom paused and then she slapped me across the head from behind. As we driving back to the station I saw the lads coming from the tip under the bridge, I pointed them out again, 'There they are.'

They knew it was me in the car so they turned and ran back over the tip. The copper who was driving pulled over, got out of the car, and ran after them. I turned around in my seat to face the inspector. 'I told you the truth,' I said to him. 'You haven't told me all off it Peter, come on tell me what happened with Terry Williams?' he said to me. 'I don't know sir! I want to go home, I'm hungry, Mom let's go home.' Mom looked at me and said I needed to tell the truth and then we could go home. I started to feel sick, I tried to be sick in the car. The copper came back panting, he obviously hadn't been able to catch the lads. When he got back into the car he look at me and said that if I was going to be sick I needed to do it in the gutter. Soon after that I got out the car and ran straight towards the tip. I knew where the lads were running to. The copper came running after me. There were a few people over the tip and when they saw him they all ran off while I ran towards the railway. I looked back as I was running and I could see that the copper was watching to see where I was going. I made believe that I was going towards the railway crossing, but I jumped aside and on the canal bridge where I could watch the copper. When he'd disappeared I slipped out from my hiding spot and ran along the canal towpath till I got to Dartmouth Street. I tried to climb up to the top of the bridge, but I missed my footing and fell back down, really I hurt myself. I lay there for bit and then decided to try again. I made sure I got my footing right and eventually got to the top. Then I ran all the way to Granny Pegg's.

When I arrived Gran was sitting in same place by the radio. The first thing she said to me was 'What the hell you are doing here? You should be at the police station. If you don't behave yourself my lad they'll putting you away.' When I simply replied that I was hungry Gran sighed and said that she didn't have much, but that she'd find me something. She eventually came back with lumpy mash potato and a slice of bread. At least it would fill me up for a bit.

A little later when I'd almost finished eating Gran told me that I had to get myself home at once when I was done. I asked if I could stay a little bit longer, but she said I couldn't that, I'd get her into trouble with the police and with Mom. A few minutes later, when I'd finished, this big bloke came in, Gran asked him to get me home safely in case I ran off on the way, I think I remember her calling him Wally. When he asked what I'd been up to Gran said that I was in some sort of trouble with the police. I went with the bloke and as we were going through the gully towards EastHolme he asked me if I wanted to go with him to his house to hide from the police. He went to grab my arm, but I shouted 'No Mister!' and ran off. He started to run after me; I was going along the edge of the gardens while he was running in the road. I got to the block before him but as I was going inside he tried to grab hold of me again. I shouted up to my Mom to help me. Mrs Bloomer and Mrs Price must have heard me because they came out of their houses to see what's going on. I was halfway up the stairs to our door when the police came out to see what was happening. At first nobody asked me why was the bloke chasing me, it was Mrs Bloomer who asked me what was going on. I said that the bloke had tried to grab hold of me and that he wanted me to go to his house to hide from the police. Mrs Bloomer looked at the bloke and asked if what I'd said was true. He replied that it wasn't and that Mrs Pegg had just asked him to see that I got home safe because I was in some kind trouble. Mrs Price looked carefully and the bloke and then said, 'I know you don't I?' He shook his head and then he quickly left. Mrs Price turned to the police and said that she was sure that she knew the bloke from somewhere. As I went into the house the copper told me that I had to go to the station again the next day. Mom asked what it was this time and the copper replied that inspector Davies wanted to speak to me again because he wasn't satisfied with me, that I must have known something because I'd run off. By now I was hungry and fed up and I wasn't really listening. I heard Mom say that the coppers had kept us waiting for over two hours and that they'd better tell the inspector if he wasn't there at ten o'clock the next day we wouldn't be staying.

As the coppers were leaving Mrs Price came running into the house. 'I've remembered who that bloke is!' she said to the coppers, 'his name Wally and he's no good. You better tell Peter to keep away from him, if you don't tell him I will.' She pushed her way passed them and repeated what she'd said about the bloke. The coppers were standing in the doorway when they asked Mrs Price how she knew him. 'He went out with my niece,' she explained, 'he's no good, always in trouble. He lives round Milk Street or thereabouts, I know he came from that part.' The copper look at me; 'Peter where do you know him from?' I replied that I didn't know him and just that he arrived while I was at Granny Pegg's and that she asked him to get me home. I went on and said that he'd tried to grab hold my arm then I ran away from him. 'We will talk tomorrow,' the copper said, 'I hope you are telling us the truth this time Peter.' After Mrs Price and the coppers had gone Mom gave me some food, although it wasn't enough so I ask for more. While I was eating I told her that I didn't want to go to the station again, that I'd rather go to school instead. Mom said that I had to go to see the inspector again, but she did say that I could sleep by the fire when I said how cold I was.

It was different the next day when I woke up really warm. As I got up I asked Mom again if I really had to go to the station and that if I went to school maybe the police could fetch me from there later. Mom looked at me and then said 'Okay, go have a wash and get yourself off to school, I will be down later to see that you've been.' A little later I was running out the block when Mom lifted the window up behind me so that she could wave to me. As I ran I turned back and wave to her. I was going down Garrison Lane and remember feeling pleased with myself because I wasn't going to the cop shop. I was running over the canal bridge but stopped when I saw that Tom, Dick, and Harry was waiting for me. They grabbed hold of me and took me down the path to the canal. We went under the bridge and they asked me what I'd told the cops. I replied that I'd told them nothing and that I only showed them where they lived. 'You're coming with us,' they said.

I was made to walk in the middle of the three of them so that they could keep an eye on me. We walked for some time along the canal footpath and when we turned off I didn't know where we were. We went through some park, then through an entry coming out in some street. We went up another entry and came out in yard which went into a house. We went inside and sat about for a while, no one spoke. They gave me a sandwich to eat, but I just kept telling them that I wanted to go home. Tom grabbed hold of me and said, 'If you don't shut up I will put my fist in your face, now keep quiet, you're coming with us later on tonight.' The house was starting to get cold so they lit the fire. I looked out of the window and I could see it had started to get dark; I was getting scared. A little later the three lads went out but they locked the door behind them so I couldn't get out. I looked around but there wasn't a front door. I couldn't understand what was going on so I sat down on the couch. I must have fallen asleep because the next thing I knew they were waking me up. When I sat up I could see three blokes in the room, I knew two of them, but not the third. I was looking round the room then the door open to run through when another bloke came in. He was a big with a scar on his face and he was doing all the talking. He kept looking over at me and he whispered something to Tom who kept nodding his head.

Shortly after we all left the house but the bloke with the scar stayed behind. I got to the bottom of the entry and the lads hurried me up and onto the back of lorry. They pulled the sheet down on the back so I couldn't see where we were going. We drove around for a while but eventually the lorry stopped. I was getting really frightened. I heard a knock on the side of the lorry and then the sheet went up. We all jump down from the back and went around the back of a building. There were some railings and because I was small I was made to crawl underneath. I scratched my leg as I was crawling and it started to bleed a lot. Once I'd got under the railings and stood up they told me to told open the gates. I looked around but the only one I could open was a little side gate. They all came in carrying big iron bars which they used to break open the lock on the big gates. The lorry backed in and they told me to close the gates behind them and to keep watch out. I saw them carrying boxes out of a nearby building and then putting them on the back of the lorry. When they'd finished they shouted to me to quickly open the gates and then get in the back of the lorry. Once I'd closed the gates and the lorry had gone through I ran to the back and was pulled me up.

      We drove off to a new place where they unloaded the boxes from the back of the lorry. The bloke with the scar on his face was waiting there when we arrived and he was shouting to get the boxes unloaded quickly, he kept saying, 'Come on come on.' Some of the boxes were a bit heavy and I had to push the boxes to the back of the lorry instead of picking them up. The bloke who was shouting kept looking over at me, I was getting frightened by him. When the lorry was unloaded we got back in and went back to the house where I was locked in again. I said I wanted to go home but they wouldn't let me. I explained that my Mom would be worried about me, but the bloke said 'I will tell your Mom that you're are okay.' I looked up at him and I knew he was lying to me. A little while later a lady came down the stairs and when she saw me she said, 'Hello little boy. What have you done to your leg, come to the sink and sit down.' She bathed and cleaned it where I had scratched the skin. I asked the lady to take me home, but she simply replied that I'd be going home the next day. She left me in the kitchen saying that she'd go to get us some food, she opened the door and locked it behind her. A little later Tom told me to lie down and get some sleep; little did I know we would be going out again later.

Before I could go and lie down the lady came back and started talking quietly to the others so I couldn't hear what she saying to them. Then they all went out again and left me on my own. The lady locked the door behind them all. Once they'd gone I went over to window to see if I could climb through and get out. I climbed onto the sink but I couldn't push the window up from the bottom, it only pulled down from the top. I started to climb through the window but as I looked out I saw two blokes standing over on other side of the yard and when they spotted me they shouted to me get back in. I quickly jumped off the sink and went over to the couch, I lay down and went to sleep.

I don't know how long I'd been asleep for when the lady woke me up. She started to shout at me saying that she told me I'd be going home the next day, the blokes outside had obviously told her what I'd try to do. She went back out with Dick, and Harry, but Tom stayed with me. Once again the door was locked behind us and Tom sat down on the floor by the door. I went to lie back on the couch again and Tom kept quiet. I must have fallen asleep again, when they woke me up the light was on I could see it was dark. Shortly after I woke up the lady gave me a sandwich and cup of hot milk which was very good. Once I'd finished she offered me another half-sandwich. While I was eating they all came back into the house, the bloke with the scar on his face whispering to one of the blokes. He kept looking over at me, then the bloke nodded his head and the other bloke looked across at me. I was getting worried and frightened and soon enough we all went out to the lorry again. I went to get in the back but the bloke with the scar said I could sit in the front with him, I had to sit on his lap. The driver was going fast again, the streets were very quiet. I had no idea where we were going, but when we stopped I realised it was the same place the last time. The lorry pulled up and then we waited for a while before I had to do the same thing as the previous night. I was made to crawl under the railings and climb through the window into room. The door in the room was bit tight but I managed to open it. All the men came in and bust open the lock on the gate again, the lorry backed in and I had to shut the big gates while the lorry was loaded. A bloke came out from the other side of the building and started to shout very loud. I came to have look what was going on but I was told to get back and keep watch. Then they started to beat the bloke up. I went back over to them and screamed at them to leave him alone. One of the men came over and grabbed hold of me, he took over to the gates while they dragged the bloke into building at the top of the yard. A little while later, after they'd finished loading the lorry, they told me to open the gates again. There was just enough room for all of us to get into the back. We drove off to same place where we unloaded the boxes before and the man with the scar was shouting to the men to get the lorry unloaded quickly; there was another two blokes helping that night. I went to jump up from the back of the lorry but the bloke with the scar told me to stand by him and to not to move. When the lorry was unloaded we got back in, it was quiet and nobody spoke.

We stopped when we got back to Adderley Street and went back into the house. The bloke with the scar followed us all in and he started talking to the others, then one of them looked over at me. 'Peter, it's time for you to go home,' he said. The he gave me a bag of money, as I took it from him I realised it was bit heavy. As soon as I got out the house I ran as fast as I could go. I was running up Adderley Street then all of sudden some bloke came out of one of the entries. He grabbed hold of my neck and took the money off me. Then, still holding me tight, we began walking towards the tip. I told him that he was hurting me, but he didn't stop. It was pitch black and it started to rain, it was coming down heavy and it was very cold.

The bloke was looking around to see if there was anybody over the tip and then he turned to me around, with his hands still on my neck, and he slipped down by the edge and finally let go of me. I think he expected me to follow his lead, but instead I ran off. Of course he came running after me and he grabbed hold of me again. I kicked him where it hurts and shouted 'You bast**d!' to him. While he was on the ground I ran again, but he wasn't down for long. He was running after me again when I hid in some shadows. The bloke was running all over the place but he couldn't find me. I was crawling along the ground trying to stay low, but my knees began to hurt so I got up and ran for bit. As I was running I tripped and fell to the ground. I must have landed on my face and my nose started to bleed. I got to Venetia Road but found that the gates to the tip were closed. I had to climb over the top and I ripped my trousers and scratched my leg as I went. Although I was hurting I didn't stop and I ran straight across the horse road and got to our block door. I made a lot of noise as I ran up the stairs and then began banging on the door. Mom was already up and she opened it for me. I pushed past her and I told her to 'shut the f**king door!' 'What have you been up to? Look at the state you're in, where have you been for the last two days? The police have been looking for you.' Mrs Bloomer was knocking on the door, but Mom said to ignore her. 'Answer me,' she said, 'have you been in some sort of trouble?' I didn't reply but told her to let Mrs Bloomer in. When she came in Mrs Bloomer, like Mom, asked where I'd been. 'I'll go up to the caretaker and tell him to phone the police,' she said. Mom told her not to and Mrs Bloomer nodded. 'I'll get the old man to put the boiler on so that Peter can have a bath,' she told Mom.

A little later it was Mrs Price who went to the caretakers to phone police. Mrs Bloomer must have told her what was going on. The police came over and they asked me question after question. As they were talking to me Mrs Bloomer came up to tell me that the bath was ready. Despite all their questions I never said anything to the coppers. I went down to the Bloomers house and one of the coppers came with me. 'You have been in the wars haven't you?' he said as we went down the stairs. I got undressed in the bathroom and the copper sat on the nearby toilet so he could keep asking me questions. I still never said anything in reply, I just carried on washing myself. My leg was covered in scratches and it hurt to keep it under the water. After a while, I got out and dried myself while the copper stood outside the bathroom door. I stood thinking for a moment and then I went to climb out the bathroom window, but then I heard Mr Bloomer outside talking to Mrs Price, so I decided against it. I was hurting all over as I went back up the stairs to our house. The copper was walking right behind me so I couldn't run away. When we went through the door I just went into my room, I was so tired. I heard the copper behind me saying, 'Peter you have been missing for two days, you had your mother worried and people have been looking for you. Where have you been?' 'I'm hungry and I'm tired,' I said in reply. The copper told my Mom to give me something to eat because it might open up to me talking. Mom told him that we didn't have any food and that she'd used all her coupons up. One of the coppers said he'd would go up to the station and see what the inspector had.

As the copper left Mrs Bloomer came back in with some stuff to bath my leg; it stung really bad. The copper that had stayed behind started to ask me questions about what went on over the last two days, he trying to be nice to me. 'Come on Peter we know where you've been we just want you tell us in your own words.' I looked over at Mrs Bloomer and said 'I'm very hungry.' Mrs Bloomer paused and then told the copper that she needed to speak to him outside. They both went out and Mom said 'You better come up with the truth my lad, you don't know how I've been sick with worry about you. You've made me ill!' The she went into the kitchen and I went to my room, I threw the overcoats over me and quickly fell asleep.

A while later Mom came into the room and shouted 'What are you doing? Get them clothes off so I can wash them, they are really dirty.' The room was so cold I started to shiver as I took my dirty clothes off so I jumped back into bed and put the overcoats back over me to get myself warm. Once again I quickly fell asleep. When I woke for the second time I could see it was still dark. I came out of my room with one of the coats pulled around me. Mom was drying my now clean clothes by the fire and there was a different copper in the house, he told me that he'd brought me some food. Mom did me some toast with some fresh milk with hot water and the copper gave me some sort of cake. He'd brought us bread, fresh milk, two tins of meat, some potatoes, two tins of dry milk, and a small jar of jam which looked really old. After I had eaten the questions started again. I looked at Mom but she told me to talk to the police and to tell them the truth.

In the end I started talking to them. I explained that I'd bumped into three lads on the way to school and that although I didn't want to go with them at first, I eventually followed them to a house. I told them about the old lady at the house who said that I had to stay there for the night. Just then Mrs Bloomer came in and asked if I'd started talking yet. I jumped up and went back into my bedroom. Mom came straight in after me and told me to get back out there and tell the truth. I simply replied that I was too tired, then I rolled over and slept till the next morning.

When I woke up the next day Mom came in with my clean cloths and told me to get up and get dressed. When I came out of my room there was a different copper waiting for me. 'I'm here to take you to the police station Peter,' he told. 'I'm not going anywhere, I haven't done anything wrong,' I replied. 'All we want to know is where you have been for last two days, we know something happened to you.' I told him that nothing happened to me and that I wanted to go to school. 'Sorry Peter but you have to come to the station with me and you need to tell us what really happened. You are in some serious trouble Peter, if you tell us what happened we can help you.' I looked over at Mom and she said that I had to go with him, but that she was going to and so was Mrs Bloomer. We all left the house together and the copper asked if I had a big coat to put on as it was cold outside. Mom replied that I was standing in the only clothes that I had. As we were going down the stairs Mrs Price came out of her house and asked me if I was alright. I said I was and then she told me 'You better tell them the truth now.'

On the way to the police station I had to walk side-by-side with the copper so I didn't run off. When we got to the station I saw the bloke with the scar on his face standing on the other side of the road watching me. I think he was with the bloke who grabbed me and took me over the tip. When I saw them standing there together I began to get scared. Inside the station the inspector was waiting for me and we all went into his room, he pulled a chair out so I could sit by him. 'Okay Peter,' he started, 'you can begin by telling me the truth.' I just sat there for bit and never said anything. 'Peter if you don't start talking to me I will have to put you in a cell, you don't want that now do you.' I paused and thought for a moment and then I started to tell the inspector everything. I told him what had happened over the two nights and how they beat up a bloke. 'Do you know their names Peter?' I was asked. I shook my head in reply. 'Peter we need you to take us to the place where that bloke was beaten up, we'll go now the car is waiting.' Mom wasn't happy about going with me so I found myself getting into the back of the police car with Mrs Bloomer and we left the station. I directed the police to the right place and we got out of the car. I led the way round the side of the right building and pointed out the railings I'd crawled under. The inspector took me inside the yard and I showed him the gate I'd had to open and the place where the boxes had been loaded. After a while the inspector told me to get back into the car, 'now you're going to show us where those three lads live,' he said. I directed the driver to Adderley Street and when we got out of the car again I took the inspector to the house. When the inspector knocked the door two old women came out. One of them was really deaf and she couldn't hear what the inspector was staying to her. People were coming out of the other houses nearby to see what was going on, most of them were old. The inspector looked around, 'are you sure the three lads brought you here Peter?' I nodded yes in reply. With the two old women not helping we went back to the police station where the inspector told Mrs Bloomer to take me home. 'We're finished with you for now Peter, we'll just have to see how it all goes.'

As soon as we got back home Mom asked if I'd told the truth. 'The inspector was pleased with him,' Mrs Bloomer said, 'and they've finished with him for now.' Mom nodded, she seemed pleased it was over, for now at least. 'Have you seen your Tommy?' Mrs Bloomer asked, sitting down. 'I haven't seen him for over week,' mom replied, 'Christmas is coming up and we've got no money. I've used all my coupons up. Run over to Able's Peter, ask her if she's got any candles. Tell her to put them on the slate till Tommy brings me some money.'

I left the house and ran to cross of the horse road. On the other side, standing by Twigg's shop, was the bloke with the scar. I stopped suddenly when I saw him and waited for a bit and thought about what to do. I decided to take my chances and run straight to the shop, but I when I passed by him he grabbed hold of me. 'You're coming with me!' he growled. 'I can't!' I said struggling, 'I've got to go get my Mom come candles from the shop'. I asked me what I'd told the coppers and when I said nothing he let me go. I ran all the way to the shop. I was waiting for Mrs Able to come out from the back and when she finally appeared I said that Mom had sent me for some candles. Mrs Able rolled her eyes and went back behind the counter to get them. While I waited for her he bloke with the scar came in. When Mrs Able reappeared he asked her how much are the candles were. 'Who are you?' she asked. The bloke replied that I was his 'kind uncle' and he stood with his arm around my shoulder. 'The candles are two shillings and sixpence,' Mrs Able said holding the candles out for me to grab. The bloke paid her the money and we walked out, he still had his arm tightly around me. He left me when we got back to the block, but he watched me as I walked in.

I never said anything to Mom when I got in. A little later she was making me something to eat when there was a knock at the door. Mom told me to go and see who was there and when I opened the door the inspector was looking down at me. Before I could shout to me that the copper was here, he had pushed his way inside; he was carrying a bag of food. 'You've got no gas or electric have you? How long have you been cut off?' he asked my Mom. 'About three weeks,' she replied. 'I'll see what I can do for you,' he said. I remember he only came to drop off the food, he never did help us again.

The next morning mom shouted to me to get up and when I went into the kitchen I couldn't believe what Mom had done for me. She gave me a cup of hot, fresh milk with no hot water mixed in it and I had toast with some jam. Then, she said she would be coming with me all the way to school. As we were going down the lane we crossed over by the rail bridge and standing on the corner of Maxstoke Street was the bloke with the scar; he was watching us. He started to walk down the lane in the other direction when he met up with another bloke, I think he was the one who drove the lorry those nights. When we got further down the lane to school gates Mom went in first and I stopped behind her. I looked over to see the two blokes walking away I wanted to see where they was going. Mom came back out of the gates and said she hoped I wasn't going to run off again. I shook my head and followed her inside to the headmistress' office. I'm glad to see you Mrs Round,' the headmistress said, 'Peter will be having his dinner today and after that we will be sending all of the children home, the school will be breaking up for the Christmas week. They will be back to school on Tuesday the 8th of January. We heard that Peter went missing for a couple of days? I do hope everything is okay now?' 'Everything is fine,' Mom replied then she turned to me, 'Peter, you go straight to Granny Pegg's when we finished today. I'm going to find your brother Tommy, I'll see you later.'

Dinner in the hall that day was lovely! We had mashed potato, meat and cabbage and afterwards we had rice pudding, which was very lumpy so I left most of it. Once we'd all finished eating and were getting ready to go home the headmistress came into the hall to talk to us. Nobody was listening to her as she carried on, I turned to Johnny and said 'Let's go'. We both ran out of school and when we got out of the gates I looked around to see if the bloke was about. I couldn't't see him and said to Johnny 'Come on I'll race you up the lane.' I was a little faster and when we got to the railway bridge I stopped and waited for Johnny to catch up. When he finally did we ran together to Granny Pegg's and I went inside. Gran gave me slice of bread with jam on it, 'Don't tell your Uncle Billy you had bread with jam on it, he don't want anybody know he's got jar jam,' she said (Bill was Granny's son.) Mom came to pick me up about four o'clock. When I asked her about whether she'd seen Tommy she just shook her head.

    I got up later the next morning as I didn't have to go to school. I was just getting the fire going when Mom told me that she was going out to look for Tommy and that I was to stay inside till she got back. I did as I was told, I kept the curtains closed and stayed inside. A little later Johnny came calling for me but I told him I couldn't go out. He asked me about what had happened with the police and where I'd gone for those two days. I told him what I'd told the coppers and that I kept seeing the bloke with the scar around and that he was scaring me. Johnny said he thought he knew who the bloke was but he wouldn't say anymore when I asked. Mom came home later in the afternoon and she'd brought four potatoes and half a tin of dried egg powder. The coal had started to run down, but she hadn't brought anymore of that. Mom mashed up the potatoes and made the eggs from the powder; they tasted awful! Mom made me go to bed early to save the coal that we had left, but my room was getting colder by the minute. I slept with my clothes on again, to try and keep myself warm.

    A few days later things were getting really bad. The coal was running out and we no food left at all. Come Tuesday Mom went out during the afternoon and didn't come back. I got very late and I was getting worried. Finally she came back with some food but it wasn't a lot and she said it had to last us until Friday. I asked her where she'd got the food from, but she didn't reply, she just went and sat by the fire and started to cry. She never told me why she was crying when I asked, instead she made me two pieces of toast with the bread was left over from two days before.

On Christmas Day morning Mom came into my room and gave me a pair of stockings. I can remember to this day they were grey and they came over my knees, but at least they kept my legs warm. We had only two buckets full of coal left, but Mom lit a fire and said she'd sort it out. The food mom made was a mixture of everything, but I ate it anyway. When I got into bed that night I lay there thinking; no gas, no electric, only a pair socks for Christmas, and no Tommy. I started to cry and think how I was in trouble with the police and that it wasn't my fault. I got up and went into my Mom's room. 'Mom,' I said still crying, 'Mom it's not my fault I'm in trouble with the police, it's them three kids who got me in trouble.' I remember Mom looking at me and sighing. 'Okay, when you go back to the police station you can tell that to Inspector Davies. Now go back to bed.'

The next day was the same as Christmas Day, I stayed in bed till the afternoon and only got up when Mom shouted at me. I had to clean fire grate out even though we only had enough coal to last for one more fire. We only had three slices of bread left and there was only enough egg powder for one of us. We shared the bread and Mom put the egg powder on my slices. While we were eating I asked Mom if she had any money. She got her purse out and opened it to show me the three pennies inside. We were also running out of candles so Mom soon told me to go back to bed again.

I felt like I didn't sleep for long before I got up and looked out of the window. It was dark and I don't know what I was thinking but I picked up my shoes and tiptoed to the front door so I wouldn't make any noise. I closed the living room door behind me just in case the front door made noise. I put the catch on and went out and sat on the cold stairs putting my shoes on. I stayed there for bit but the next thing I know I was running down the stairs straight out the block running and down Garrison lane. There was nobody about, I kept on running and I finished up outside Wilson's bakery in Montaque Street. The bakery gates were closed but they weren't too high. I could see the door was open ajar so I started to climb. A lady came out and when she saw what I was doing she shouted out to me. I was at the top with my leg over the gate when she told me to get down before I hurt myself. 'Can I have some bread?' I asked, 'I haven't eaten for two days.' 'Where's your Mom and Dad?' she asked back. I replied that I only had a Mom. The woman looked at me for a second and then turned to go inside saying that she'd see what she could do for me. I climbed back down to the street side of the gate and a little later the woman came back out with two small loaves. 'Does your mother know you're here?' she asked. I lied and said that she did. 'Here you are,' she said passing the bread through the gate to me, 'now hop it and don't come back.' I was running away when she shouted at me not to tell anyone where I'd got the bread from. Further down the street I slowed to a walk and started to pick lumps out of the bread, I was so hungry. I walked to Mitchell's grocery shop and stopped to cross the horse road when two blokes suddenly came from the side of Mitchell's. One of them recognised me. 'Peter what are you doing out at this time in the morning,' he asked. I told him that I'd gone to the bakery to get bread for my Mom. The bloke told me to wait here I was. He went back up the opening by the shop and came back with two bottles of milk. He passed them to me (I think milk was still on ration at the time) and then he told me to get off home.

    When I got back to the block I ran up the stairs. I crept inside, closing the door quietly behind me. Mom was still in bed so I put the milk and bread in the kitchen. I went back to bed my bedroom and although I was warm from running I put the coats over me as the room was still cold. I slept for a little while but then Mom was shouting and shaking me. 'Has your brother been here?' she was saying. I told her no and that it was me who'd got the bread and milk. I explained what had happened because she thought I was getting myself into trouble again. 'I will have to go find Tommy, see if he can help us,' Mom said, 'You go back to bed and keep yourself warm, don't open the door to anybody do you hear?' I lay there waiting for her to come back but I must have fallen asleep because next thing I knew there was a loud bang on the door. I was getting frightened, but I stayed in my room. The banging was going on for some time and then the shouting started; someone was shouting my name on the other side of the front door. I didn't know what to do, I was on my own. 'Come on Peter open this door I know you are in there!' I heard a voice say. Slowly I went to the door and I opened it a crack. I saw who was on the other side; it was the bloke with the scar on his face. He pushed against the door and grabbed hold of me, dragging me into the living room. He never spoke to me but he did put a bag of money on the table. He grabbed hold of my collar and lifted me of the floor putting his finger in my face. Suddenly Mrs Bloomer came running in; 'What do you think you are doing to that poor lad? Put him down right now!' The bloke slowly put me down and let me go, then he turned and left. Next, in came Mrs Fleetwood and Mrs Price to see what was happening. Mrs Bloomer came over to me and gave me hug. She was holding me saying that she was going to stay with me until my Mom got home. 'Where is your Mom Peter?' 'Out looking for Tommy,' I replied. 'Come on, you're coming with me down to my house, it's bloody cold in here.'

A little later I was sitting in front of the Bloomers' fire when Mr Bloomer came in and asked if I'd been in the wars again. Mrs Bloomer gave me a cup of hot milk and some toast, I was just finishing the milk when Mom came in with Tommy. When Mrs Bloomer told Mom what had happened Mom started to shout. 'I can't go on like this! You need to start telling the truth Peter otherwise they will put you away for good.' 'Shouting at him isn't going to help,' Tommy said. We all stood silently for a moment and then Mrs Bloomer asked Tommy if he'd step outside to have a word with her. When they came back in a few minutes later Tommy told Mom to let me stay with the Bloomers for the night. I followed Tommy upstairs to our house and he saw the bag money on the table; he picked it up shoved it into his pocket. He went straight back out and Mom shouted after him asking where he was going. Mr Bloomer came walking in with two buckets of coal. 'Mrs Bloomer said you didn't have any and to give you some of ours,' he said. Mom made some mashed potato where she got it from I don't know and she made me some toast and a cup of powdered milk.

    When I'd finished Mr Bloomer came back up for me to go band told me to go downstairs to his house. It was lovely and warm inside; I sat by the fire while Mr Bloomer made me up a bed on the couch. When he was finished he came and sat next to me on the floor. 'I won't ask you any questions Peter, just tell me what really happened when you went missing, everybody was really worried about you.' I pulled my legs up to my chest and with my hands around my legs I stared into the fire. I started to tell him everything, I was completely honest. I must have started to fall asleep because I can remember him picking me up putting me on the couch then waking me up to ask just one question. 'Peter I want to ask you one thing, who was the bloke with the scar?' 'I don't know his name Mr Bloomer and that's the truth.' 'All you have to do is tell the police what you told me. You've been very brave and don't have to worry about the police, they are there to help you and they will. I was quiet for a minute and then I told Mr Bloomer about the money that the bloke had put on the table and how Tommy had taken it. Mr Bloomer told me to go back to sleep, that it wasn't time for me to get up yet. A little later I heard a knock on the door and then there was a whispering voice, I remember thinking that it was Tommy. Mr Bloomer closed the living room door and I got up to try and listen but all I could hear was sharp talking and not actual words. I got back on the couch just before Mr Bloomer came back into the room. 'Peter that was your brothers Tommy, when you're ready you're to help him carry the coal up here.' I put my shoes and before I went out Mr Bloomer pulled me towards him and put his hands on my shoulders. 'Look here Peter don't be frightened of your brother. Remember I'm here to help you if that bloke with the scar comes around again, you shout for me and if the police want to ask you more questions you come for me is that understood? I nodded my head in reply. I went down the stairs and started to get the coal ready to take up when Johnny appeared. He offered to help me with the coal.

After a while Mr Bloomer came out, he'd obviously been watching us; we were almost finished. Mr Bloomer looked at Johnny and put a hand on his shoulder. 'Johnny I want you to look after Peter, keep him out of trouble and that goes for you to,' Mr Bloomer said smiling. 'I will Mr Bloomer, I will,' Johnny replied. Mr Bloomer went back inside and Johnny and I started to laugh. Then Johnny started to moan because his clothes were getting dirty. 'My Mom will kill me for getting so filthy,' he said. When we had finally finished we went upstairs and washed our hands in cold water. I asked my mom if I could go out. She wasn't happy about it at first, but eventually said it was okay. Johnny ran out the door and I happily followed him.

Once we'd got to the top of the Holme Johnny turned to me and asked why we didn't have any hot water at home. I explained that the gas and electric had been cut off because my Mom had broken into the meters. We were walking through the gully to WestHolme when I saw Granny Pegg putting the washing out. She spooted Johnny and I and shouted at us to come over. I told Gran that we was off to the park, but she asked if I'd do an errand for her first. 'Go down to the shop and get me some snuff,' she asked. Once she'd finished putting the washing out, Johnny and I followed her into her house where she got her purse out and gave me six pennies. 'Tell the woman in the shop that I want half an ounce of snuff, tell her who it's for.'

Johnny and I went down St Andrews Street into Sarah Street and as we were turning the corner into Dartmouth Street I saw the bloke with the scar on his face. He was with two other blokes and they were walking in front of us. I stopped suddenly, turned around and ran back up Sarah Street; Johnny came running after me. Johnny asked me what was going on, but I never replied. He left me after that to walk back home on my own. I went back down Sarah Street and when I got to the end I looked round the corner to see if I could see any of the blokes. Thankfully I couldn't so I ran across the horse road as fast as I could go. I ran into Barwell Road and was still running when I got to the shop. The woman behind the counter asked who was chasing me and to slow down so I could get my breath. She came from behind the counter and went outside to see if anyone was about. When she came back in she asked me what I wanted. 'Half ounce of snuff, for my Granny Pegg please,' I said handing over the six pennies. She weighed the snuff out from a tin box, it didn't quite come to half an ounce so she gave me two pennies back. I left the shop and ran all the way back to Gran's. When I passed her the snuff and the two pennies, explaining why there was money left, she said I was a good lad and that I could keep the two pennies.

I went to run out but Gran stopped me and asked what I'd been up to. 'I know you've been up to something, you were missing for two days. Come on tell your Gran,' she said kindly. I went over to the window and I saw the bloke with the scar coming into Holme. 'Gran who is that bloke?' I asked pointing him out. 'Nobody,' Gran snapped back, 'get away from the window.' I could see that there was copper coming out one of the blocks from the other side of the Holme, the bloke saw the copper and he turned ran. The copper never ran after him. Gran was standing behind me, watching what was going on. Afterwards I ran straight home without stopping. When I got back I explained to Mom where I'd been and I offered her the two pennies. She looked at me and then took the pennies from my hand. 'Go clean out the fire so I can get it going,' she said. Dinner was the same lumpy mashed potato and powdered milk. There wasn't even any bread to go with it.

At 8 o'clock Mom said it was time for bed. 'It's so cold in my room, can I stay out here?' I asked. Mom nodded yes. We sat together looking at the fire, Mom was only putting one lump of coal on at time. She would break it up and throw it on, just enough to keep us warm. When it was time for Mom to go to bed she put two small pieces coal on the fire and told me not to put any more on. The next thing I knew Tommy was waking me up. 'Nip come with me.' I got up, put my shoes on and we left together. Downstairs Tommy had a pram loaded with two bags full of coal. 'Nip go and get the coal bucket and start carrying the coal up, don't make any noise, keep very quiet.' I had to carry all the coal on my own and it took me ages! I was nearly finished when Mr Bloomer came out to see what I was doing. 'Peter what have you been up to?' he asked. 'Nothing Mr Bloomer,' I replied. He asked where the coal had come from and when I explained that Tommy had brought it Mrs Bloomer said, 'Okay, put two buckets aside in the coal, you owe me.' When I went back up the stairs Mom was up and asked what had been going on. 'Tommy brought us a load of coal,' I said to her. 'Where's Tommy now?' she asked me. I told her that I didn't know and that   Tommy had left me to sort all the coal out by myself. I went back out to the stairs and looked over the railings on the   landing. The pram had gone. I quickly ran down the stairs looking everywhere for the pram, but it was nowhere to be found. I ran back upstairs shouting to Mom that someone had nicked the pram. She didn't seem very bothered and told me to go and clean out the fire again. I had to be very careful with the warm ashes especially when I was putting them down the shoot on the veranda. This time I didn't realise that some of the ashes was still light. After a while Mom heard shouting out the back; it was Mr Bloomer. 'The bloody shoot is on fire! Throw some water down it!' The fire was really going bad and as Mom was throwing water down on our side of the shoot Mrs Fleetwood was throwing water on her side. Mr Allen was also throwing water from the top flat it, but it still took a while for the fire to go out. Mr Bloomer couldn't open the shoot door because it was too hot. After the fire was eventually out Mom had right go at me, she'd done nothing but moan at me all day. 'Run over to Able's to see if she has had any bread delivered yet,' she told me. 'Come on Mom you've already got some bread.' 'Shut up and go do as you're told!' she shouted back. So I went running down the stairs and nearly bumped into Mr Bloomer as he came out of his front door. 'What do you think you're playing at Peter?!' 'Sorry Mr Bloomer I've got over to Able's before she sells out bread,' I said. I carried on down the stairs while he shouted at me that I could get into trouble for what I'd done. I went running straight over the horse road without looking back. When I got in the shop Mrs Able came out from the back, she took one look at me and asked what I wanted. When I told her that Mom had sent me for some bread she replied that Mom hadn't ordered any bread. I must have started to be cheeky with her because she told me to get out of her shop; 'wait till I see your mother,' she said, 'go on, get out!'

When I got back home I told Mom what Mrs Able had said. At first she wanted me to go over and ask for the bread again. 'What have you done now?' she said, 'I'm may as well go over myself.' She started to put some food together, but it wasn't much. I had to eat it because I was hungry, I was getting one meal day. Mom went to bed early that night and told me not to put too much coal on the fire. She also took what food we had left to bed with her so I wouldn't try to pinch any. I was lying on the floor looking at the fire wondering when we were going to get the gas and the electric back on, it was still very cold outside. I started to fall asleep when there was load knock on the door. I went to Mom's room and told her that there was somebody at the door. 'Well go and ask who's there before you open the door,' she told me. I went to the door and slowly opened the letter box. I couldn't see anybody out there. Suddenly I heard Mr Bloomer's voice; 'Open the door Peter, it's only me.' I went to Mom's room again and told her who it was. She got up and opened the door. Mr Bloomer was standing there with a copper. 'I've come to take Peter up to the station the inspector wants to have word with him,' the copper explained. 'He'll have to wait till morning, he's not coming at this time night,' Mom replied. 'I'm sorry Mrs Round I've got to take him now.' Mom turned back inside to get dressed when Mr Bloomer stopped her, 'I'll be coming with you Mrs Round,' he said. I sat on the stairs waiting for Mom, the stairs were cold on my

85

bum. Mom came out of the house and we all started walking down the stairs. I was at the back of the group and when we got out of the block I turned and ran through the garden into the lane. I ran down the lane as fast as I could go, but the copper was chasing after me. I got to the canal and saw that gates were open. I ran down the slope along the canal path and I kept on running even though it was really dark. When I got to the locks I couldn't see the copper behind me so I decided to stop for bit. I had wee in the cut and then I started to climb to the top. I heard voices so I stopped until they passed, then I started climbing again. When I got to the top on the canal bridge I saw two blokes walking towards the railway crossing, they were carrying bags over their shoulders. A horse and cart was waiting for them, they put the bags onto the cart and covered them up. They carried on walking down Garrison Street and the horse and cart went in the other direction. I sat on top of the bridge wall for a minute then I jumped down and made my way across the crossing. Some bloke shouted to me from the signal box, I stopped and looked up at him. He asked me what I was doing out at this time of night. I didn't respond instead I just ran away and turned into Wolseley Street. I stopped running and saw two old ladies walking towards me. I suddenly started to cry so they stopped and asked me what was wrong. I told them that two blokes was chasing me. They asked where I lived and when I told them they offered to walk me back home. We started walking and they asked my name. 'Are you Dolly Round's son?' one of the ladies asked. I nodded in reply. When we walked up the lane to the railway bridge I saw Tommy pushing the pram, it was full of coal again. I ran from the two old ladies and shouted back to them that this was my brother. When I got to Tommy I explained about the copper and said that he wanted me to go with him to the police station. Tommy told me to run back to the house to check if the copper was still there.

When I got back to the block a little later Mom was standing with Mrs Bloomer. As soon as she saw me she started to shout, 'That copper has gone off with Mr

Bloomer to look for you!' she screamed. I felt scared and ran back to Tommy. I helped him to push the pram back to the block and when Mrs Bloomer saw the coal she asked Tommy if there was any for her. Tommy looked at her and then handed over one of the bags. 'Come on nip help to get the rest of the coal up quickly before the copper comes back.' Mrs Bloomer, Mom and I were running up and down the stairs as quick as we could go with the buckets of coal. Tommy didn't help at all he just went left us to it and walked off. A little later Mr Bloomer and the copper came back but they never said anything, I was standing at the top of the stairs and Mr Bloomer just looked up at me shook his head and went into his house. The copper left after that.

    The next day I was lying on the floor in the living room. It was early in the morning and there was knock on the door. I got up and walked over to the door. When I opened it I could see that there were two coppers standing there. 'Peter this time you're coming with us to the police station.' One of them got me by the arm, he was holding me tight. I tried to shout to Mom and about halfway down the stairs Mr Bloomer came out in his long johns. Mrs Price also came out to see what all the noise was about. 'Why are you taking him down to the station at this hour? The lad had done nothing wrong,' Mr Bloomer said, 'I'm going to get dressed and then I'm coming to, I'll make sure he's okay.' Mr Bloomer went back into his house but the copper never waited, they got hold of me and dragged me the rest of the way down the stairs. Mrs Price ran into Bloomer's to tell Mr Bloomer to hurry up. By the time he came down the stairs we was at bottom of the Holme walking up Garrison Lane. Both coppers were holding me, Mom and Mr Bloomer eventually caught up with us, running up the lane. As we were walking up Tilton Road I noticed two of the blokes from those two nights on the other side of the road. Mr Bloomer waved over to them, I remember thinking he must have known them. 'What's going on?' they shouted back, we just kept on walking. We got to the police station and went straight into the inspector's room. 'Peter I want to ask you few questions,' the inspector said, 'I will promise you all I want from you Peter is the truth, 'yes sir I will tell you the truth,' I replied. Then he asked me what the lads names were, if I knew the man with the scar, where was I for the two days I was missing, could you show me? I told him everything that I could, that I thought Johnny knew the lads and maybe the bloke and then I tried to explain the place I'd been taken to. Mr Bloomer came in when I'd finished speaking and told the inspector that it was time for me to go home. 'I haven't finished with Peter just yet,' the inspector said. Mr Bloomer looked over at Mom and when she nodded her head he left, closing the door behind him. I remember feeling really hungry and that I started to hold my stomach. 'What's up Peter?' the inspector asked me. When I told him how hungry I was and that I had pains he got up and told me to follow him. We went to a kitchen where there was a lady working, the inspector asked her to look after me and give me as much as I wanted to eat. She told me to sit down, at the table, which I remember was very wobbly. She gave me a sandwich made from thickly cut bread and a glass of fresh milk. She didn't really speak to me and once I'd finished she took me straight back to the inspector. He asked if I felt better and when I nodded yes he said he just had a few more questions, then I could go home. All of a sudden I was sick over his desk and the papers he had on there. He stood up quickly and then I was sick all over him too. 'Mrs Round you better take Peter home,' the inspector said. But before I got out of the room I was sick again on the floor, Mom started to do her nut. 'What have done to my son?! Look at him, just look at him!' I started to double-up with pain so the inspector he got me some water, but when I drank that I was sick again. 'You must have given the lad some bad food, he wouldn't be sick like that otherwise,' Mr Bloomer said to the inspector. When we got outside I was sick in the yard. 'Come on Peter let's get you home,' Mom said.

  When we got back I started to feel a little better and asked Mom if I could go to Granny Pegg's. 'No you can't, you can get in bed and stay there.' She started the fire in my bedroom but suddenly a load of soot came down the chimney and went all over the place. The room was full black smoke so I ran out of the room and went next door to Mrs Fleetwood's, the door was open so I went straight in. 'Can you come help Mom,' I asked her. She came straight away and went into my bedroom. Mom was covered in soot. 'Dorothy this will take a while to clean up you know,' Mrs Fleetwood said. Mrs Bloomer and Mrs Price came to see if everything was alright. When they went into see Mom they stood silently for a moment and then they all burst out laughing, including Mom. 'Come on Dorothy it's not going to clean itself,' Mrs Bloomer said, then they all helped Mom out. They fetched buckets from their houses and started filling them with water. It was my job to put the soot down the shoot but as I did the wind kept blowing it back on me, I was getting filthy. A little later Granny Pegg came round, she heard I was at the police station. When she saw the state of the bedroom she burst out laughing (it was very rare to see Gran smile let alone laugh). I got my mop bucket and we all helped to clear out my room. Mrs Fleetwood and Mrs Bloomer took my over coats to be washed. 'Where are Peter's blankets Dorothy?' Mrs Fleetwood asked as she picked them up. Mom simply replied that they were at the pawn shop. 'He can't go without any blankets,' Mrs Fleetwood replied.

Later that day I was standing in my bedroom look at the clean bed when I heard Mom crying from her room. I went into to her room and I sat alongside her. 'Don't worry Mom,' I said putting my arm around her, 'I'm going to be good boy I promise.' She looked at me and gave me big hug then she smiled. 'Go get dressed now.' As I was getting dressed there was a knock at the door. I was standing there naked by the warmth of the living room fire when the knock came again. 'Are you going to open this bloody door?' a voice said. Mom shouted to me to answer the door and when I opened it up I saw Granny Pegg standing there. She took one look at me and asked why I was standing there naked, 'Go and get yourself dressed!' She brought some food round, it wasn't lot but it would fill me and Mom up. 'What's Peter been up to now, why did he have to go the police station again? You should have fetched me I would have gone with you.' Gran was doing all the talking and Mom never got word in, she was just sitting there   listing to her. As Gran was leaving a little later she turned around and pointed her finger at Mom. 'You fetch me if Peter goes to the cop shop again Dorothy.' When she'd gone Mom sent me off to bed.

The next morning Mom gave me some food and as I was eating she was looking through the curtains. 'The inspector is coming into the block,' she said suddenly, 'go open the door for him, this time he not going to take you the station.' I opened the door as he came walking up to our door. Before he could speak Mom shouted that he wasn't going to take me away again, not after what had happened the day before. 'Mrs Round sit down, I'm not here to take Peter to the station and I'm not going to ask Peter any more questions. He has done very well. We asked his mate Johnny the same questions to see if Peter was telling us the truth. Johnny knows who they are we will take it from there. I have brought you some food to make up for yesterday. Is Peter ok now?' 'Yes,' Mom said, 'he will be going back to school shortly I think on the 8th of January.' After that the inspector got up to leave and told Mom to let him know if she saw any of the lads hanging about.

On Saturday morning Tommy came with bag full of food and when Mom asked where he'd got it from he didn't answer her and just said that she should be thankful. 'I hope you haven't pinched all that food,' she said. 'Look Mom, I'm doing my best for you and Peter,' Tommy replied. Mom started to cry; 'I've got the police coming for him [she pointed at me], the inspector's not long been here. I can't cope with what's going on all the time.' Tommy told her not to worry. 'You two will put me in early grave,' was her reply. Tommy told her that he wouldn't bring trouble to her door so that she could look after me. He left shortly after that. I ran after him and shouted down the lane for him to stop. 'What's do you want nip?' 'I don't want you to go, I want you to stay,' I said to him. He gave me a big hug and told me to go back home. I stood watching him go down the lane and when he got to the railway bridge he turned around and waved to me, I waved back.

When I got home I told Mom I was hungry. She told me that the food had to last and that I'd have to wait. 'But the pantry is full!' I said. She wasn't too happy with that, I could tell, so I ran out of the house fast I could go. I was running out the block when Mom shouted from the window 'Don't stay out too late Peter!' I ran around the corner to Granny Pegg's and as I went in I bumped into a big bloke. He pushed me out of the way, but he fell over me and hit his face on the floor. When he looked up at me his face was bleeding. When Gran came to door she shouted at him give her the purse back. I kicked him hard when I realised what he'd done. When he got up his face was still bleeding badly, he look at me and then he hit me across the head really hard. He threw Gran her purse back and when he saw two blokes coming up to see what was up, he ran off. 'Are you okay Mrs Pegg?' one of the blokes asked her. 'Yes if wasn't for this brave lad I would have lost my purse,' she replied. The blokes asked who the thief was, Gran replied that his name was Wally. I told them that I thought he lived down Coventry Street. 'We'll go and find him for you,' the blokes said as they left.

I told Gran that I was hungry; I always seemed to be hungry back then. She gave me some mash potato, two horrible sausages from a tin and a thick slice of bread. Gran sat there watching me eat and when I finished she gave me a glass of fresh milk. 'Need to fill you up till tomorrow my lad, then you can come back and have some more. You've been a brave lad you wait till I tell your uncle Billy.' Just then I heard Auntie May calling from her room next door. 'Right off you go now, I'll see you tomorrow.' As I left I told her that I didn't have to go to the cop shop again, that I'd told them the truth. 'You're a good lad peter,' Gran said to me.

I didn't notice Wally waiting for me as I turned into the archway near EastHolme on my way home. He grabbed hold of me and started to march me round the back away from my house and towards the bottom Holme. I was trying to get away from him, I tried to kick him twice so he stopped and hit me across the head; it really hurt and I started to cry. We went around the back away from NorthHolme and as we neared the gully I saw two blokes standing there. When they saw me with Wally they shouted at him to let me go but they couldn't get hold of him because there was wire netting between us. Wally let me go and he ran off. One of the blokes ran up the gully and the other ran down the gully, I think they were trying to go after Wally. I didn't hesitate; I ran all the way home.

When I got back Mom started to shout at me. 'Where the hell have you been Peter?' I explained that I'd been to Gran's and that when I was there Wally had tried to pinch her purse. I told her that I've stopped him; I'm not sure if she believed me. 'Okay,' she replied, 'go have a wash now and make sure you do your neck.' The water was cold water again. 'I'm going to make you something nice to eat,' Mom said, 'how about mash potato and sausages?' 'Are the sausages from a tin Mom,' I asked. 'Yes how did you know Peter?' I couldn't tell her that I'd already eaten, so I said that I'd seen the tin in Gran's kitchen. Mom had to cook the food over the fire, she only gave me a bit of mash potato and one sausage, which was good because they still tasted horrible. 'Who was the bloke who tried to pinch Gran's purse then?' Mom asked as we ate. 'I told you Mom, it was that bloke Wally who Mrs Price knows.'

That night Mom let me sleep in the living room again, it was a lot warmer than my bedroom. I was fast asleep with the coats pulled over me when Tommy woke me up. 'Come on nip wake up,' he whispered, 'go get the coal up from downstairs.' Mom must have heard the noise because she came out of her bedroom to see what's going on. 'Mom I got you some coal,' he said when he saw her. Before she could reply Tommy left and I had to bring the coal up by myself again. When I finished Mom looked at me and asked if I knew where Tommy was getting the coal from. I told her that I honestly didn't know. That was last time we saw Tommy for a while.

On Sunday Mom told to me go next door and ask Mrs Fleetwood if she could borrow the small tub so she could wash my school clothes ready for the next day. I had to knock on Mrs Fleetwood's door and shout through her letter box before she answered. 'What do you want?' she asked when she finally opened the door. I asked to borrow the tub and she pointed through her house towards the veranda, 'it's out there,' she said. Coming back through her kitchen with the tub Mrs Fleetwood stopped me. 'What's your Tommy been up to? Coming to your house during the night,' she asked me. I just shook my head in reply. 'He is going to get you into trouble my lad,' she said, 'what did the inspector want too?' I told her that I told them the truth and that he wasn't going to ask me anymore questions. Then I quickly left carrying the tub.

Mom got the tub on the hob and I had to fill it half full with cold water, then Mom would fill up the rest with hot water from the fire. Then all of my school clothes went in and now and then Mom would get the clothes with the tongues and lift them up and down. When the clothes were clean Mom started to dry them by the fire. She singed my trousers and my shirt, but luckily I had another pair of trousers. I still had to go to school with a singed shirt but good job I had overcoat to cover it. Mom let me sleep by the fire again that night and the next morning she made me breakfast. Johnny was waiting at the bottom of the block for me, it was a really cold day. Johnny looked very smart, he had a suit on and an overcoat. On the way to school he told me that I had to tell his Dad that I was lying. I didn't answer him, I was shivering with the cold so I started to run to get myself warm. Johnny ran after me and when he caught up with me he said again, 'tell my Dad that you're lying   Peter.' 'I'm not lying Johnny, you know who them kids are and where they live, I think one of them is your cousin,' I replied.

When we got to school one of the teachers was standing by the main door. Instead of going straight to the playground we had go through the main entrance. As I was going through the door the teacher told me that the headmistress wanted to see me in her office right away. I went to the office and walked straight in without knocking. The headmistress told me off and asked me to go back out and wait for her to call you in. While I was waiting outside Johnny came up to me and asked what I'd been called in for. I just shrugged and said that I didn't know. Just then I heard her tell me to come in and Johnny followed me. 'Are you in this together?' she asked when we got into the office. Johnny didn't reply he just stood there, I went to walk out but the headmistress stopped me. 'No Peter stay here. Johnny you wait outside, I'll call you in afterwards.' Johnny closed the door quietly behind him. 'Peter are you telling the truth?' the headmistress asked me. I promised her I was and explained that I wasn't in any trouble and that she could check with inspector Davies. 'I'm not lying,' I said, 'but Johnny is, he knows those lads.' 'I don't want any trouble from you Peter,' she said looking down at me, 'if you give me any trouble at all I will give you the cane.' I looked up at her and I started to laugh. She got the cane from the cupboard and showed it to me. 'If you hit me with that I will hit you back,' I said to her. 'Don't talk to me in that manner!' she shouted, 'who do you think you are? You are going to be my first lad to feel my cane, I will hurt you.' She banged the cane on her desk and told me to get to class before she gave me a 'taste of the cane.' She told me to send Johnny in as I left.

When I got into class everyone was sitting with their coats on, they all look clean and smart whilst I was in rags. Our teacher asked where Johnny was and when I told her she asked me to go and sit down. The classroom was so cold. Our teacher started to do some sums on the blackboard and then she turned round. 'Peter, come up here and work out these sums please,' she asked. I got up from my desk and went to the blackboard, I started to shiver with the cold. I did the first two sums and was just working on the third when the headmistress came in. 'You are all to go home please,' she said. I asked here where Johnny was but she never answered me. The class all got up and I went to follow then. 'No you don't,' the headmistress said, 'I want a word with you.' When all the kids has left our teacher stayed and closed the classroom door. 'Peter Round I want the truth from you, Johnny said you're the one who's lying.' 'No miss it's Johnny,' I promised her. 'I believe Johnny, not you,' she replied. 'What happened when you went missing?' 'I'm not going to tell you, you can piss off. The coppers believe me and they're not going to ask me no more questions. I'm going home now, if you don't let me go I will fetch my big brother to you! I'm getting hungry, I want to go to the toilet, and I'm going to wet myself,' I said angrily. She took a long look at me and then she opened the door. 'You are still lying to me Peter,' she said as I passed her. 'Piss off,' I said and then ran all the way out of the school.

    I ran straight across the horse road without looking and when I got to the corner of Witton Street I looked back and saw the bloke with the scar. He was with Johnny's Dad, they were going into the Garrison pub together. I started to shiver with the cold so I ran all the way to Granny Pegg's house. I went running straight inside; 'Gran they are all lying about me!' I shouted. 'Peter? Come and sit here, get your breath. Who is lying.' 'That bloody Johnny from top Holme he's been telling lies to the headmistress about me and she believes Johnny and not me.' 'Come on,' Gran said, 'we're going back to that school, I will tell her who is lying' and off we went, Gran was holding my hand and I remember thinking that I never saw her walk so quickly. We got to the end of the gully and she stopped, she was out of breath. 'Go back and get the wheelchair Peter, go on hurry up.' I ran up the gully as fast as I could, I went running in the back, Gran never locked the door when she left. I went straight into Auntie May's room. 'Hello Auntie May, I've come for the chair for Gran, she's out breath.' I grabbed the chair and was leaving the room when she raised her arm for me to go over to her; she wanted me to kiss her on the head. I did kiss her and then I heaved the chair out of the room and outside. I finally made it back to Gran, though she wondered why it had taken me so long. The chair was running away from me when I was pushing her down the lane, I had to really hold it tight. When we got to the school Gran got up and I had to hold her. As we went up the steps she asked where the office was, I led her in the right direction. We got to the office and Gran never bothered to knock, she just went walking straight in. The headmistress looked surprised and asked what was going on. 'My grandson has been telling you the truth all along,' Gran said, 'it's that bloody Johnny who's been lying to you, you leave my grandson alone. I don't want to come here again, but if I do come back you will get a taste my tongue.' We were going out the office when the headmistress said 'Mrs Round?' Gran replied 'Do I look like his mother? You should know his mother, I'm not Mrs Round, I'm his Granny Pegg.' I stood there laughing 'Come on Peter, take your grin off your face and let's go,' Gran said. Outside Gran got in the chair and I started to push her again. We were passing the Garrison when Johnny's Dad came out. I started to push gran up Garrison Lane, we had just got to the canal bridge when he caught us up and started pushing Gran. I was waiting for Gran to say something to hi, but she never said anything. We got to the gully and we both said thank you. I looked back as we left and Johnny's Dad was just standing there. He pointed his finger at me so I pulled my tongue out to him then he showed me his fist. I showed him my tongue again and then carried on pushing Gran up the gully. Further down she told me to stop, she said to me to come and stand in front of her. 'I want you to look at me Peter, I want you to tell me the honest truth.' I started to shiver with the cold, 'I'm telling the truth Gran! You can ask the bloody copper he's not going to ask me no more questions, he knows I was telling him the truth.' 'Which copper Peter, that inspector Davies?' she asked. I nodded yes and then said I was hungry and asked if we could go home.

    Once we got back Gran found me something to eat. I didn't have long though, before I knew it she told me we were going back out to the police station. Before we left she went into Auntie May's room to see if she was alright. I went to run out but Gran stopped me and asked where I thought I was going. I had to get the chair and bring it to the steps at the back of the house. I pushed Gran all the way up Garrison Lane then into Tilton Road, up the hill then into Cattell Road. We went through the gully where there was some back-to-back houses then into Greenway Street then onto the Coventry Road where the police station was. Gran got out of the chair went through the station door and went straight to the copper who was behind the desk. She pointed her finger at him; 'I demand to see that bloody inspector now,' she said. The copper behind the desk replied, 'He's not here at the moment. What's your name?' 'Never mind who I am just go get the inspector out here now.' I stood there looking at the copper, he and Gran was making me laugh. The copper told Gran to go and sit down, but she refused to. The copper came from the behind the desk and stood in front of her. 'Madam if you don't sit down and keep quiet I will throw you out.' Gran wasn't having any of that, but after a few minutes the copper got Gran to understand and she eventually sat down. The copper went back behind his desk and although she was sitting down, she carried on grumbling at him. The copper looked over at me and asked what my name was. 'Peter Round sir,' I told him. 'Now we are getting somewhere,' the copper said. 'Now Mrs Round you tell me.' 'I'm not his mother, I'm his Gran,' she shouted at him. She got up from the chair and went back over to the desk. 'Look here young man, I want to know if my grandson is telling the truth or not.' Before the copper could say anything the inspector came walking in with another copper. Gran looked him and asked the same question that she'd just asked the copper behind the desk. 'Mrs Pegg your grandson Peter is telling the truth. He has been a good lad.' Gran stood silently for a moment thinking about what she'd just heard, then she nodded and turned to me. 'Right come on then Peter, we're going down to that bloody school of yours.' 'Mrs Pegg there's no need we have just come from there. All we want Peter to do when them three kids come and start to hang around the school is to go tell the teacher,' the inspector said. Then he turned to me and asked if I was hungry. I told him that I was and then Gran said she was too. 'Follow me then, we will go to the kitchen and see what we've got in there.' We followed the inspector to the kitchen where he found us some eggs. He got the other copper to cook them for us while he sorted out some bread. Gran and me had an egg sandwich each, the bread was cut really thick so I couldn't eat it all. The inspector wrapped up what was left and handed it to me as we left.

We went out of the station and Gran got back in the chair. On the way home I stopped and went to stand in front of Gran. 'I told you I was telling the truth all the time,' I said to her. 'Peter I have known you was telling me the truth, I will always believe you, you are good lad and I hope you grow up to be good man. Now come on, get me home it's getting really cold.' I stood there looking at her for a moment and then I kissed on the forehead. 'Come on Gran, I'll get you back.' This time we went different way home, around Kingston Road the way down long St Andrews Road and then into Ada Road. As we went passed the school on Ada Road Gran said, 'You will be going to that school, I can keep an eye on you. I can see you going to school every morning and then back when you pass my house.' I finally got Gran home and settled and she told me to make sure I told Mom where I'd been as soon as I got back. 'Here take the sandwiches home with you too,' she said handed them to me.

When I got home Mom wasn't in but the key was behind the door so I let myself in. Before I could close the door Mrs Price came running in. 'Are you in trouble again Peter?' she asked. 'I saw you and your Gran going into the police station, there's been copper looking for you. Come on Peter we are all here to help you.' I stood there shivering, the house was really cold. I looked up at Mrs Price and I told her to piss off. 'What do you say? You heard me, go!' I shouted at her. Mom came in just then and she heard must have heard what I said to Mrs Price because she slapped me across the head twice and it really hurt me. 'Say you're sorry to Mrs Price!' she shouted in my face. I ran into my bedroom and slammed the door behind me. Mom came after me and banged on the door. 'Get out here now! You better say sorry or you will get another slap!' I heard Mrs Price telling Mom about the copper who came to the house, she also told her she saw Gran and me going into the police station. 'I'm sick of this!' Mom shouted and I heard her bang the   table with her fist. 'What have you been up to now Peter?' 'Mom if you listen to me I will tell you the truth,' I called through the door. 'I'm in no trouble. Yes Gran took me to the cop shop but only because the headmistress said I was lying, she believes Johnny and not me about them three kids who keeps hanging around the school.' There was silence for a minute and then Mom said, 'You still haven't said sorry to Mrs Price.' I opened my bedroom door and went into the living room. I looked at Mrs Price and, in low voice I said, 'I'm sorry Mrs Price.' She nodded at me. 'Come on now, clean out the grate Peter,' I told me. Shortly after Mrs Price went back to her house and as I was cleaning out the fire I told Mom that the headmistress said she'd give me the cane if I didn't start telling the truth. 'I'm coming to that school in the morning, I'm going to give her a piece of my mind you wait till I get there.' I could tell Mom was really angry.

    During the night Tommy arrived outside with another of load coal. He was with another bloke who also had pram full of coal. Once again Tommy woke me up and then left me to carry all the coal up from two prams by myself. The coal house was getting really full by then. I hardly got any sleep that night and come the next morning I was lying by the fire trying to keep warm. When Mom woke me I asked her if I had to go to school explaining that I was so tired because Tommy had come with more coal. Mom went to have look how much coal we had and then asked, 'Did Tommy bring all that coal last night?' I nodded yes. I went into the kitchen and had a quick wash. Mom had followed me and told me to wash behind my ears and to give my neck a good wash. When I finished I got ready for school and then Johnny came calling for me. He knocked our door and Mom called out asking who was there. When Johnny shouted back Mom said, 'Oh it's you, you got my Peter in trouble with the headmistress you know.' 'No Mrs Round I never said anything to her, I was told by my Dad to keep my mouth shut or I would feel his back of his hand. All I said to her was ask Peter and that's the truth Mrs Round.' 'Come on you two, I want to see that bloody teacher of yours.' Mom walked to school with us and when we got there the headmistress was waiting by the main entrance. As soon as she saw us she shouted over for us to come to her office. When we got there Mom said to her, 'Look here what are you accusing my son of? You told Peter that he was lying to you and you said that you believe Johnny! I'm going to tell you now, Peter is in no trouble with the police. Tell me what you are accusing him of? Come on I haven't got all day.' Mom stood looking the headmistress straight in the face. 'Mrs Round if you let me speak for a moment. The police have confirmed that Peter isn't in any trouble, but he has been very cheeky. He pulled his tongue out to me.' 'You can't give my son the cane for that!' Mom replied. 'You better watch out or you will be hearing from me and his Gran, do I make myself clear?' I stood behind Mom while they were talking, Johnny was making me laugh and was pulling faces behind Mom's back. She looked in the mirror in front of her and she saw what Johnny was doing. Mom turned right around and gave both me and Johnny a slap around our faces. 'Now you pair say you're sorry to the headmistress!' 'That's okay Mrs Round, they can just go along to their classroom now.' As we left the office the headmistress told Mom that she'd be sending the whole school home after dinner. Mom turned to me and told me to go straight to Granny Pegg's when we'd finished.

    We never did any school work that day and before we ran out of school at dinnertime the headmistress came into the classroom and announced that we didn't have to come in the next day. After that we all ran out of the gates, I looked over the road and saw Johnny and his dad with the bloke with the scar standing on the corner of Witton Street by the park. They were looking at me and Johnny's dad shouted over to me. I ignored him and instead I ran up the lane fast I could go. I kept looking around to see if they were following me as I made my way to Granny Pegg's. When I got there she asked if I'd been to school, so I explained that we got sent home early and that we didn't have to go in the next day. Gran had made some cakes so we sat together and ate some. A little later when Mom arrived Gran told her that she really needed to sort it out. 'The poor lad is never going to learn anything if they keep sending him home from that school.' Mom didn't reply to her and just told me that it was time to go home. 'Thanks for the cakes Gran,' I said as we went out of the door.

As soon as we got home I had to clean out the fire again. The, once she'd got the fire going, Mom toasted some bread and made me cup of oxo (where she got the oxo from I don't know). It was very good, nice and hot and I dipped the toast in to the cup. Mom had one piece of toast with the powered egg on it, she gave me the rest of the bread that we had left. Time was getting on and Mom told me that I could sleep out in the living room that night. When she went to bed I piled the coal onto the fire right up to the start of the chimney and then I got down on the floor and put the overcoats over me. Next thing I knew Tommy was kicking me awake because piece of coal had fallen from the fire. If Tommy had not come home when he did the house would have gone up. When Mom came out of her bedroom she did nothing but shout at me, she kept on all night long even when I was getting the coal up Tommy had brought another pram full of the stuff.

It was getting towards end of January of 1947 and when the snow came it was pretty heavy. Tommy was looking after us and also the others in the block. He made sure we all had enough coal to last through the winter. We had no food, no gas, and no electric so Tommy could only leave us enough food to last for one meal. One Friday morning I looked out the window and I could see that it was snowing. I crept out to the kitchen to see if there was any food in the pantry, but it was empty. I stood by the kitchen door thinking what I could do, then I crept out of the house and went down the stairs. When I got to the entrance to the block the snow was coming down pretty heavy but I went out into it and started to walk down the lane. I don't know where I was walking to, I got to the horse road and started to get really wet, but I kept on walking. I eventually got to the school which seemed to take me ages. I stood by the school gate for a while; there was nobody else about. After a while I said to myself 'I'll go to the bakery.'

    The snow was still coming down, but I carried on walking and it seemed easier to walk in the horse road. I got to the bakery and found that the gates were open and the door was also open a crack. I opened bit more and went in. I was standing by the door shivering when this old lady came up to me and took a look at me. Then she shouted to somebody inside and a bloke came over. 'Oh it's you again,' he said to me. The old lady asked the bloke to help me, 'Look at hime,' she said, 'he's shivering with the cold.' The bloke was having go at me though, 'You shouldn't be out this time in the morning nor in this weather.' Then he went outside and came back in straight away. 'It's stopped snowing, if you want some bread you've got to work for it,' he told me. He went away again and came back with a shovel. 'Go on, move the snow away from the bakery.' He showed me where I had to shovel the snow to and as I started the old lady came out and told me to come back in once I'd finished so she could dry my clothes off for me. Then she asked why I was out so early, if I had any brothers or sisters, and what my parents were doing. When I explained that we didn't have any food, gas or electric at home the old lady sighed and told me to get the snow shovelled and that she'd 'sort me out.' She was walking away when she turned and asked if my mother worked. I replied that my Mom has been very ill lately.

    I work very hard shifting the snow and when I'd finished the bloke came out and said, 'Well done lad, come on now let's get them wet clothes off you, follow me.' It was nice warm in the bakery and I followed him into an office. 'Take your clothes off and put this around you,' the bloke said passing me a white coat. He went out of the office with my clothes and came back with cup of hot milk and two pieces of thick toast with some butter on. I was there for some time when the bloke came back with my dry clothes, two loaves, a tin of dried egg powder, a tin of powder milk, and two tins of meat. He wrapped the bread up and put it all in a bag together while I got dressed. As I went to leave I thanked the bloke for the food and for drying my wet clothes for me. He said it was no problem and told me to get home safely. He stood watching me as I walked away, staying in the horse road as I went.

There were a few blokes about as I walked and they kept looking at me. When I got to Gordon Street there was a copper on the corner. As I passed him he look at me, 'Come here lad, what are you doing out this time in the morning?' 'I went to get some bread from the bakery,' I replied. The copper asked to look in the bag and when he did he asked if I'd nicked it all. 'Come on, you are coming back to the bakery with me,' he said, despite me swearing that I was telling the truth. When we got to the bakery he led me to the front door, he kept knocking but nobody answered. 'Sir, you've got to go around the back.' He grabbed me by the arm and we went round the back together. The gate was still open but this time the big door was closed, so the copper banged on it. The old lady opened the door and she looked at us standing on the door step. 'What are you doing with that poor lad?' she asked the copper. 'I have come to see if this lad has stolen the bread and the other things he has in the this bag,' he said holding the bag up. 'Look here copper,' the old lady said, 'that poor lad has worked really hard moving all the snow out the front there, the gaffer gave him all what he's got in his bag as a thank you.' The copper looked down at me sheepishly, 'Go on lad get yourself home then.'

It started to snow again as I was walking away and I heard the copper shout to me to wait where I was. I waited for him to catch me up; 'Come on lad I'm going to see you get home safe.' He carried my bag for me and he asked me where I lived. I told him the flats and he said 'Let's get you home then, I bet your mother will be worried about you when she finds out you been out in this weather.' When we got to the Holme I said, 'Thank you for seeing me home sir,' then went to take the bag from him. 'No you don't I'm coming to your house, which block do you live in?' I pointed to the last one on the right. Walking up the Holme Mrs Bloomer came out of our block, 'Your mother is going out of her mind worrying about you!' Then she looked up at the copper, 'What's the little b***d been up to now?' she asked him. I stood there shivering while they talked then Mrs Price came out and looked at me. 'Have you been trouble again Peter?' she asked. Before she could say anything the copper said in loud voice, 'He's in no trouble at the moment, it's up to his mother.' Mom must have heard what was going on because she suddenly came out of the block. She looked at the copper she shouted, 'Take him away! I don't want to know him, I'm not going to the station with you. Get him out my sight now!' She walked back into the house and the copper shouted after her, 'Mrs Round can I see you for minute, it won't take long.' 'You can come up, but he can stay out there, I don't want to see him.' The copper went up while I sat on the cold stairs shivering and waiting. Mrs Bloomer and Mrs Price kept on asking me what I'd been up to. 'Come on Peter tell your Auntie Bloomer, if you tell me I'll try fix it with your mother.' I just sat there shivering saying nothing and just looking at them. 'Looks like your Mom is going to have you put away this time,' Mrs Price said. I still said nothing and then the copper came out of the house. 'Come on Peter, your Mom wants to speak to you.' I went running up the stairs and Mrs Bloomer and Mrs Price followed me, but the copper closed the door on them before they could come into our house. When I got into the living room Mom look at me, 'Is that the truth Peter what the copper said to me?' I nodded yes. Mom started to cry, 'I have been worried about you, going out in this weather.' The copper said that he was going and that I was a brave lad for going out in the snow to find some food. 'Peter look after your mother and don't go out again in this sort of weather,' he said to me as he left. As the copper was going out of the door Mrs Bloomer, Mrs Price and Mrs Fleetwood pushed past him nearly knocking him over. Then they all came in and asked Mom what was going on this time. They barely gave Mom a chance to reply to their questions. 'Come on give Dorothy chance to speak,' Mrs Price eventually said. Mom looked at all three of them and said, 'Look at my brave son.' I was standing by the fire shivering trying to get warm and trying to dry out. Mom told them the story and when she had finished they all said, 'well done' and how brave I'd been. A little later, as they left and closed the door behind them, Mom came over to me and she slapped me straight across the head. You don't know how I was worried about you!' Then she slapped me across the head again and she started to cry. Then she sat down by the table and she started to take out what was in the bag. She couldn't believe what was in there. 'I can't believe how brave you've been getting all this food,' then she got up from the table and she came over to me by the fire. She pointed her finger at me, 'You don't go out again in that weather, you could have been killed do you understand me? What made you go out in the first place? You wait till your Granny Pegg hears about what you've been up to. Please Peter be a good lad for me? Every time you go out I get worried about what trouble you are going to get up to. You and your brother Tommy will be the death of me. I'm worried where he is getting all the coal from he must be nicking it from somewhere,' she started to ramble on. 'I don't know where he is living; has he told you?' I shook my head 'no.' 'I don't know when you are going to start back to school, the sooner the better then I know where you are.'

I was off from school for two or three weeks because of the snow it was very bad come February when we started back. Mom was taking me there every day making sure I went in. That didn't last long, she must have started to trust me to go by myself and that I'd go straight to Gran's afterwards. After about two weeks being back at school the three lads started to hang around again and this time the headmistress saw them too. The class never went out to the playground at break time because it was really cold. One day the headmistress came into the classroom and asked to see me outside. I went out with her to the main entrance of the school and we stood by the door. She pointed to Tom, Dick, and Harry who were standing in the park. 'Are they those three lads the police want to question?' she asked me. 'Yes miss,' I replied straight away. We went back inside and she told me to go back to class.

Later, at home time Johnny came out with me and as we left the school gates we saw the three lads on the opposite side of the road. I think they were waiting for me. Johnny and I tried to get lost in the crowd leaving the school but the lads caught up with us. They wanted me to go with them. I ran away when they said, I ran all the way to Granny Pegs. Johnny came running after me, he caught me up and he got me by the collar. He was taller than me and he pushed me over, he got on top of me and he was going to hit me. 'You're coming with us all tonight Peter.' I waited a moment and then I nodded in reply. I slowly got up, there was still snow on the ground and my clothes were wet from been pushed down. 'I've got to go to Gran's first,' I said. 'Okay, but I'm coming with you.' I asked him where we were going that night, but he didn't really reply, he just said, 'You're going to be a look out Peter.'

When we got to Granny Pegg's we went straight in and found her sitting in her usual place by the window. 'Are you two both hungry?' she asked us. When we told her that we were because we hadn't had any at school again Gran rolled her eyes. As she got up to go the toilet I asked her, 'Gran I want a wee is that okay?' 'Of course it is, go on then you know where the toilet is.' This was my chance. I went out the living room and I closed the door behind me. I crept to the front door and slowly opened it, trying not to make any noise. Once I was outside I ran out the block as fast I could go. I ran straight home but when I saw that Mom wasn't in I banged on Mrs Fleetwood door instead. 'What's up Peter?' she asked when she saw me standing there trying to catch my breath. 'It's them three lads, they're after me again!' 'Okay, you can stop here till your Mom comes home. Don't you worry, come on in.' It was nice and warm inside. We were sitting by the fire together and she started to ask me questions about Tommy and where he was getting the coal from. 'I don't know Mrs Fleetwood and that's the honest truth,' I told her. She gave me a cup of hot milk made with powder, it was really nice and tasted better than what I usually had at home. A little later Mom came back. Mrs Fleetwood saw her coming up the stairs and called out the window to her. When Mom came in and saw me there she asked why I wasn't at Gran's, 'You should be waiting there for me to pick you up.' Mrs Fleetwood told Mom it was them three lads chasing me again. 'It's true Mom I was going round to Granny Pegg's after school and Johnny was playing about, he pushed me over, see look at my clothes!' Mom took one look at my dirty clothes and said, 'Pushed you over did he? Oh did he wait till I see him.'

The next day Johnny came calling for me, he came up to our door and Mom called him inside. 'Come on Johnny I want the truth from you,' she asked once he was in the living room. 'Are those three lads hanging around the school again yes or no?' Johnny looked over at me and then replied, 'Yes Mrs Round they are.' 'Okay, I will take both of you to school and if them three lads are there then God help them.' On the way to school Johnny whispered to me asking if I'd said anything to my Mom, I replied that I hadn't. 'I didn't want to go with you Johnny, that's why I ran away from you and left you at Gran's,' I told him. I paused for a moment and then asked, 'Did you go with them last night?' Johnny looked at me, 'No I wanted you to come with me, I don't want to go on my own.' As we approached the school gates we didn't see Tom, Dick, and Harry. In fact we didn't see them for a while.

It was a Friday night and it was late when there was a big bang on the door. I went to open it but Mom said, 'No they will go away, just leave it.' Then there was another big knock so I slowly walked up to the door and opened it very slightly. Standing outside was my other brother, Albert. He was in his army uniform and when I saw him I jumped up and down with joy. I put my arms round him and he said, 'Okay nip, you can let go now.' He came inside and I closed the door behind us. He look around, 'What's going on Mother have your lights been cut off?' Mom nodded in reply. 'Okay,' Albert said, 'we'll see what we can do on Monday for you. Where's Tommy?' 'He comes and he goes, he's never here half the time,' Mom told him. Once Albert had dropped off his bag he told Mom he was popping out for a bit. He wasn't gone for long and and when he came back, Tommy was with him. It was very late when they returned and we all slept on the floor together. I lay between them, I remember feeling overjoyed that my two big brothers were with me that night. Come Saturday morning I kept following them round the house, I just wanted to be nearer them as much as I could. They kept on talking to each other, but they were whispering so I couldn't hear what they were saying. On the Saturday evening they both went out but Albert came back first. He came out on to the veranda and in a very calm voice he said, 'Peter give me my rifle back.' I had been playing with it pretending to fire from the veranda. He looked at me, he had real calm way about him. 'Peter don't you ever let me find you playing with this again, it's not a toy it's very serious weapon.' Once I passed it back to him he went into Mom's room and said, 'Mother I got something to tell you. I'm getting married next month, we've set the date for 22 March.' I was shocked and didn't know how Mom would react. She was quiet for a minute and she jumped up and hugged Albert. She was very happy and had started to cry. Mom told Tommy the news when he got back later that night. Tommy congratulated Albert and then asked when he had to leave. 'I've got to go back by 6 o'clock Thursday morning,' Albert replied.

    Monday morning came and Tommy was up first. I thought he had already gone but he came out of the bedroom in his R.A.F. Uniform. It was the first time I had seen him in his uniform and it was the last. Tommy and Albert left together, but Albert returned a little later. 'Mother I've got some good news for you, your gas and electric will be back on by the end of week me, and Tommy have fixed for you.'

Come Wednesday afternoon Mom and I went to see Albert off from New Street Station. Albert's future wife was already there and we stood on platform 7 with a number of soldiers. When the train arrived at the platform there lots of pushing with the soldiers trying to get on the train first. Albert got on, put his kit bag and his rifle on the train then he came back over to me. He got me one side and he put his hands on my shoulders, he look straight into my eyes and said, 'Nip you look after mother, don't get into any trouble, I don't want Mother worried about you do understand me?' I look at him and nodded my head, he put his arm around my shoulder, 'I'm going to trust you nip.' We walked back to Mom together and then he went over to his future wife. He kissed her goodbye and then he got on the train. He'd managed to get by the window and we all waved him off. Together Mom, Iris (Albert's future wife), and I walked up to Queen's drive. We stood there for while Mom and Iris were talking. When we eventually got to the top of the bull ring Iris said her goodbyes and left us. Mom and I had to walk home because we only had money to get into town and not back again. As we walked Mom asked me what Albert had said to me at the station. 'He told me to look after you and to keep out of trouble,' I said to her. It was still cold out and when we got to Great Barr bridge the old lady from the bakery she shouted over to me. 'I've got something for you at the bakery,' she said, 'you've got a good lad there.' We walked over to the bakery and we waited outside until the old woman appeared. She came out with an overcoat, a loaf, and a tea cake. Mom took the food and I put the coat on, it was a bit big on me but it was warm so I kept it on. Mom thanked the lady for her kindness and we left. As we were walking away the old lady shouted out again, 'Come back to the bakery on Saturday and I will find you job lad.' 'You're not working for nothing Peter,' Mom said as we walked away.

A little later we passed the school and Mom stopped. 'I'm going in to see what's going on,' she said. When we got to the headmistress' office she was just coming out. 'Mrs Round what's been the matter with

Peter? He should have started back on Monday.' Mom looked at her and said, 'Look here you have been sending Peter home, you close the school for days and now you're saying he should have started to school on Monday. What's going on here? He's not learning anything!' 'I'm sorry Mrs Round I can't say anything, my hands are tied,' the headmistress replied. Mom shouted back, 'There's something going on here and I'm going to find out!' The headmistress looked at me, 'Peter we will see you in the morning,' and then she went back into her office. On the way home Mom kept on saying, 'I know there's something going on at that school of yours.' When we got home it was so cold inside that I cleaned the fire out straight away so we could get a new one going. As I got the ashes up I tripped over the grate, the ashes went all over the floor. 'Look what you've done,' Mom shouted when she saw the mess I'd made. 'Get this tidied up quickly.' I had to clean the floor with a wet rag but I was making it worse. 'Get out of the way, I'll do it myself,' Mom said. 'Go and have a wash and then I'll make you a tea cake.' I had to wash in cold water again and a little later, after we'd eaten we sat by the fire together. All of a sudden Mom looked at me and she started to laugh, then I started to laugh. When I asked her what was funny Mom said, 'You, your neck's filthy, you washed your face but you forgot to wash your neck.' A little later, when it was quite late Mom said that she was going to trust me to sleep out in the living room, 'Don't pile the coal up and be very careful,' she warned me. After she went into her bedroom I got up and went into the kitchen where I washed my neck properly. Then I went into my room and fetched all the overcoats. Before I got down on the living room floor I put three lumps of coal on the fire.

During the night Tommy came in very quietly. 'It's only me nip, go back to sleep,' he said when I sat up and looked at him. He lay down by my side and I got really warm and cosy. The following morning Tommy did me some toast and then said he was off. 'Can I come with you/' I asked him. 'Not this time nip, you've got to go to school. Tell Mom that I will back tonight and that you will have your gas and the electric back on today or tomorrow.' As Tommy was walking out of the door Mom opened her bedroom door. She ran out after him and shouted to him, asking when she'd see him again. Tommy shouted back that he'd be home that night. When Mom came back in I could see that that wasn't too pleased. She left the front door open behind her and Mrs Fleetwood followed her in. 'Everything alright Dorothy?' she asked. 'It's Tommy,' Mom replied, 'I don't know what's he's is getting up to, I'm getting worried about him. And as for him,' she pointed her finger at me then, 'them pair are a right double act. You better get ready for school Peter and make sure you have a proper wash this time.'

Mom walked me to school and we met Johnny at the gates, but it wasn't only him waiting there for me. I saw two coppers standing just inside the playground. When they spotted me I went to run away, but Mom shouted to me to come back. Johnny Mom and I walked up to the coppers and I asked what all the fuss was about. 'I'd like to know that myself,' Mom said, 'what's Peter done this time? Whatever he's done I want to know.' The coppers looked at each other and then one of them turned to Mom, 'I want to ask Peter and Jonny a few questions about three lads that keep hanging around the school, follow us to the headmistress' office,' he said nodding towards the entrance. When we got inside one of the coppers stood by the office door and the other copper stood in front of the desk. Johnny and I we had to stand in front of him while he spoke to us. 'Okay boys, were you with those three lads the other day?' Before I could answer Mom shouted at the copper, 'He was with me all day, we saw his brother who's in the army off at new street station.' 'Mrs Round I would like Peter to answer the question,' the copper said calmly. The copper turned back to me and waited for my reply. 'My Mom is telling you the truth sir,' I told him. 'I saw Peter with his mother, they were here yesterday although Peter hadn't been to school for three days,' the headmistress confirmed. The copper turned to her, 'We've got three lads down at the station and all three of them said Peter and Johnny were with them all day.' Mom asked when they arrested the lads and the copper told her it was the previous evening. 'Two lads were seen running away after we arrested the other three,' the copper said. 'Well it wasn't Peter!' Mom pushed me away and approached the copper, she pointed her finger at him. 'Peter was with me all day, the old lady at Wilson's bakery gave him an overcoat,' she pointed to the coat I was wearing, 'I can take you there now, they told him he can go on Saturday morning and they will find him a job.' The coppers looked and each other again and the one doing all the talking sighed. 'Okay Peter you can go.' As I was leaving Johnny began to follow me, but the copper stopped him, 'Not you Johnny, I want to ask you some questions.'

Outside the office Mom left and I went to my class, but before I sat down I asked the teacher if I could go to the toilet. As I was going down the corridor towards the toilets I saw the coppers coming out of the headmistress' office with Johnny. I started to walk up to Johnny, but one of the coppers pushed me away and told me to go back to my classroom. I watched the coppers take Johnny out of school and I went to follow them. The headmistress said, 'Where do you think you're going Peter?' 'Nowhere miss,' I replied, then I added 'are they taking Jonny to the cop shop miss?' 'Yes now go back to your class.' At dinner time the whole school was sent home yet again. I walked home on my own and as I was walking up the lane I saw the bloke with the scar on his face coming out of Grey Street. He looked over and shouted to me, 'Come here Peter.' I went over to him and he put his hand on my shoulder he asked me where Johnny was and I explained that the coppers had taken him away. 'I want you to come with me,' he whispered. 'I can't my mom is waiting for me,' I replied, I was starting to get scared. He got hold of me and put his hand around my neck starting to lead me away; he was hurting me now. We walked down the lane over the canal bridge and then as we were coming around the corner from Wolsely Street I saw two coppers. When the bloke saw them too he quickly let me go. I turned around and ran back up the lane as fast as I could go. When I got to the gully I ran up it and who was coming into the gully from the other direction but Wally. When he saw me he started to run towards me so I turned back on myself and ran back the way I came. 'Run Peter, run fast,' I said to myself. Wally was starting to catch up with me and I had a good idea. 'I'll just go to Mrs Bloomer house, I can get in round the back,' I thought. I banged on the back door of the Bloomer's really hard and I heard a voice shout, 'Hang on a minute!' Wally was about to grab my collar when Mrs Bloomer opened the back door. 'What's going on here?' she asked when she opened the door. By then Wally had grabbed my collar, 'This little bast**d is coming with me,' he growled. He started to drag me along the ground when Mrs Price came running out of her door. She ran up to Wally and told him to let go of me, but he just pushed her out the way and she fell to the ground. Mrs Bloomer shouted to Mr Bloomer to come quickly. When Wally saw Mr Bloomer come running he finally let go of me and ran off. Mr Bloomer asked me what I'd been up to this time and I explained that I was just walking home from school as we'd been sent home early when Wally grabbed me. 'Come on Peter let's go inside,' Mr Bloomer said. I went into their house and he gave me cup of hot milk, then he asked me why the school sent us home again. 'My Mom asked the headmistress yesterday but she wouldn't tell her,' I said.

When Mom came home and passed the Bloomer's front door Mrs Bloomer spotted her and called her inside. 'The school sent him home again,' she explained, 'oh and some bloke tried to drag him off earlier.' Mom looked at me and asked who it was. 'It was Wally Mom, he was the one who try to steal Gran's purse.' She said that she'd go to the police station and report him. 'No don't do that Mrs Round,' Mr Bloomer told her, 'leave that bloke to me, I'll see no harm comes to Peter. When I see this Wally again he won't bother Peter anymore.' I looked at Mr Bloomer, 'You never mentioned the bloke with the scar, he was after me too you know.' 'Don't worry about him either Peter, just make sure that you stay out trouble.'

We left the Bloomer's after that and walked up the stairs to our house. Once we got inside I told Mom about the coppers taking Johnny to the cop shop. 'So Johnny was with them and he tried to get you in trouble,' Mom said, 'you stay away from him Peter.' I tried to tell her that he was my mate, but she shook her head and just told me to keep away from him and then to clean the fire out. I must have left the front door open because as we were talking a big bloke came walking in, he never knocked he just walked in. Mom was in the kitchen and when she saw him she asked who he was. 'I'm here to put to your electric on,' the bloke told her, 'it's going to cost you a shilling.' He put the electric on very quickly and as he was going out the door he turned to Mom and said, 'Don't get breaking into the meter again Mrs Round, I will be back in two weeks' time to empty it. I see you had the gas cut off too, why was that?' Mom didn't reply except to tell him to piss off. After three months of having no electric it was great to walk around the house without having to carry a candle.

The following Friday I was on my way out the house to school but when I opened the door there was a bloke standing there. 'I'm here to put you're gas,' he explained. I called to Mom and she let him in the house to get the job done. When he finished he turned to Mom and said, 'It's only going to last you short time and if you're thinking of breaking into the meter when it's full, don't, you could gas yourself. I'll be back in a week to empty the meter and every week after that.' He left and Mom shouted at me to get to school or else I'd be late. Even though I ran all the way there I was still late so I went straight to my class. 'Peter Round go sit down I will speak to you when school finishes,' our teacher said when I went in. As I walked to my desk I looked around to see if Johnny was there, but his seat was empty. No surprise but at dinner time we was told to go home again. I was ready to run out of the class, but our teacher stopped me, 'I want a word with you Peter,' she said. Nancy was standing by the door singing to me,

'You're in big trouble Peter Round,' pulling her tongue out as she closed the door behind her. 'Right Peter, I have been worried about you,' the teacher said to me, 'what kind of trouble you are in?' 'I'm in no trouble miss and that's the truth.' 'Your friend Johnny is in trouble, do you know what it's about?' 'No I don't miss,' I replied, 'I know that my Mom is wondering why we keep getting sent home from school,' I asked her. She just looked at me and said, 'You can go home now Peter and I'll see you on Monday and don't be late.'

    I went running out of school and saw that Tommy was waiting for me at the gates. 'Tommy! Tommy we got the gas and the electric back on,' I told him happily. He put his hand around my shoulder, 'Come on nip, let's go home.' He was carrying a bag on his back, it looked heavy. As we were walking up the lane Wally was standing by the entrance of the canal and I pointed to him. 'Tommy see that bloke over there? He's been trying to get me to go with him.' Straight away Tommy dropped the bag and ran after Wally who turned and ran down the slope to the cut. He had a good start on Tommy who couldn't catch him. Tommy came back and I told him about Wally trying to pinch Granny Pegg's purse. When we got home Tommy passed Mom the bag and said, 'There's plenty of food in there for you and Peter.' 'So where have you been staying,' mom asked putting the bag of food onto the table. Tommy never answered but just said, 'I'm going now Mom.' 'That's it, off you go again! You're never here when I need you!' Mom told him. She was getting all the food out, there were potatoes, tins of meat, powdered milk, powdered egg, tinned sausages and two loafs of bread. Mom looked at Tommy, 'Are you sure you haven't pinched all this food?' she asked him. Tommy said he hadn't and that she should trust him and then off he went to the front door. I ran after him and asked if I could go with him. 'Not this time nip,' he replied, 'next time you can come with me.' I followed Tommy out of the block and ran to the end of the Holme, I watched him go down the lane and I kept waving to him until I couldn't see him anymore. Come Saturday morning I was still sleeping on the floor by the fire. Once I was up and washed I shouted to mom and said that I was going to the bakery. At first she wasn't keen to let me go, but eventually she said, 'Okay you can go, but watch what you're doing and don't let them pick on you.' I ran all the way to the bakery and when I got there the gates was open so I went straight in. The old lady was there and told me to come in and start sweeping the floor up first. There was flour everywhere but I managed to get it all up. Then I had to sweep the yard and tidy some boxes up. The gaffer came out with the old lady and said, 'You've worked hard today Peter.' Then he gave me three shillings, two loaves and two tea cakes. He put them in a bag and told me to bring the bag back when I finished school on Monday. I was pleased as punch as I was walking up the lane heading home when I saw Wally again. He was standing by the entrance of the canal but I was on the other side of the horse road. I couldn't run because the bag was heavy, so I kept looking round, he was watching me all the way up the lane. I got home safe and thankfully he never follow me. The front door was open and when I walked in Mom said that I looked pleased with myself and asked how much they paid me. I showed her my two shillings and the food. I explained that I'd swept the floor in the bakery and the yard and tidied a few boxes up. 'As long they didn't pick on you,' Mom said, then she went into the kitchen asking me to give her the money as she went. 'I worked for that Mom,' I said. 'You've got to help your poor Mom, those two shillings can go towards the gas and electric.' I didn't give her the money instead I hid it in my bedroom when she wasn't looking. Mom started to cook on the stove while I stood by the kitchen door watching her, she was doing mashed potato and meat. When I started to eat it a little later, but soon told her that it smelt and tasted horrid. 'You're right,' Mom said, 'I'll open another tin and mash in your potato.' I ate all of the second plate she made me.

      That week the same thing happened every day; we got sent home from school after dinner. Come Saturday morning I shouted to Mom because she was still in bed, 'I'm off to the bakery now.' She shouted back that I wasn't to let them pick on me. As I walked about of the door a felt a sudden pain in my stomach, but I carried on down the stairs. When I got to the railway bridge the pain seemed to be getting worst but I still didn't stop. I was by the Sportsman Pub when I fell to the ground with the pain, I was doubled up. Mrs Kilby saw me and came over, she asked if I was alright. 'Come on Peter, I will get you home,' she said. I told her no, that I was going to work in the bakery. She helped me up and said she was taking me straight home, no work today. I leant on Mrs Kilby on the way home, but she smelt very bad. I tried to be sick on the side of the road, but found that I couldn't. As Mrs Kilby and I were going into our block Mrs Price came out, she could see straight away that I was in pain. 'Take Peter upstairs quickly,' she told Mrs Kilby, 'I'll go and find the doctor.' When we got upstairs Mrs Kilby told Mom what was going on and then I was made to get into bed. Doctor Linley arrived a few minutes later, I heard him say to Mrs Kilby that she needed a good bath. Then he came into my bedroom and asked me where the pain was. I told him and he said, 'I know what it is, I will make the pain go away.' He gave me some thick black stuff, it was really horrible but I had to have two big teaspoons of it. 'I'm going to stay with you for a while and make sure that stuff works,' he said sitting next to me on my bed.

    A little later, with the front door still open, a copper from Digbeth police station and the gaffer from Wilson's bakery walked in. Mom asked the copper, 'What the bloody hell do you two want?' 'There was some money taken from the office,' the copper said, 'Peter was seen running away from the bakery.' Mrs Kilby piped up then, 'Who's accusing Peter? They are bloody liars, fetch that bloody liar to me and I will give him piece of my mind.' She explained to the men what had happened and the gaffer apologised to Mom. The Doctor came out of the bedroom, 'Everybody stand back Peter's about to run out.' I couldn't get to the toilet quickly enough, it was running down my leg and in my trousers. When I was finished the Doctor stood by the toilet door and asked me if the pain had gone. I told him yes it had. 'Good,' he replied, 'I'll leave the bottle with your Mother, take two spoons of it tomorrow then the pain will go away for good.' Doctor Linley left and the copper and the gaffer was about to go but Mom stopped them and asked who it was who said they saw Peter running away. They didn't answer and just left. Mom finally came into the toilet with some rags and hot water to wash me down. Mom told to me that I wasn't to go to the bakery again, not if they were going to accuse me when something went wrong. When I was all clean Mom thanked Mrs Price for fetching the Doctor and then Mrs Bloomer came running in and asked Mom what was going on. 'I thought I saw was Mrs Kilby here, smelt her too,' she said. When Mom explained Mrs Bloomer said, 'It was a good job I wasn't there, you know what those blokes would have got from me.' I later found out Mrs Kilby had a problem with her water works, she even wet herself in the pub.

    Johnny came calling for me and Mom went to the door. 'Come on in Johnny, you're just the lad I want to see. What's all this about you getting Peter into trouble?' Johnny frowned at her, 'It's not me Mrs Round, it was them three kids.' 'Why did they take you down to the police station then?' Mom asked him, 'I was told you're in   trouble.' 'No Mrs Round, the coppers have let me go.' Johnny didn't stay long after that, he just said a brief hello and then went home. That was the last time I saw Johnny for a while.

    Mom made me stay in on Sunday, even though I asked if I could go out. On Monday morning I got ready for school, I couldn't wait to get there. I made sure that I washed my neck clean while Mom made me some toast and hot powdered milk. Mom checked me over before I left and then I ran out the house, down the stairs, and out the block fast as I could go. I'd started to walk down the lane and there was this kid standing on the corner of NorthHolme. He asked me where I going and I told him the school in Garrison Lane. I told him my name was Peter Round and he said he was called Jimmy and that he lived in the third block on the left. 'I'm off to the

118

school in Ada Road tomorrow,' he said, 'but I'll walk with you to your school.' We got to the canal bridge and we jumped up   looking at the barges. 'Come on,' I said, 'let's go down the cut and have a good look.' There were two more kids sitting on the canal bank and they waved to us to come sit by them. When we sat next to them they said their names were George and Jack. There were five barges waiting to go through the locks, George ran over to the lock gates to get a closer look. He jumped up on the gates as they were opening, but he slipped and fell over. Luckily one of the blokes who worked on the boats was standing by the edge and caught George by the collar, then the bloke really told him off. George came back and sat by us, Jack put his arm around him and he started to cry. Later on in life both George and Jack became boxers.

One off the ladies from the barges came over and gave us all a hot drink, 'When you've finished bring the cans back,' she said to us. The drink was potato peel soup. We watch all the barges go through the locks, then George said, 'Come on, we can go back to my house.' On the way he said he'd show us some horses, we walked down this long road and George said that the horses were at the bottom of the road. We watched them under the railway bridge for a while, but we couldn't get too close. We walked up to George's house on Windsor Street together, we went up this entry into the yard and there were ladies sitting outside their houses all chatting away with blankets around their shoulders. We went over to George's Mom and he introduced Jimmy and I as his 'new friends.'. We went into the house and George's Mom followed us in, 'Sit yourselves down,' she said. I went over by the fire and sat on the floor, she started to toast thick slices of bread by the fire. George said that his dad worked over at the bakery and that's why they had plenty of bread. His Mom shouted at him to keep his mouth shut or he'd feel the back of her hand. She gave us a cup of hot fresh milk each and then said that we were all to go home when we'd finished. I was the last one out and as I left I heard George's Mom say to him, 'When they've all gone your Dad wants you to go over to the bakery to help out.' Outside Jimmy asked me if I knew the way home and I told him yes. I stood waiting on the corner of Windsor Street and said that I was waiting for George to come out. He eventually came running down the road and I asked him if he wanted Jimmy and I to come to the bakery with him. 'No my dad will kill me I've got to go by myself, now piss off,' he replied. I turned to Jimmy and said, 'Come on, I want to go home.' 'Are you sure you know the way home?' he said as we started walking.

We went down Lawley Street to Garrison Street and there was a horse and cart waiting on the corner. Who was sitting on the cart was but the man with the scar? He shouted over us to and asked who my friend was. 'Get in the cart,' he said to us both. I shouted no and started to run away but Jimmy got on the cart and shouted over to me to come back. I kept on running and arrived at the school gates just as all the other kids were coming out. I saw Nancy and she called over to me, 'You been playing the wag again Peter Round?' I walked with her for a bit and she told me that they sent everyone home again. We went up by the canal together and we saw a barge coming so we ran down to the canal path and started to wave to people on the boat, they waved back. When they passed us Nancy said she was off home so we walked up the slope and when we got to the entrance of the canal Nancy kissed me, then she ran off. I walked home by myself and when I got in Mom was already in. 'Have they sent you home again?' When I nodded yes Mom said, 'That's it, I'm coming to that school tomorrow to get some answers.' She never knew I played the wag that day.

On Tuesday morning for the first time in ages I really enjoyed my breakfast that Mom made me. Johnny came calling for me again, he shouted up to me and Mom opened the window. 'He's coming down now, you wait there,' she called to him. I ran downstairs and saw that Mom was still by the window, she shouted to us, 'You two better get off to school and go straight there!' On the way Johnny and I saw the man with the scar on his horse and cart coming up the lane. He pulled his horse up, but we never waited to see what he wanted we just ran. When we got to school and we went straight in through the gates. Nancy was standing by the classroom door, 'Hello Peter Round, not playing the wag today then,' she said. Then she kissed me again and went into the classroom. The teacher came in behind us and said good morning. Then she looked over at me, 'You're all going to stay in school today and that goes for you too Peter Round, no more going home early.' She asked Nancy to pass some textbooks around and we had to put our names on them. It was about eleven o'clock when the classroom door burst open and in marched the Mothers. My Mom was the first in she said come on Peter I'm taking you out of this school you are going to another one. Johnny's Mom was also there that day, he ended up going to a different school to me. There were eight Mothers who took their kids out of Garrison Lane school. We were walking away from the school when Nancy came running up to me, she kissed me again and didn't say anything. Mom said, 'That's nice of her she likes you, what's her name?' I didn't reply.

Chapter 2
Tilton Road School

'Gran you got to help me, I'm in a lot of trouble.'

Mom and I went straight from Garrison Lane school to Tilton Road where we had to wait outside the headmaster's office. We waited for some time before the headmaster came out and called us in. Mom and I sat down and the headmaster introduced himself as Mr Watson. 'Now Peter,' he said, 'I have been in touch with your previous school, the report I got back is good and bad. I see you like playing truant a lot. I don't like giving the cane,' he held it up to show me, 'you don't want me to give you the cane do you Peter?' 'No sir,' I replied quickly. 'We will have to wait see how it goes,' he said (it was true I never got the cane at Tilton Road, but I did play up sometimes). Mom said she would make me behave or else I'd be answering to my big brother Tommy. I was the only kid from Garrison Lane to go to Tilton Road school. 'You start tomorrow,' I was told, 'report to Mrs Barton in the morning and she'll show you to your class.' The headmaster gave me a good talking to, the last thing he said to me was that he was told that I liked going down to the canal on the way to school to watch the boats. 'There's no canal up here,' he looked at me and smiled.

As we left the office Mom turned to the headmaster and asked if he knew what was going on at Garrison Lane school. 'I'm sorry Mrs Round I have no idea and even if I did I wouldn't be allowed to tell you,' he replied. Mom and I left and I asked her if I could go round to Granny Peggs and tell her about starting my new school. 'Go on then,' she said, 'but don't be long, I'm going to do you something nice to eat for tea.' I went running round to Gran's and for the first time she wasn't sitting in her usual place, instead she was sitting by the window. I thought she was dead for a moment, she was sitting with her mouth open, very still. I shouted, 'Gran, Gran!' but she didn't move. I went over and started to shake her. I was shaking her hard when she suddenly woke up, 'What's going on?!' she shouted. I told her that I thought she was dead. She laughed and said, 'I'm long way off throwing my clogs Peter, now tell me what trouble you're in today.' 'I'm in no trouble Gran, but I'm going to Tilton Rod school tomorrow.' 'Let's hope the teachers aren't too soft like they are down Garrison Lane,' she said, 'I bet you're hungry.' I nodded and told her I'd like some bread with jam. 'Your Uncle Bill brought some jam from work, but you never tell him,' Gran said winking at me. She gave me two thick pieces of bread with jam and while I was eating she looked at me and said, 'One day you will come in here and you won't be hungry, then I'll pop my clogs,' we both laughed. 'Gran, can I have some fresh milk too?' I asked. She said I was being cheeky, but she still brought me a glass of hot, fresh milk. I looked at her and laughed, she smiled back. 'You're sitting there all innocent like butter wouldn't melt in your mouth, now tell your Gran are you in any trouble?' 'No Gran and that's the truth.' I replied. 'I believe you,' she told me. 'Before you go you can run down to the snuff shop to see if they got any snuff for me?' I went out the front way and I ran down the gully. I saw Jimmy at the end, he was watching the trains through the opening. I stayed with him for bit and we chatted. Then I said that I had to go and get my Gran some snuff from the shop. As I was going out the gully and over the railway bridge I saw Wally coming over from the other side. He saw me and he shouted so I turned started running back up the gully towards Gran's. When I got there I went straight in and told her that the shop hadn't got any snuff left, but I promised to go the next day.

    A little later, before I left, I looked out the window to see if Wally was still hanging about. 'Who are you looking for?' Gran asked coming over to the window. I didn't reply and told her I was going home. I ran round the back way in case Wally was there. When I got home safe and sound Mom told me to take all my clothes off as she was going to wash them so they were all nice and clean for my first day at my new school. Mom did me nice tea that night and then a good breakfast the next morning. When it was time for me to go to school Mom looked me over to check I had washed myself properly. On my way out the block Mrs Price and Mrs Bloomer both came out to see me and told me to behave on my first day at my new school.

Off I went up the lane to the school with Mom watching me from our window, I turned round and waved up to her. I went up to a copper who was on the crossing, when I got to him he looked at me, 'Are you the new lad?' he asked me. I told him, 'Yes sir.' I crossed the road and he stood watching me so I turned round and pulled my tongue out to him, he shouted to me to come back but I ran into the school. I bumped straight into a lady at the entrance and said, 'Sorry miss can you tell where I can find Miss Barton?' 'You've found her, are you Peter Round?' I nodded and she said she'd show me to the classroom. Miss Barton gave me some textbooks and told me to go and sit at the back of the room and put my name on the books. As I sat down in came the rest of the class, a girl came and sat by me. 'My name's Ann, what's your's?' she asked. 'Peter,' I replied. 'I like you Peter,' Ann said, I said nothing back. The teacher was doing some sums on the blackboard and we had to copy them into our textbooks and then add them up. Ann said she'd help me. The classroom was quiet as we worked and then the headmaster came in followed by the copper I'd seem at the crossing. The copper pointed to me and the headmaster called me to the front class. 'This is your first day and you are already in trouble with the police, pulling your tongue out to this policeman,' the headmaster said. The whole class laughed at that and he shouted to the cat them all to be quiet. Then he took me out of the classroom, the copper was close behind me. I got a right telling off outside. I stood there looking at the headmaster and I never said anything. 'Do you have anything to say to this policeman Peter?' Mr Watson asked me. 'Not even sorry?' he said when I shook my head. 'You pulled your tongue out at a policeman I could give you the cane you know.' I looked up at the copper and said, 'Sorry sir, I will never do it again sir, sorry.' 'Thank you Peter, now go back to your classroom.'

When I got back Miss Barton told me I'd have to stay in at break time to catch up on what I'd missed. 'I'll stay in with him miss to show him what to do,' Ann said. Two lads also put their hands up and told Miss Barton they'd help me too; they became my mates. 'Did you really pull your tongue out to that copper?' Ann asked. I nodded my head and she put her arm round me. The teacher shouted at Ann to be quiet and she called me out in front of the class, she ask me to read if I could. I stood there all quiet with the book looking around the classroom, then I started to read. I made few mistakes and the class started to laugh at me, Ann stood up at her desk and shouted to everyone to leave me alone. One of the kids shouted that I couldn't read at all, Ann jumped up from her desk, went over to the kid and slapped him hard across the face. The teacher shouted at Ann, 'I'm not going to put up with that sort of behave in my class, you stay in after school.' Then Ann came and stood by me and although Miss Barton told her to go and sit down Ann said, 'No miss I'm going to help Peter to read.' Miss Barton grabbed hold of Ann and took her back to her desk. 'I'm not sitting down miss I'm going to help Peter to read,' Ann said again. Miss Barton sat on edge of her desk looking at me, she folded her arms, 'Peter you have only been here for half a day and you have already caused trouble.' I looked away from her and nodded, 'Yes miss, I mean no miss.' 'Okay Peter, well go ahead and read.' I couldn't believe it but I did read the book and Miss Barton told me 'Well done' when I'd finished. Next she got the kid up who Ann slapped across the face to read the book, but he couldn't do it properly. Ann shouted to him, 'You took the mickey out of Peter and you're no better!'

The bell went for break time and I had to stay in, but Ann, David, and Dennis stayed with me as they'd promised. Ann showed me what to do, I had to copy from her textbook then I had to add the sums up, there were four pages full of sums but the three of them was helping me and I managed to do some myself. When break time was over Miss Barton called me out in front again to read from a another book which was a bit harder but I managed to read ten pages with only a few mistakes. Miss Barton never said anything to me she just took the book from me and told me to go back to my desk. At dinner time some kids ran home, but I stopped and went into the playground, I started to feel hungry there wasn't anywhere to sit down so I just walked around. I found myself looking through the kitchen window when another kid came up to me, 'You never get anything from them old bags,' he told me. I don't who the kid was he wasn't in my class. David and Dennis came over to me and asked what the kid had wanted so I told them what he'd said about the dinner ladies. 'Keep away from him,' Dennis said, 'he'll get you into trouble.' David and Dennis shared what food they had with me and David asked if I had a ticket which would get me something from the kitchen. When they'd finished eating Dennis left us for a bit and David told me to, 'Go get some food from the kitchen, tell them that your Dad was killed in the war and they will give you a free ticket. They give me free food every day and Dennis doing the same, go on go to the headmaster's office before the kitchen closes.' I went running to the office and I knocked on the door and waited for bit. I knocked again and after the third knock the headmaster called me in, 'What you want Peter,' he asked when I walked in front of his desk. 'My Dad was killed in the war sir, can I have free ticket so I can get some food from the kitchen?' Mr Watson looked at me and said, 'Are you lying to me Peter?' 'I'm not sir it's, the truth sir. You can ask my mom.' 'Oh I will Peter, I know you are lying to me and I could give you the cane for lying to me.' 'Sir I'm hungry,' I replied simply. Mr Watson looked at me and then said, 'Come with me, we'll go to the kitchen and see if there's any food left.'

There was bit of mashed potato left and a slice of bread left, Mr Watson stayed with me until I finished and then we went back to his office. 'I want the truth from you now Peter, have you got a father?' I shook my head and he asked, 'What happened to him?' 'I don't know sir, but I've got two big brothers though I hardly ever see them. They don't live with me and they was away in the war.' There was a knock on the door of the office and in came Inspector Davies. He looked, 'What trouble are you in now Peter?' 'I'm in no trouble sir,' I told him. 'Peter go back to your class now, I'll see you after school has finished, come to my office then.'

When I got back to the classroom Miss Barton said I was late and asked where I'd been. 'I've been in Mr Watson's office miss,' I told her. Dennis and David said they saw me in the kitchen with Mr Watson, Miss Barton said it was okay and that I could go sit at my desk. As I passed David he asked if I'd told Mr Watson what he suggested and I nodded yes. Later that afternoon the bell went for home time and I went to run out but then I remembered that Mr Watson was waiting for me, so I went along to his office again. When I got there I knocked and he invited me in, telling me to sit down. 'I want you to tell me the truth have you got a Father? And are you're brothers really in the army.' 'I really don't have Dad,' I replied, 'and both my brothers are in the army, one of them is getting married soon.' 'Peter I want you to go home and ask your Mother to come see me tomorrow can you do that?' I nodded and told him that I could. 'Now Peter, you've only been here for one day and you have been in a bit of trouble with the police. I hope you're not going to cause me anymore trouble now.' He got up from his desk and put his hand on my shoulder then he looked at me and smiled, 'Don't forget to tell your Mother to come and see me tomorrow. I'll see if I can help you, off you go now, go straight home okay?' 'Yes sir,' I said and I ran out of there as fast as I could. I ran all the way home going straight across the horse road. I ran up the stairs and when I got inside Mom was talking to Mrs Bloomer. Shortly afterwards Mrs Price came running in and asked what was going on, she said she'd seen me running down the road and wondered if someone was chasing me. 'Come on Peter what   trouble are you in?' she asked. I looked at them and then I started to laugh, 'I'm in no trouble, the headmaster wants to see you tomorrow morning though

Mom,' I said. 'What for?' she asked walking over to me, 'are you in some trouble? You've only been there for a day and you're already in trouble!' I promised her that I was in no trouble and said that Mr Watson just wanted to talk to her. Mrs Bloomer said, 'Do want me to come with you Dorothy?' Mom shook her head and said it would be alright.

I had leftovers from the night before for dinner and then it was time to go to bed. I lay down on the bed and all of a sudden the bed broke. With no bed to lie on I decided to go and sleep in the living room by the fire. The next day Mom gave me a bit of breakfast and she checked me over to make sure I'd washed myself properly. 'Come on let's go and see this headmaster of yours and find out what trouble you are in,' she said as she closed the front door behind us. I never said anything in reply, going down the stairs Mrs Bloomer and Mrs Price came out of their houses. Mrs Bloomer asked if Mom wanted her to come too, Mom looked at her then she nodded and said yes.

The copper on the crossing was the same one from the day before and as we walking across he looked at me, 'You're not going to pull your tongue out to me today are you Peter?' he asked. 'Why did you do that?' Mom asked me, I looked away and didn't reply. Mom asked the same question to the copper and he replied that, 'It was the devil.' As we walked away from the copper he shouted, 'Keep out trouble today Peter!' Mrs Bloomer started to laugh Peter and asked if I'd really pulled my tongue out at him, I said yes I had. The headmaster's door was open when we got there so we all walked straight in. Before Mr Watson could speak Mom asked, 'What has he been up to and what sorted trouble he is in?' 'Mrs Round before you get carried away Peter is in no trouble,' Mr Watson replied, 'the reason I asked you come and see me is to check if I can help you with Peter's free dinners. Have you got a husband?' Mom said no and she didn't reply when Mr Watson asked what had happened to him. 'Mrs Round I can't help you if you can't tell me what happened to your husband.' Again Mom never answered, she just sat there. Mrs Bloomer piped up and said, 'Just tell him Dorothy.' Mom stayed silent so Mrs Bloomer blurted out, 'Peter is a bastard.' Mr Watson looked at me and quickly said, 'Peter go to your class please.' Before I went I asked Mom Mr Bloomer had meant, she didn't reply and Mr Watson told me to leave.

A little later just before break time Mr Watson came into the classroom and handed something to Miss Barton. 'Your dinner ticket is here Peter.' I put my hand up and asked him, 'Mr Watson, why am I a bast**d?' Some of the class burst out laughing. Ann said, 'Because you haven't got a proper Dad.' Afterwards, in the playground, this lad Foster came up to me and started to call me names. I went for him and we both fell to the ground, he got on top of me and started to punching me. David and Dennis pulled Foster off me and I got up, my nose was bleeding. I gave him a good kick and somehow I also gave him a good punch on the nose, so hard that his started to bleed too. I jumped on him and we fell to the ground again, this time I was on top of Foster and I started to punch him. One of the duty teachers came over to us and told us to stop, but I kept on punching him. Then another teacher came over and he got hold of my collar, he pulled me off Foster and told us to report to the headmaster right away. After a good telling off from Mr Watson made Foster and I shake hands, after that we became sort of friends.

School was going well and I was getting some sort of school meals at dinner time. When Miss Barton asked me a question sometimes I gave the wrong answer, I made the class laugh and I made Miss Barton laugh. On the 22th March 1947 Albert got married at St Andrew's church he held the wedding reception up at my school on Tilton Road. The week before Easter break a new family moved in to the next block to me, but they didn't stay long. Shortly afterwards another family came, they were named Murphy and there was a young lad called David. I got to know David quite well, we walked to school together and came home together. His bedroom was next to my mine and he would bang on the wall and I would open my bedroom window and he would open his. This happened a few times before he banged on the wall and I opened the window and David whispered, 'Shall we climb out?' I climbed out of the window and down on the drain pipe. After climbing down we went running round the flats, we were laughing the whole time. Eventually David and I climbed back up to our bedrooms. I still had no bed, I'd been lying on my bedroom floor. One day on our way to school a lad named Jimmy White was standing on the corner of EastHolme and he said to us, 'I saw you two running round, I'll come with you next time, are you going out tonight?' We never said anything instead we carried on going to school. David and I did go out that night and Jimmy was waiting for us this time. We all went running out the flats together and went over the railway bridge into Maxstoke Street. Jimmy picked up a stone or a brick and he threw it at a window and smashed the glass. We ran up St Andrews Street as fast as we could go to, once we got to WestHolme we split up. Jimmy went to the left through an archway and David and I went through archway on the right, we met up again at the back of our houses.

It was May of 1947 and David and I were coming home from school when we bumped into Tom, Dick, and Harry coming up the lane. They stopped and spoke to us, one of them knew David. They wanted us to go out with them that night, David said yes but I said no. 'Johnny's coming with us,' Tom said. I shook my head and said no again. That night Johnny and David shouted up to my bedroom window to come with them. I looked outside and shouted down 'No!' I didn't see the man standing in the dark until he came up stood by them both. It was the man with the scar, he called to me in a stern voice, 'Come on down Peter.' In the end I did go down and we followed the man to a lorry, Jimmy came running shouting, 'Wait for me!' Three blokes were standing by the lorry and Tom, Dick, and Harry were there too. We all got in the back of the lorry, but none of us really knew where we was going. We drove around for some time then the lorry stopped all of a sudden. When we all got out David ran off down into the darkness. We were in some road, the man with the scar got hold of me and told me to climb up on another man's back and smash a window in a nearby building. Then I had to climb through the window, it wasn't big but I managed to climb through it because I was small. 'Go open the gates,' the man with the scar called up to me once I was through. I was getting very frightened and I remember it was very dark. I found the gates and they were easy to open, then the lorry backed in and I had to close the doors and stay there. The lorry backed all the way up to the building, I think it was a factory, and the blokes started to load it up. Suddenly the night watchman came from nowhere. He stood in front of the lorry and asked what was going on. The blokes jumped on him and started to beat him up. I went up them and tried to tell them to stop. The night watchman looked at me, 'I know who you are, your Peter Round, I know where you live.' I started to run, but one of the blokes got hold of me and told me that I wasn't going anywhere, once I twisted free and I ran fast as I could go. Johnny was following after me shouting for me to wait. He caught up with me eventually but we were running around in circles. We stopped for a bit to catch our breath. Johnny said, 'I think we are lost.' We started walking along this road I think it was Anderton Street and we got to the bottom Johnny realised that he knew where he was. When we got to Coventry Road I started to run again and Johnny followed. I ran all the way to Granny Pegg's and banged on the back door when I got there, Johnny had already run home. Gran opened the door and asked, 'What's going on at this time in the morning Peter?' 'Gran you got to help me I'm in lot of trouble.' I told her what had happened and she said that we were going straight to the police station. I said no at first but Gran told me that we were going whether I liked it or not.

When we got to the police station it was closes so Gran started to bang on the door and after while a copper came and opened it. 'Where have you been?' Gran asked him, 'I bet you been asleep, we need to see the inspector.' 'Inspector Davies is not on duty,' the copper replied. 'I don't care!' Gran shouted, 'get him down here now and tell him it's Mrs Pegg with her grandson Peter Round, I want him here now quickly.' After Gran kept on at him the copper finally rang the inspector. Gran grabbed the phone off him and told the inspector to, 'Get your arse down here right now.' After about an Inspector Davies finally arrived. 'Peter what trouble are you in now?' I started to tell him but he stopped me and told me and Gran to come into his office. Once we were sitting around his desk I told the inspector everything, what went on at the building I thought was a factory and all the names of the blokes that I knew including Tom, Dick, and Harry. Inspector Davies asked me a load more questions and then he looked at me and sighed. 'Okay Peter you can go home for now, I'm glad you've told me everything.'

Later when we got home Mom was doing her war dance, but Gran told her not to worry saying that Inspector Davies was going to look after me. I never went to school that day and towards the afternoon a copper came to the house. 'I'm going to take Peter down Cheapside for two weeks in case the blokes come after him, not to worry Mrs Round he will be taken care of.' I stopped with two old people and when I found out the old man's name was Davies I had to laugh. When I returned home I found out that all the blokes had been arrested and I never went to school for two more weeks. I had to report to the police station every day and so did Johnny, David, and Jimmy. It was about August time when we had a date to
appear to the juvenile court in October, only Johnny and I was the only ones who turned up to court in the end. Inspector Davies told Mom not to worry, 'Mrs Round leave it to me,' he said before we went into the courtroom. As we was waiting Violet Pegg came running up to us. The inspector said asked who she was and Violet said that she wanted to speak with her cousin. We told her that she couldn't come in but when the doors eventually opened she was the first one into the courtroom. The talking went on for some time but it finally came to an end Johnny and I had to stand up in

132

front the woman, the judge, who gave us a right telling off. 'Both of you would have been put away if haven't been for Inspector Davies,' she told us, 'if you end up back in court within two years you will be sent away for very long time.'

It wasn't until that day that I found out that the night watchman who the blokes had beaten that night had died. I asked Inspector Davies why Jimmy and David weren't in court too. 'Both of them have left the flats and we don't know where they've gone,' he told me, 'don't worry about them Peter we will find them. I'm going to trust you and Johnny not to get into any more trouble, I'm going to let you go. You haven't got to report to me every day now, that's where the trust comes in.' He turned to my Mom, 'I hope I've made myself clear to you too Mrs Round.' Mom smiled and thanked him. From that day to this day I still don't know what happened to David and Jimmy nor Tom, Dick, Harry and the man with the scar.

It was getting towards end of 1947 and all was going well. I was enjoying school and my brother Tommy was still getting us some food and coal every now and then. At the end of November that year I was on my way to school one day, it was a Wednesday and it was cold. When I got into school I had to go to Mr Watson's office, I had to report to him every Wednesday. Every week he asked me the same question, 'Are you keeping out of trouble Peter?' I always replied, 'Yes sir,' I wasn't going up to the copper on the crossing and I wasn't playing the wag. This particular day it was a different copper on the crossing, he looked at me and asked if my name was Peter Round. At first I said no and carried on crossing the road, but when I got across the horse road I went to run and the copper shouted to me to come back. I went back to him and he asked again if my name was Peter Round. Two girls from school went passed and shouted, 'Are you in trouble with the coppers Peter Round?' 'So you are Peter Round,' the copper said with smile, 'you have to report to Inspector Davies at six o'clock this evening with your Mother and don't be late.' I carried on

133

to school and I went to Mr Watson's office, knocked on the door and went straight in. 'Peter I've told you to wait until I say come in, now go back out and wait till I call you in.' I did as he asked and went back out closing the door behind me, then Mr Watson shouted for me to come in. We had our usual talk and then I went to my classroom.

The day went well, I was making the class and our teacher Mr Simms laugh. The bell rang at 4 o'clock and I got up from my desk and went to run out of the class. Mr Simms said, 'No you don't Peter you stay here, I've got a message from Mr Watson for you.' When all the class had gone Mr Simms asked, 'Do you know where you've got to be at six o'clock today.' I shook my head in reply and Mr Simms said, 'I think you do Peter, you've got to report to Inspector Davies, the policeman on the crossing told you this morning didn't he?' 'Yes sir,' I said. 'Please tell me in the morning what the inspector wanted,' Mr Simms said. I told him that I would and then I went running out of the classroom. As I was running down the corridor I didn't see Miss Barton coming towards me and I knocked her over, she fell to the floor. I didn't stop, I just looked down at her and ran out of the door.

When I got home Mom was already there, I went and joined her where she was sitting by the fire. 'Can I have something to eat I'm hungry Mom,' I said. 'I think you've got something to tell me haven't you Peter? Haven't you got to be somewhere to be by six o'clock?' I looked at her, 'No Mom.' 'You bloody liar!' she shouted, 'you've got to be at the police station? I saw Johnny's Mom and she told me, you weren't going to say anything were you?' 'Yes Mom I was, but only after I had something to eat.' We had some rough food and then we went to the cop shop, Johnny and his Mom were already waiting there. We had to wait for the inspector to arrive, he was never on time. When he came in our Moms went into his office first and Johnny and I had to wait outside, we never spoke to each other we just sat there silently. Then Inspector Davies called us in without our Moms. He gave us a good talking to and told us that he was leaving Coventry Road police station, he told us that if we got into any more trouble we'd be put away straight away without our Mother's permission and that we wouldn't see them for a very long time. 'The inspector who is taking over from me is not a nice person like me,' he said, 'he will put you away without telling your mother's and if he wants to see you, you have to come to the police station straight away. I hope I have got through to you two?' Johnny and I looked at each other and said, 'Yes sir.' Inspector Davies called our Mom's and said that they could take us home. As we were leaving he said, 'I hope I don't hear from the other inspector about you two.' On the way home Johnny and I were walking in front of our Moms and we kept looking at each other and laughing. We said our goodbyes and Mom and I walked into our block. I was walking up the stairs in front of her and when I got to the house Mom slapped me across the head, 'What was that for?!' I shouted. 'I was watching you and Johnny laughing, I hope you are not going to get into any more trouble,' she said.

    It was almost Christmas of 1947 and it was still very cold, we had some coal and some food and thankfully we still had the gas and the electric on. Come Christmas Day I was standing by the window hoping my two brothers would come and see us, but they never did. I think it was over week before Tommy visited but it was some time before Albert came over. They never bought me any Christmas presents that year.

    At the beginning of 1948 I was going to school every day and was reporting to Mr Watson every Wednesday, the copper on the crossing was watching me to see I'm going into school. Nothing happened in January of 1948, it was just the same thing day in and day out. One Friday in February when I arrived home from school Tommy was waiting for me. I ran up to him and hugged him hard, 'That's enough nip,' he said, 'there's something in the pantry for you.' I had a look and found a small tea cake then I saw that Tommy was heading for the front door. 'Aren't you going to stay till Mom comes home?' I shook his head and then said,

'Bye nip,' and off he went. On Saturday morning the 21st February Mom went to do her cleaning job and I went round Granny Pegg's where she gave me a thick piece of toast to eat. Gran was walking round the house talking to herself and I kept asking her what she was saying. I finished my toast and left shortly afterwards. As I walked into the block I bumped into Mom who was walking up the stairs. I told her I'd been to Gran's and that she kept talking to herself the whole time I was there. 'I talk to myself all the time worrying about you, 'Mom said. She went straight into the kitchen when we got inside and I went over to the table, 'Mom there's a letter for you here,' I said passing it over to her. The letter said, 'Mom I'm getting married this morning,' and that was it. Mom was fuming and told me to hurry up as we were going back out into town. We got to the registry office but we were too late, Tommy was already married and gone. Mom went walking round few pubs near the registry office to see if we could find him, but we had no luck. We had to walk all the way home, it was very cold and I was shivering. Walking through the bull ring we bumped into my Uncle Harry and he asked Mom what we were doing in town. 'We're looking for that son of mine,' she told Harry, 'he's just got married today.' Harry told me that we better get home and carry on looking. When we got home the first thing I had to do was to clean out the fire and get it ready for Mom to get a new one going. We were starting to run out food and we were on our last bucket of coal. I went to the toilet and when I came back I saw that Mom was about break into the meters, 'Mom don't do that or you'll be in big trouble,' I told her. She didn't listen to me, instead she went ahead and broke into the meters anyway, they were full.

I went running round to Granny Pegs, when I got there I banged on the door but it was locked. I was shouting through the letterbox for her to open up and when she finally the first thing she said was, 'What trouble are you in now Peter?' 'I'm not in trouble,' I told her, 'Mom is breaking into the gas and electric meters again. We've got no food or coal, oh and our Tommy got married today.' Gran laughed for a bit, 'That's your Tommy all over!' she said, 'so what do you want me to do about your Mom then?' 'Come round the house and stop her Gran! You're the only one who can,' I told her. Eventually I persuaded her to come down later and I went running ahead and got back to the block first. I was about to run up the stairs when Mrs Bloomer came out of her house, 'What's up Peter?' she asked me as I passed her door. 'My Mom is breaking into the meters again, I've told Granny Pegg and she's coming up now.' Mrs Bloomer started to run up the stairs ahead on me, 'Get out my way Peter,' she said as she went. I didn't go in when I got to our door, instead I sat on top of the stairs which was very cold. I heard Mrs Bloomer shouting at Mom, in the meantime Gran came into the block and she heard the shouting too. 'Who's that having go at your Mom,' she asked when she reached me at the top of the stairs. When I told her it was Mrs Bloomer Gran went past me and into the house. I heard her having go at Mom too and I sat there thinking of running away but then realised I had nowhere else to go. Suddenly the shouting had stopped and Mrs Bloomer and Gran came out of the house. 'Go on Peter you can go in now,' Gran said. I went inside and Mom told me to shut the door, then she starting shouting. 'I owe Mrs Able some money,' she said, 'she won't let me have anything on the slate until I pay her!' Then she started to have a go at me about going round to Gran's and for telling her and Mrs Bloomer what she was doing. I didn't want to hear it anymore so I ran out of the house, it was dark outside. I ran to the railway bridge and as I ran it started to rain. There was bit of an opening in the fence and I managed to squeeze through the fence. I slipped down the embankment and hurt myself so I went under the bridge where I sat on the floor shivering with cold. I must have been there for some time when I heard someone shout to me to come down. I followed the voice to a bloke, I was still shivering as I walked up to him. When he asked what I was doing I told him that I was running away from home. He laughed at me and told me to follow him. We went across the railway tracks to the signal box, I saw a big stack of coal and told the man, 'You've got a load of coal there Mr,' but he didn't reply. We went up the stairs inside the box and the bloke told me to go and sit by the fire and get warm. He gave me a very hot drink and told me to go and lie down in the corner once I'd finished.

I must have fell off to sleep in that corner because the next thing I knew I was awoken by two blokes talking. I sat up and I looked around. The bloke I didn't recognise said, 'I think that's Tommy Round's son or brother, what's your name kid?' I didn't answer him even when he asked a second time. 'Okay Arthur,' the bloke said turning to the other one, 'call the police.' I still didn't answer, instead I got up and said, 'I'm going home now.' 'No you're not, you're not going anywhere till you tell us your name.' 'It's Billy Brown,' I said making something up on the spot. Then I lied again and told him I lived on the Tilton Road by the school when he asked me. 'Arthur call the police he's lying to us and if we can't get the truth out of him they will,' then he turned back to me, 'are you Tommy Round's son or brother?' I stayed quiet again, the man sighed I could tell he was annoyed. He asked the bloke called Albert where he'd found me. 'I saw him under the bridge he was shivering like mad,' Albert said, 'he told me he was running away from home.' 'Why are you running away, are you in any trouble?' I was asked. I never answered again so they said, 'Right let's get you home, I know you are Tommy Round's brother and I also know where you live, I won't be long Arthur.' I didn't have a choice but to go with him, but as we were walking towards NorthHolme I ran off. I ran up NortHolme to the top of the Holme and when I looked back he was still standing there at the bottom where I'd left him. I got to the block and who was standing at the entrance of the block but Mom Mrs Bloomer, and Mrs Price. I stopped suddenly and just stood there looking at them. Mrs Bloomer had her say first, 'You wait till the inspector hears about this, you have been in trouble again Peter.' I just stood there saying nothing, I was getting good at keeping quiet. Mrs Price said, 'Give the lad chance to say where he's been. Have you been in trouble Peter?' I shook my head in reply. 'You should know your own son Dorothy,' Mrs Price said, 'come on Peter tell us, your Mom has been very worried about you, you will put her in her early grave!' 'I've been looking for you all night,' Mom said, 'me and the Bloomers, come on Peter tell us right now.' I explained that I wasn't in any trouble and that I'd been at the signal box all night in the warm. 'Don't lie to me,' Mom said, 'the only way to find out is to go down there.' 'I'll go,' Mrs Price said, 'I know if Peter is telling the truth or not.'

Off Mrs Price and Mrs Bloomer went together while I stayed home with Mom. 'You can wait till they come back,' Mom said, 'and if you're lying to I tried to tell her how hungry I was but she just got angry, 'You can wait,' she told me, 'and if I find out that you've been lying to me I'm going to take you straight to the police station and let them deal with you. I've had enough of you all I'm doing is worrying about you.' Mrs Price and Mrs Bloomer came back after a short while, 'Peter was telling the truth.' Mrs Price said while Mrs Bloomer started to laugh. 'He gave the wrong name,' she said, 'where he got the name from I don't know he must have a mate called Billy Brown, that's the name he gave to the bloke in the signal box. He had to laugh he said Peter stood there and couldn't have cared less even when he threatened to call the police.' 'I told you all long Peter was telling the truth,' Mrs Price said turning to Mom, 'now give him something to eat the poor lad must be very hungry.' Mrs Bloomer came out of the kitchen, she'd gone in there while Mrs Price was talking, 'You've got no food in the pantry Dorothy, how are you going to feed the poor lad?' she asked Mom. 'I've got no money and I owe Mrs Able, she won't give me any more on the slate till I pay her what I owe. That's why I broke into the meters so I can pay her,' Mom explained. Mrs Bloomer went over to the cupboard where the meters were kept and asked Mom how much she'd taken out. Mom denied that she'd opened them at all and said she hadn't taken anything. Mrs Bloomer told Mrs Price to go get her husband so he could try and fix the locks, 'They are due to be empty the meters any day now,' she told

Mom. A few minutes later Mr Bloomer came up, he gave one look at the locks and said to Mom, 'You're lucky Dolly, I can get these fixed for you. Are you sure you haven't taken any money out?' Mom shook her head in reply. 'By the looks of it you haven't but we will see when they come to empty them,' Mr Bloomer said. While Mr Bloomer worked Mrs Price and Mrs Bloomer went to find some food. They came with just enough for Mom and I.

We still had no coal and my two brothers hadn't been around for weeks. Tommy did eventually visit with his new wife, but there was an argument between him and Mom. His new wife took me on to the veranda and she told me her name was Irene, from that day she took me into her heart, she was always there for me whether I was in trouble or not. While Irene and I were talking outside the argument had stopped so we went back in. Mom asked where Tommy and Irene had met and Tommy told her it was at New Street Station. I could tell that Mom wasn't too happy. I changed the subject and explained to Tommy that we had no food or coal, 'Mom was going to break into the meters again,' I said, 'so I had to run around to Gran's to stop her. Mom owes Mrs Able money too.' Irene asked how much she owed and Mom replied that she thought it was £2 17. 6d; I knew she owed more than that. Irene and Tommy gave Mom the money to pay Mrs Able and shortly afterwards Tommy turned to me and said, 'We're off now nip, make sure Mom goes over to pay Mrs Able.' After they went Mom did her nut at me, she kept on at me about telling Tommy about breaking into the meters and couldn't believe that I'd told him in front of Irene. I got by the front door and told her that if she didn't stop yelling at me I'd run away again. 'I don't bloody care what you do!' she shouted, 'go on get out my sight.' I went down to Mrs Bloomer's, the door was open so I walked in. I asked if I could stay there with her as Mom wouldn't stop shouting at me. 'I told Tommy that Mom was going to break into the meters,' I said, looking down. 'Don't worry Peter you did the right thing,' Mrs Bloomer said, putting her arm around me, 'now tell me what's Tommy new wife like?' I told her that Irene was very nice and that her and Tommy had given Mom the money to pay off her slate at Able's. Just then Mrs Bloomer heard Mom coming down the stairs, she was watching her out of the window as she walked over to Able's. Mr Bloomer gave me a cup of hot milk, I thanked him and told him it was very nice.

A while later Me saw mom coming out of Able's, she seemed to have a bag of food with her. Mrs Bloomer and I left and met Mom as she was coming up the stairs. Once Mrs Bloomer had said her goodbyes Mom and I went inside. 'Shut that bloody door and listen to me,' she said, 'what goes on in this house stays in this house. You don't go round telling the Peggs' and the bloody Bloomers' nor her underneath us.' I nodded my head and promised I wouldn't talk again. During the night Tommy came with a pram full of coal, I had to be very quiet getting the coal up the stairs. I remember that after that night he came four or five nights in a row and that each time he had a pram full of coal. Things seemed to be going well, Mom got two cleaning jobs and although food was still on ration Tommy and Mom seemed to be getting quite lot of food in. In August of 1948 when it was my birthday on 9th I didn't get any presents. Mom didn't buy me anything but couple of days afterwards Tommy and Irene and Albert and Iris came to visit. I got a white shirt and a pair of trousers and some socks. I thanked them a lot during that visit and when they all left they told me to keep out of trouble.

Johnny kept on calling for me every day and sometimes Mom would say I couldn't go, but on this occasion she said it was okay. Before I went out she called Johnny up and she told us both not to go over the tip, 'There's big rats over there they can bite, a little girl got bit by a rat and she died.' Were told her we wouldn't go over there and then we said our goodbyes. Johnny and I went down to the cut and this long barge which was full of coal was going along. We shouted to the bloke on the barge, 'Eh mister give us some coal?' and he threw six big lumps up to us. We carried the coal up to the canal bank and decided we needed to hide it. I told Johnny to stay where he was while I went to find the pram. I ran up the lane and I saw a pram outside a house in Maxstoke street, I took it and ran Johnny. 'Where did you get the pram from?' he asked me, I told him that I 'borrowed it from lady.' Together we hurried up to the barge before it went into the locks and I shouted to the bloke again, 'Eh mister, can we have some more coal? I got a pram here.' The bloke looked over at us, 'Okay you cheeky beggars, bring the pram alongside the boat.' He filled the pram up and then told us to piss off before we got him into trouble. Once Johnny and I got all the coal together we started towards Johnny's house. I admitted that I'd actually pinched the pram and that I needed to take it back when we'd finished. When we got to Johnny's house we shared the coal out and I helped Johnny to take his share inside. Luckily his Mom and Dad weren't in otherwise they would have done their nut at him. Next we hurried to my house and we ran up and down the stairs as quickly as we could go taking a bit of coal at a time. Johnny helped me to clean the pram out and then I asked if he was going to come with me to take it back. He told me no and then ran off towards home, turning to wave as he went. I took the pram back by myself; when got to the house where I'd taken it from some lady appeared from the front door. I stopped a few steps from the door and she looked at me, 'Did you nick my pram young man?' 'No lady honest, I saw the pram in the gully by the flats and my Mom told me to take it and go get some coal.' 'Oh did she now? That's my bloody pram! Go on piss off before you feel the back my hand.' I turned and ran as fast as my legs could take me.

Come September it was time to go back to school. On my first day back I got to the copper on the crossing and he told me that he wanted a word with me. I stood on the corner waiting and once he'd seen the other kids across the horse road he came over to me. 'Now Peter, what have you been up to in your school holidays? Have you been in any trouble?' I shook my head in reply. 'I think you have Peter. Come on, I will come to Mr Watson's office with you.' As we were walking I thought to myself, 'What trouble have I been in?' I ran off ahead of the copper and went straight to the office where I banged on his door until Mr Watson told me to come in. 'Sir, I've been in no trouble but that copper said I have! He's coming to see you now.' 'Peter get your breath back and tell me what's going on?' Mr Watson said gesturing at me to sit down. 'That copper said I've that been in trouble. but I haven't been in no trouble sir and that's the honest truth.' Mr Watson looked at me for a moment, 'Okay Peter,' he said, 'go to your class and I will see the policeman and find out what all the fuss is about.' Later that day, before break time Mr Watson came into the classroom and asked Mr Simms if he could see me for moment. Outside in the corridor he told me that I didn't have anything to worry about and that I wasn't in any trouble.

I think it was the last Saturday in October (of 1948) when I had to take the wheelchair down to the Acorn pub to fetch Granny Pegg. When I got there people were running out of the pub, the word was there was some party going on at the Hen and Chickens and that there was plenty of food going there. I had to push Gran up Barwell Road to the Hen and chickens and when we got there we heard that the party was a celebration for home coming of a sailor. We was about to cross the horse road towards the pub when a fight broke out on top of the stairs on by the fire exit. I think two blokes was fighting the sailor who ran down the stairs to get away from the. The sailor was in the middle of the horse road as the fight continued. A crowd had gathered and they were shouting trying to break up the fight, but all of a sudden everyone went quiet. The sailor had been stabbed. The two blokes ran off up the horse road, a few men ran after them while the rest of the crowd went towards the sailor. I remember hearing later that the sailor had died right there in the middle of the horse road.

In December 1948 Mom lost one of her cleaning jobs and unfortunately it was the one that paid the most. I came home from school and there she was breaking into the meters again, by the time Christmas came we had no gas nor electric, it had been turned off again. We had the cold weather come Christmas day and I never had any Christmas present from Mom nor my two brothers. Albert and Tommy didn't come to visit until the new year. One evening Albert came round, I think he was still in the army at that time. He brought me some new shoes and when he found out that we had no gas or electric again he wasn't too happy. He asked Mom if we had enough coal left, she told him that we had enough to last us the day. Albert went to the coal house to check, 'I will go see if I can get you some more,' he said and left shortly afterwards. After about hour he came back with a coalman and between them they were carrying three bags of coal and some food. Within a week Albert got our gas and electric back on. How he came to do it in week I don't know. I remember that I found out later that Albert had borrowed the money from his father-in- law.

Chapter 3
Moms New Job

'I was told that I would be getting one final chance.'

In 1949 Mom found a job in the vinegar factory in a packing warehouse. I think it was round about April of 1949 when Johnny and I found ourselves in trouble again. We went down to Wilson bakery one day and found that the gate and the sliding door was open. At first we just stood there and then we went in, there was nobody about. There was plenty of bread in wooden trays sitting on the tables inside so we nicked two loaves each and ran out as fast as we could go. When we got to Garrison Lane park there were some ladies walking about. As Johnny and I were walking past them one of them asked where we'd got the bread from. We explained that a bloke had given it to us. 'Here give us the bread and I will give you a shilling,' one of the ladies said. Johnny handed over one of his loaves and he got a shilling in return. We ran back to the bakery and there still there wasn't anybody about, so we went in and took another two loaves each. Johnny and I got back to the park, it was a nice afternoon and there were a few more ladies about. We sold four loaves for a shilling each and off we went back again to the bakery. Johnny and I went to walk in as we had before but the gaffer came running out, 'Hello Peter, what are you doing here?' he asked. 'I've to see if you got any spare bread for my Mom,' I told him. He looked at Johnny and I carefully, 'Have you seen anybody about on your way here?' he asked us. At first I said, 'No' but then Johnny that we'd seen two lads running up Lawley Street carrying some bread. The gaffer nodded and asked if we were sure, Johnny and I both nodded in reply. He told us both to leave, but as were turned to go I asked the gaffer if we could have a loaf each. 'I've already told you no, now piss off!.' the gaffer said. As Johnny and I were down the street outside the gaffer shouted to us, 'I think it was you two anyway, little bast**ds.' He stood watching us walk away for a few minutes and then he started to follow us. When we got to Derby Street the gaffer caught up with us and grabbed us both by our collars. 'I'm taking you back to the bakery and then I'm going to fetch the police,' he said. Johnny and I tried to explain that it wasn't us, but when we got back to the bakery he locked us in an out-building, we were shouting to him and banging on the door. The gaffer ended up keeping us locked up for a while, I think he was trying to frighten us. After what seemed like ages he came back and unlocked the door. 'Right you two I believe you this time, but if I catch you here again I will fetch the police, now piss off.'

Mom fell ill and lost her job at the vinegar factory, shortly after our gas and electric was cut off again and we were behind with the rent. It was about two weeks before Mom got her job back at the vinegar factory, but I think it only lasted for only about two or three weeks before she came ill again. Some woman came round from the factory and told Mom that she was sacked, I remember her passing Mom a little envelope. A little later that day Mom told me that Tommy may be coming to live with us. Tommy did come to live with us at the end of September, he came with Irene and their baby daughter, Joan. He brought his own bed and a couch for me to lie on, it was long and hard. Before they came I had to do something, had to go out and get some money. I was standing at the bottom of the Holme when I saw my mate David, he was pushing a pram with some tat on. He asked to help him to push the pram to Raggy Allen's. When we got there we put the tat on the scales, the whole lot came to 1pound and 5 shillings. David started to argue with Raggy Allen and said, 'You have done me out of 10 shillings Mr.' Raggy Allen got us by our collars and told us to piss off and not to come back again. I got 5 shillings out of that little job so David came with me to get some coal. We walked down the Garrison Lane together until we got to the railway bridge. We went into the gully alongside the flats where there was an opening to the rail bank. 'This is where I get coal for my Mom from,' David said, 'but you gotta watch out for the bloke he can run!' We started to carry the coal up to the pram, I kept running up and down the embankment with the coal while David kept watch so nobody nicked anything. I filled the pram up to the top it was so heavy that we struggled to push it. We managed to get the coal to my house, I ran upstairs banging on the door, I was proud of my efforts and wanted to show Mom what I'd brought for us. When she finally opened the door her first words were, 'Where have you been.' I was so excited to tell her that I got whole pram full of coal for her and she said, 'Where have you nicked it from.' I explained the story, that I was working for David, pushing the pram and getting shouted at by Raggy Allen and she said, 'How much money did David give you?' When I told her it was 5 shillings Mom was incredulous. 'You bought all that coal for 5 shillings?' she said, I could tell that she didn't believe me. David tried to back me up but Mom wasn't having any of it and she told David to piss off. Just then Mrs Bloomer came out to see what all the commotion was about. Mom told her that David and I had stolen a whole pram full of coal. 'Shall I go up to the caretaker to phone the police?' Mrs Bloomer asked. As soon as David heard that he ran off and left me to carry the rest of the coal upstairs, thankfully Mrs Bloomer never did call the coppers.

It was a Saturday when Mrs Bloomer shouted up the stairs to Mom and asked if she wanted to come down for the cup of tea. Mom went down to her, Mrs Bloomer lived in one of the flats of the ground floor, the front door was left open so I sat of the stairs to hear what they was saying. Mom told Mrs Bloomer that she was seven weeks in arrears with the rent and they were coming on Wednesday to cut the electric off, they'd already been the day before and cut off our gas. Mom never told me that she'd had a letter from the council saying that if she didn't pay £2 by the next day we would be evicted, but I overhead her tell Mrs Bloomer. 'Don't worry Dorothy, if Peter nicked the coal he is trying to help you, have you anything to pawn?' Mrs Bloomer asked. Mom told her that she didn't, Okay,' Mrs Bloomer said, 'I will lend you two of the old man's suits.' A little later Mom came out of the house with Mr Bloomer's suits, as she did Mrs Fleetwood was coming into the block and she could see that Mom was upset so she asked her what was wrong. 'I've got to find 35 shillings for the rent man when he comes on Monday and you know what he's like, moaning old git.' Mrs Fleetwood came in to our house and brought Mom some sheets and towels to pawn. While they were talking I went round to Granny Pegg's and I told her what was happening. Gran had a good moan about Mom, she always had to have a moan, after that she gave me Uncle Bill's suit for the pawn shop. The she gave me half-a-crown to buy some food and told also told me to tell Mom that she needed the suit back by next Saturday morning. When I got back home Mom was doing her nut again and she said that Gran was the last person she wanted to know what was going on.

Mrs Price lived next door to Mrs Bloomer and Mrs Allen lived in the top flats above the , they used to work on the boats and they lived above us. They all helped Mom over the weekend, it was nice that all of our neighbours tried to help us out. There was a real sense of togetherness and community. Mom gave me the half-crown back that I'd passed over from Gran and told me to go over to Able's and get some bread and butter. I was coming out of the block and I heard my mate Dennis was calling for me. He asked me where I was going and when I told him I was off to the shop he said he'd come along with me. We walked off together and we bumped into David, pushing his pram again. He was on his way back to the railway tracks to get some coal so we all decided to go together. Dennis saw a coal bag hidden in the bushes and he brought it down to us. It was almost half full so we dragged the bag up. There wasn't enough for all of us and we stood wondering what we were going to do. Dennis came up with a brave idea of nicking some coal from outside the signal box, doing so when the bloke wasn't looking. Taking in turns to push the pram over the railway bridge, I went down the steps first and got three lumps of coal from outside the box. David was next and then Dennis. It was going okay and we managed three turns each, it was our fourth attempt that when we came unstuck. The signalman got me by the scruff of my collar and shouted, 'I'm going to call the police!' He was about to take me up the stairs to the box when he looked and me and said, 'Aren't you Dolly Round's son?' I nodded in reply. 'What are you doing nicking the coal?' he asked me. I told him my sorry tale, 'My mom has been very ill and she wasn't able to work so we've got no money to buy anything sir.' He looked at me and said, 'You have ten minutes before my relief comes, go on and get your mates to help you out.' We moved like lightning to fill the pram up and the bag and just has we were leaving the bloke came to the top of the stairs and said, 'Come and see me tomorrow afternoon, I will show you where you can get load of scrap copper wire from, now piss off before my relief comes.'

All three of us pushed the pram to my house and when we got there I ran up the stairs first. Mom knew straight away where I got the coal from, she never said anything about it but she did ask for the half-crown back. Once we got my share of the coal upstairs I helped David to push the pram up to his house. We got to the corner of Tilton Road by the Royal George pub and David's uncle came out. When he saw us he agreed to help David push the coal the rest of the way. I went back home where Mom said told me to fill the kettle, 'You can have a wash Peter, you're bloody filthy!' I put the kettle on by the side of the fire, while I did so Mom was very quiet and never said a word. The night was drawing in and all we had was two candles. 'When you've had a wash run over to Able's and see if she let you have half dozen candles,' Mom said to me. Able's was on the corner of Venetia Road and Garrison Lane, I ran over but I had to go round the back and knock on the door. 'It's Peter Round Mrs Able,' I said as I knocked, 'Mom said can she have half dozen candles please?" Mrs Able came out with four candles and said, 'That's all I've got, tell your Mother to pay me on Monday.' I can remember on that night Mom and I had two baked potatoes and a slice of bread each for our dinner. I had to draw the curtains so nobody could see we had no electricity, Mom put two candles on the table so we could see what we were doing. As we sat staring at the fire sitting on two hard chairs (that was all the furniture we had) I smiled at the fire, all my hard work getting the coal was worth it.

On Sunday morning Mom handed me the bit of money she could find in her purse and she asked me go over to the fruit shop and get something for dinner. The fruit shop owner's name was Mr Howard, I can remember he said to me, 'What do you want Mr Trouble,' when I walked in. 'Mom sent me over to get some veggies for today's dinner,' I told him. Mr Howard put a load veggies in a bag and said, 'That will be three shillings and 6 pence.' 'I've only got half-a-crown sir,' I told him. 'Okay, tell your Mother she owes me and don't forget,' he replied. I ran out of the shop and back to the house, but I never said anything to Mom I kept the 6 pence. We never had enough money to pay the rent. Around two o'clock on Sunday afternoon David and Dennis came calling for me, I'd forgotten we had to go and see the signalman again. Mom lifted the window up and shouted down to me, 'Watch what you're doing and keep out of trouble!' We got to the signal box and he was there waiting for us. He took us to where the copper wiring was, there was wooden door and it was half broken. We pushed the door open, it nearly came off the hinges, inside there was a mountain of scrap copper wire and lots of small oily bags lying about. The signalman told us not to wander off and o keep by the door in case the night watchman saw us. David, Dennis, and I started to fill the small bags with the copper wire, there were twenty-two bags in all. We had to find somewhere to hide them, David found a place up in the corner of the railway bridge behind some thick bushes. It was right in front of the signal box where the signalman could see us. We were lucky because we never saw any trains, we had to carry the bags over the railway tracks taking them one-by-one. Some of the bags were heavy and once we'd got them to the first spot we then we had to drag them up the up embankment. When we finished we waved over the signalman and we started to walk under the bridge. The copper wire came from the G.P.O, it was a very big place, it started from the railway bridge and finished at the canal bridge then it went right way back to Carr's Paints. When I got home mom did her nut again, 'You're filthy Peter! What have you been up to all afternoon?' I couldn't tell her I'd been nicking copper wire, she'd only have got even more angry.

    On Monday morning I had to be at the pawnshop by eight o'clock so I was first in the queue. Mom got me up at seven o'clock and I had a swill in cold water. 'When you've finished your toast go and borrow Mrs Price's pram,' Mom told me, 'put an old sheet on the bottom of it so the suits and the sheets and the towels won't get dirty.' I got to the pawnshop about ten to eight and I could see the workers going into the pie factory Bywaters. By nine o'clock came there must have been at least twenty or more people in the queue for the shop. When it opened I pushed the pram inside and gave the bloke behind the counter the three suits and the sheets and the towels. He look at them and asked how much I wanted for them. 'My Mom said she wants two pounds for them because she wants to pay rent,' I said. The man thought for a minute and then said 'Thirty bob.' I told him again that Mom wanted two pounds, but he said again that it was thirty bob and then he told me to piss off. When I got home I gave Mom the money straight away, I knew the rent man was due around eleven o'clock. Once I'd handed the thirty bob over I ran out of the house, got the pram and ran down to the railway get some bags of copper wire. I got through the opening and slid down the embankment and I went under the bridge. I looked across at the signal box and saw a different signalman, Billy wasn't there. I wondered what I was going to do. I went back under the bridge and waited until the signalman wasn't looking. I had to lie down on the wet ground and when he had his back facing me I crawled up the embankment to where the copper wire was. I got two full bags of the stuff but they were so heavy. I had to drag one at a time under the bridge and up by the embankment till I got seven bags then I had to drag all of them up the embankment. When I got them all to the top I was shattered, but I kept on going, all I could think off was getting the rest of the rent money for Mom. I managed to loaded all seven bags onto the pram and headed straight to Raggy Allen's. On the way there I met Billy, the signalman who had helped me to get the copper wire in the first place, he asked me where I was going. I explained and he insisted he was coming with me so I wouldn't get fiddled. I couldn't believe what Mr Allen gave me, it was six pounds and fifteen shillings. Billy held out his hand so I gave him one pound, 'Give me two f**king pounds,' he said so I gave him another. Afterwards, I ran all the way home and up the stairs shouting, 'Mom I've got the rest of the rent money.' I was banging on the door to be let in when Mrs Bloomer, Mrs Price, and Mrs Fleetwood all came out to see what was all the fuss was about. 'I've got the rest of Mom's rent money, I've got four pounds and fifteen shillings here,' I told them, I was very proud of myself. They asked me where I got the money from and I told them I found some copper wire over at the tip. Just then Mom opened the door, 'I'lll speak to you later about this later, now get to the caretaker's place quickly before the rent man leaves. Pay the rest of the rent, give him the fifteen shillings and make sure he puts it down in the rent book in front of the caretaker,' she told me.

    I ran up to the caretaker's house in SouthHolme and thankfully the rent man was still there. I knocked on the door and the caretaker opened it and asked what I was doing there. 'I've come to pay up our rent,' I told him. The rent man came to the door and said that it would be fifteen shillings. As I passed him the money I told him, 'You've got to put in the rent book in front of the caretaker.' He told me that I was cheeky but he finally wrote the fifteen shillings in his book in front of the caretaker and then he said, 'Tell your mother she's up to date with her rent, but if she doesn't keep up with it she will lose the house next time.' When I got back home Mom started to shout at me about the copper wire. She began to cry about me telling lies, but I kept telling her not to worry and said that I would be able to get more wire so we could have the gas and the electric back on. On Tuesday morning I started to get ready for school mom came in and said that I couldn't go in the dirty clothes that I was putting on. When I told her that they were the only ones I had she said, 'Well you'll have to go and get more copper wire, but watch what you're doing and don't get yourself into any trouble. If you get any more money we'll go up to Oakley's and get you some clothes for school.' So off I went with Mrs Price's pram again, I went down to the railway line to get more copper wire. I went through the opening and down the embankment and then I went under the bridge and looked over towards the signal box to see who was there. It was Billy again, another signalman was standing there so I had to keep looking over to see if when he wasn't looking. Finally I went up the embankment to the hiding place but there was only one bag left and it was quite heavy so I had to drag it down the embankment. I managed to get to the top but it took me some time. Eventually I got the bag into the pram and I hurried all the way up to Raggy Allen's. One of his workers and got the bag out of the pram, he put it on the scales and just then Mr Allen came out of his office. He weighed the copper wire then he went away and when came back he gave me seven shillings. I looked at him and said, 'Is that all?' He nodded and then told me to hop it. As I left Mr Kettle came into the shop, he looked at me and asked what was up. I told him that I'd given Mr Allen a whole bag of copper wire but that I'd only got seven shillings for it. 'Give me the seven shillings,' Mr Kettle said, so I passed over the money and then waited outside for about 10 minutes till he came back. Mr Kettle gave me twelve shilling, as he put the coins in my hand he asked what I was going to do with it. 'I'll give it to my Mom so we can go up to Oakley's to buy me some clothes so I can go to school tomorrow,' I told him. Mr Kettle told me to come with him so we went across the road to some sort of café, it was a house made into a café and if my memory serves me right there was only two chairs and one small table. Mr Kettle bought me a cup of tea and then started to ask me lot of questions. He asked me about my Mom and I told him that she became very ill and that we was behind with the rent and had no gas or electric. 'Where's your dad,' he asked me next. I explained how Granny Pegg told me that he had died in the war, but that I wasn't sure anymore. Mr Kettle thought for a moment and then said, 'Okay I will help you to get your gas and electric back on, where did you get the copper wire from?' I told him where and he said that on Saturday and Sunday we'd go together to get some more wire.

Mom was finding it hard to live and I was being good lad going to school, I was still getting the copper wire after school and at the weekends, but only when Billy and Mr Kettle were there. Mom started her cleaning jobs again one of them was in the factory in Glover Street where she got the sack from. One Sunday afternoon I went to get some of the wire on my own, Billy was there and he let me go in like he always did, but this time I went further into the grounds looking around to see what else I could find. I must been there for some time looking round because I never saw the night watchman coming up behind me. He grabbed me by the collar and he took me into the building where he phoned the police. When they arrived they took me in the police car to Coventry Road station and they sent for my Mom. When she arrived a little later she took one look at me and started to cry, I can remember her trying to get the police to let me go with a warning. Inspector Taylor said that he wouldn't be doing this, that I'd be going to juvenile court to teach me a lesson.

So I had to go to the court again, but this time I went in front of Mrs Cadbury, everyone said that she showed no mercy and that she sent lots of people away. Thankfully my Mom won Mrs Cadbury over by giving her a letter from the doctor. I was told that I would be getting one final chance. Mrs Cadbury really told me off, I was shaking all over and I nearly wet myself I was so scared. She told me that if I appeared in front of her again I would be sent away. She ask me, 'Do you understand Peter?' In a low voice I said yes, I understood. When I got home from the court Mom gave me a big slap round the head, she really hurt me. It was first time Mom had hit me really hard and hurt me. I ran out the house and went over to the tip where I saw David and Mr Kettle, they tried to get me to go down with them to the railway to get some copper wire, but I said that I couldn't and explained that I had just come from the court. Mr Kettle asked if I got a fine, I told him no but said that if I appeared in front of Mrs Cadbury again I'd be put away. 'You're very lucky not to be sent down, Mrs Cadbury is a right cow,' Mr Kettle told me. I started to walk away but Mr Kettle stopped me and asked when I'd be going to get more wire. I told him that I didn't know and Mr Kettle told me not to wait too long if I wanted to get our gas and electric to stay on.

It was a Friday when Mrs Fleetwood came into my house and asked me if could I go fetch her some coal from Job's, which was a coal yard in Tempfield Street. I asked Mom if this was okay and she said I could go but that it would have to wait until Saturday. Come Saturday I borrowed Mrs Price's pram again and headed downstairs. When I got to the railway tracks I found that there wasn't enough coal to fill the pram, so I went over the bridge to see if Billy was there. Fortunately he was and I asked him if I could have some coal for my Mom, he said we'd have to hurry as his gaffer was coming. It was a bit heavy carrying the coal up the stairs, I went up and down the stairs about six or seven times, I filled the pram right up and then headed back home. When I was coming into the block I bumped into Mrs Fleetwood who collected her bucket and filled it with coal from the pram. She gave me one shilling and told me it was for all of my hardwork. When I got into our place Mom was sitting by the fire, I gave her the money I'd earned from passing round the coal and explained how I got it from the railway tracks. I could tell that she wasn't very happy at first, but then she was okay about it and said that I could keep the shilling Mrs Fleetwood had given to me. A little later Mom was making dinner and all of sudden there was a big bang on the door and lots of shouting. I tiptoed to the door and when I opened it some bloke grabbed me and asked, 'Where's your bloody mother?' By this time Mrs Fleetwood and the Bloomers had come out to see what all the fuss about, but the bloke shouted to all three of them to f**k off and that Mom owed his Dad two pence. The bloke still had me by the collar and everyone shouted at him to let me go. The bloke refused saying that he needed his money. Eventually Mr Bloomer gave him the two pence and the bloke left. My Mom was a little shaken so Mrs Fleetwood put her arm round her and asked if she was okay. 'Peter has been a good lad,' Mom said, 'I'll treat him to a tea cake.' Mom and I went into Twitter's together to get a teacake, as we went in Twitty came out from the back with his nose running and his glasses on the edge of his nose. He pulled out a piece of old rag which was covered with snuff and he wiped his nose with it. Twitty walked round to the back of the counter and his nose started to run again, he turned to me and asked what I wanted. I pointed to the teacake in the window and Mom put a penny on the counter and walked out. Old man Twitty shouted, 'You owe me another two pence!' Mom shouted back, 'With that runny nose not on your Nellie!' When we left Mom said she was going to go to Able's to see if there was any butter for a penny and that I was to go home to get the fire started. A little later Mom came in with a little piece of butter cut into a square then she toasted the teacake on the fire. It was getting late when Mom told me to draw the curtains and light the candles, it was about ten o'clock before I went to bed. I was lying awake thinking about Twitty for ages but I must have fallen asleep because when I woke up it was really dark outside. I got up and looked to see what Mom was doing, she was in bed so I got dressed and opened the door very quietly then I ran down the stairs and of out the block. There wasn't anybody about as I went over the horse road to Twitter's shop and looked through the window. I could see a teacake and a small loaf sitting there so I went by side of the fruit shop to find a brick to throw through the window. I found one and threw it through the window, I quickly grabbed the teacake and the small loaf and then I ran down the lane as fast as I could go. I went over the railway bridge and turned left into Maxstoke Street then I ran all the way to St Andrews Street and into WestHolme through the gully into EastHolme. When I got to our block I hurried up the stairs and closed the door very quietly behind me, thankfully Mom was still asleep. I put the teacake and the small loaf in the pantry and went to my room, Mom never knew I went out that night.

Come Sunday morning I heard Mom cleaning out the ashes from the fireplace so she could start afresh. The fire grate was only small, there was a stand which you could pull down to put the kettle on. We had an oven next to the fire and while the kettle was boiling Mom was sitting by the table counting out money. Just then Mrs Bloomer came knocking on the door and when she got in she asked Mom if we'd heard what had happened over at Twitty's. 'Somebody's only gone and smashed the shop window,' Mrs Bloomer explained. Mom asked if anything had been taken but Mrs Bloomer said, 'I don't know the old man told me when he fetched his paper this morning.' I looked over at Mom and told her that I knew who'd done it. 'How do you know Peter?' she asked me. 'I did it ,' I told her, 'I pinched a teacake and a small loaf,' then I went to the pantry and fetched the teacake and the loaf. 'Why you little   b*****d,' Mrs Bloomer said, 'you wait till I tell the old man!' Mrs Bloomer went out and then Mom came by me and gave me hard slap across my face, it stung and I knew my face was going red. Mom started to cry so I went over to her I hug her and told her I wanted to get my own back on Twitty, I tried to tell her not to worry and that the police wouldn't know it was me.

A little later Mrs Bloomer came back up to the house and when she saw that Mom was crying she said, 'Now stop that Mrs Round nobody is going to find out that it was Peter.' Mom nodded and then asked Mrs Bloomer if she had any money for our gas and electric. 'I've got thirty five shillings,' Mom explained, 'I'm going up there on Monday I got to take time off from work again.' Mrs Bloomer told Mom that she'd take the money up there for her and that she'd take me with her so that I knew where the place was.

Later that day Mom sent me over to fruit shop with two shillings to get some potatoes, a small cabbage, and some carrots. As soon I walked into the fruit shop the bloke behind the counter asked me if I'd brought him the shilling that Mom owed him. I still had money in my pocket so I gave him the shilling Mom owed and then he asked me what I wanted. When I told him he asked me how much money I had. I held out the money for him to see and then he gave me three potatoes, six cabbage leaves, and four carrots. I can remember that Mom made a meal with what I'd managed to get from the shop and with the small loaf. Although we only had a small fire Mom cooked very well, it was some sort of stew and she toasted the small loaf then let it go hard, then she cut it up and put it into the stew pot. I remember it tasted alright and it was filling, Mom said there would be leftovers for the next day.

Come Monday morning Mom got ready for work and she told me to behave myself before she left. 'Go to Mrs Bloomer's when you get back,' she told me, 'don't come here and don't get into any trouble. Granny will feed you and I'll pick you up later.' Mrs Bloomer shouted up to me so I went downstairs to meet her. Together we went down Garrison Lane and got on the tram by the park, I remember the fair for me was a penny and threepence for Mrs Bloomer. We got off top at the terminus on Albert Street and we had to walk back down to the electricity office. When we got there I can remember Mrs Bloomer saying that she wanted to see someone in charge. We had to go up some stairs where there was this big bloke standing by the door. 'Mrs Round?' he asked. 'No,' Mrs Bloomer replied, 'I'm here to pay some money for her though, this is Mrs Round's son, Peter.' The bloke asked how he could help and Mrs Bloomer replied that she'd come to pay him thirty-five shillings off Mom's bill so that he could put electric back on. I think Mom actually owed over five pounds by then. The bloke said that Mom used a lot of electric, but Mrs Bloomer tried hard to persuade him. 'Okay Mrs Bloomer, if Mrs Round can pay two pounds and ten shillings and pay one pound and ten shillings by next Monday I will reconnect the electric on Wednesday. Do you know this is the second or the third time Mrs Round has had her electric disconnected?' 'I will tell her,' Mrs Bloomer said, 'Mrs Round has been very ill and has been of work for some time. She's got no husband and money is very tight, she's also behind with her rent. It's going to be a struggle to find the money.' The bloke thought about what Mrs Bloomer had said for a moment. 'Okay,' he said, 'if Mrs Round can find thirty five shillings by next Monday morning and pay five shillings a week I will reconnect on Wednesday. I will come see her myself and explain what's got to be done. If she misses one payment then I will disconnect her electric and she won't get it back on till she pays the full amount and the reconnection charges.' Mrs Bloomer promised to make sure Mom understood. When we got back Mrs Bloomer told me to come upstairs with her so she could explain the situation. I later found out that Mrs Bloomer knew Mom never went to work that day. As we was going up the stairs Mrs Fleetwood came out of her house and asked if everything was okay. 'We'll have to wait and see,' Mrs Bloomer told her. In our house Mrs Bloomer told Mom to sit down and told her everything. Mom just sat there while Mrs Bloomer was talking. Mrs Fleetwood had followed us in and she asked me if could I go fetch her some coal from Job's, she gave me three shillings so off I went to borrow Mrs Price pram yet again. Mrs Fleetwood shouted from the landing to make sure I got three shillings worth of coal. I went down the lane towards the railway tracks and there was only few lumps of coal there. I looked across to the signal box to see if Billy standing there. I got the few lumps of coal up the embankment into the pram and then I went over the bridge to the gate and shouted to Billy asking whether I could have some of his coal for my Mom. He came down from the signal box and said, 'If I'm giving you all this coal you got to do something for me. I have found way into Lucas's so you can get me some car batteries.' He gave me some coal and as I was loading coal into the pram he told me to come back on Saturday afternoon around two o'clock. I got the three shillings worth of coal in the pram and when I got back Mrs Fleetwood said, 'You haven't been to Job's at all have you?' I told her no because a new coal yard had opened up down at the bottom of the lane, I told her that the man there said for me to help myself so I did. 'You're a good lad Peter,' she said and then she gave me sixpence to carry the coal up the stairs for her. I had to go and wash the pram out and then take it back. When I gave Mom the three shillings and the sixpence she asked if I'd got the coal from the railway tracks. When I nodded in reply she did her nut and told me to keep away from the tracks.

On Tuesday morning I was lying there thinking what Billy wanted me to do on Saturday afternoon when Dennis came calling for to go to walk to school. When I got downstairs we both looked at each other and decided to play the wag. We went running over the tip looking for some tat and I told Dennis what Billy the signalman wanted me to do that Saturday. 'I'll come with you to see how many batteries Billy wants us to get for him,' Dennis said, 'I'll bring my cousin with me too. Next we went to the railway tracks and into the gully through the opening and walked along the embankment. So the signalman didn't see us we went under the bridge and down the embankment to cross the tracks up the embankment looking for opening into Lucas's. We went all the way along top of the embankment trying to find an opening but we couldn't so we went back the same way and crossed the tracks again this time we climbed up the fence onto top of the railway bridge and jumped down. Together Dennis and I started to walk down St Andrews Street. Lucas's had whole of the street apart from a few houses and the Methodist Church. Dennis and I kept trying to find an opening into Lucas's but all we found was an archway and when we looked in we saw people working. We went along to the next gate and again we looked to check. There was no one about so we started to walk through the archway but some bloke shouted to us to get out so we ran all the way back to my house. Dennis left me at the entrance to the block and walked towards his house, he turned and shouted to me that he'd see me the next day. When

Mom came home a little later she did me tea; she never knew I'd played the wag that day.

It was a Friday when Dennis came calling for me. Mom thought Dennis was calling for me to go to school to school with him but we played the wag again that day. We ran down the stairs and headed over to the tip again. As we were going up Venetia Road there were tipping lorries and also dust carts coming up the road. One lorry driver shouted at us to get out of the way or we'd get ourselves run over. Dennis and I ran past the air raid shelter to the tip to look for tat again. We searched for a while and we found some sticks then Dennis shouted over to me to 'Come here quickly.' When I got to him he was crouched over a big bag, 'What's in there?' I asked him. Dennis wouldn't tell me but he asked me to help him carry the bag with him, it was quite heavy. We went towards the back of Tilton Road and I asked again what was in the bag, Dennis didn't reply. We got to the opening of Tilton Road where there was a framework of an old pram with two front wheels. We got the pram through the opening then we got the bag through opening and onto the pram. Dennis opened the bag and then he got some paper out of the bag and stuck up it up my jumper. He did this three or four times and then told me to get home quickly. I stood there for a moment watching Dennis running away with the pram. Then I turned I ran in the opposite direction. I rushed in through our door and pulled out the paper and put it onto the table. 'Where's all this come from,' Mom shouted. I told her that Dennis found a big bag over at the tip, that it was very heavy and that he stuffed all this paper up my jumper then he told me to hurry off home. Looking at the paper I could see that it had fancy writing on it, but that was all. Mom told me to go put some coal on the fire so I went and got the coal bucket while she started to straighten the paper then she took it into her bedroom. A little later all went quiet, Mom never spoke all she was doing was looking at the fire. Time was getting on and it started to get dark, all I had for my tea was some mash potato and one dried piece of bread. I drew the curtains about nine o'clock and Mom said it was time for bed. As I walked towards my room Mom said that we would try and get the gas and electric connected again on Monday.

Saturday morning came and Mom shouted to me from her bedroom to clean out the fire grate. After the fire was clean I got two slices of stale bread out for breakfast and Mom got up and started the fire. She gave some hot water with powdered milk and then toasted the stale bread. I ask her if I could go out and she said I could as long as I kept away from Dennis, she said he was trouble. 'I'm going up the Coventry Road to see what food I can buy,' she told me as I left. I ran over horse road into Venetia Road just in case Mom was watching me from the veranda, you could see all the way up Venetia Road from our place. I went along the side of the tip till I got to the opening of Tilton Road and then I ran to   Dennis' house. Some kids were playing in the garden next door and they told me that Dennis left in a hurry yesterday. I looked through the window and I could see that the house was empty so I crossed Cattell Road into Garrison Lane. As I was I saw Dennis cousin Jimmy, he lived in Camp Street. I ask him where Dennis had gone and he told me that his dad told him they had done 'a moonlight flit.' I didn't don't know what he meant so I asked Jimmy to explain. 'They pissed off without paying the rent,' Jimmy said. I ask him if he was coming with me to get the car batteries and he said he would so we started walking off down the lane together. When we got   towards EastHolme and I told Jimmy to run so my Mom wouldn't see me if she was looking out of out the window. Billy was waiting for me by the block and when Jimmy saw him he ran off and left me alone. Together Billy and I walked through the gully up towards St Andrews Street and over the bridge alongside Lucas's till we got to the Methodist Church. Billy had a key to open the gate and we went in, Billy locked the gate behind us. We went around the back of the Church where there was a tall wooden fence with barbed wire on top of it; Billy had a bar to force an opening for us to go through.

I just about managed to squeeze through the opening and when I got to the other side of the fence Billy pointed to a door and told me go in and fetch the batteries. The door was hard to open but I managed it and I went inside. It was very quiet, nobody was about and there was a funny smell, it was making me feel sick. Billy shouted to me to hurry up so I started to carry the batteries over to the fence. The batteries were very heavy but somehow I managed to get them to Billy through the opening. When I'd got five of them Billy told me to go back and close the door. I got back through the opening and he closed the opening in the fence behind me. We went back through the gate and Billy covered the batteries up. As he was locking the gate I realised that I smelt and that I was very filthy. Billy told me I was a good lad for helping him and he gave me four half crowns. Then he told me I could come for some more coal tomorrow afternoon. Once Billy had left I sat on the church wall for a bit looking at the four half crowns in my hand. I eventually went home, Mom was in and when she saw how filthy I was she did her nut and asked where I'd been. I told her I hadn't been in any trouble and that I'd been helping Billy the signalman get some batteries and that he'd given me ten shillings. I gave Mom the money and she went into the kitchen put the money into a jar in the pantry without saying anything else.

Come Monday morning it was time for the rent man to come. The door was already open when he arrived and I saw Mom give him one of the white papers with the fancy writing on. The rent man asked her where she got the money and she said, 'My son gave it to me, he got the money from the army fund.' Mom went on to tell him that she wanted to pay ten weeks including the three weeks she'd already paid so that would be thirteen weeks in total. Mom made sure the man put all the weeks down in his rent book and I can remember him saying that this would be three pounds and five shillings. Mom said for him to put another five shillings down and the rent man to give her the change. The rent man what army fund Mom meant, 'It's none of your business,' she shouted back, 'you've got the rent money now I don't want to see you for another eleven weeks!' After the man had gone Mrs Fleetwood came in to see if everything was alright, she said she'd heard Mom shouting. Mom didn't really explain she just said that Tommy and Albert had helped her with money to pay the rent.

A little later Mom and I went downstairs and we called on Mrs Bloomer to borrow some money for the tram fare. She asked where we was going, 'I'm going to see my son Tommy at New Street station to see if he can help us to get the gas and the electric back on,' Mom explained. Mrs Bloomer did lend Mom the fare and we got on the tram to Albert Street. When we got off we walked back to the electric office which was on the corner of Albert Street and Fazeley Street. Mom spoke to a woman and asked to see the manager about getting the electric back on. After few minutes the woman came back and asked Mom if she had any money to pay the electric bill. Mom replied that yes she did have the money and then the woman disappeared again, returning shortly after to say that the manager will be down in few minutes.

The manager eventually came down and he asked Mom how much she was going to pay. When Mom told him it would be the full amount he nodded and told us to follow him up to his office. When we got inside we sat down and the manager said, 'Mrs Round you owe eight pounds twelve shillings and sixpence plus one pound and fifteen shillings to reconnect. So, have you got that much money?' 'I've got fifteen pounds here,' Mom told him holding the money out. The manager thought for a moment and then asked, 'Where did you get the money?' Mom explained she got it from her two sons who got it from the army fund. 'Okay Mrs Round,' the manager said, 'the full amount comes to ten pounds ten shillings and sixpence.' Mom pulled two white papers from her handbag and handed them to the manager. 'Okay Mrs Round,' he said nodding, 'when the man comes to reconnect your electric give him the ten shillings and sixpence. I'm going to tell you, your electric will go up to over a shilling. The man will put another lock on the meter and it will be a lot stronger the last one. Your electric will be reconnected on Wednesday morning but Mrs Round, if this happens again your electric will go up even more, it will double to two shillings.' Mom nodded and thanked the manager for being so understanding. As we were leaving the office the manager asked if the gas was also cut off and Mom told him yes. 'How have you been coping Mrs Round?' Mom replied that she was coping just about and that she had the money for the gas too. 'You must have two great sons to help you to get the money,' the manager said. 'Well I've also got a third great son,' Mom said pointing to me, 'this one here has been a great help to me.'

Mom and I left the electricity office together and headed to the gas office which was on Edmund Street at the back of the council house. It was a big building and we had to go up some steps into a large hall, the counter was like a half circle. Mom told me to wait over by the door on the bench; I went over and sat down. I remember waiting there for quite a while. I started to get hungry so I went over to Mom to ask her how much longer we would be, she told me to go and sit back down and to be patient. After a while longer Mom seemed to finish so she came over to me and said, 'Come on we will go see your Tommy at the station now.' We got to New Street station and found Tommy, Mom told him about what I'd found. He put his arm around my shoulder and he led me away from Mom to a doorway where he asked me to tell him the truth about where I got all the money from. I explained that I'd told Mom the truth and that it was Dennis who found the bag then he stuffed big handfuls of the money up my jumper and I ran straight home to Mom. 'Where does this Dennis live up?' Tommy asked me. When I told him it was by the Atlas pub Tommy got me by the scruff of my collar and said, 'Okay I believe, now come on we will go tell Mom you're telling the truth.' We went to meet Mom at the nearby cafe where she's bought me a rock cake. It was a bit hard but I ate it because I was hungry. Tommy looked at me and pointed his finger saying that I'd better stay out of trouble because I was worrying Mom. I just nodded my head and carried on eating my cake. A little later Mom and I left Tommy at the café and we started to walk up Queens Drive. Just then Tommy came running up to us and he gave me another rock cake.

Mom and I were walking through the fish market towards home, you could smell the fish it was so strong. When we got to the end of the street we bumped into my uncle Harry again and Mom asked him how he'd been keeping and how Nellie was. Harry replied that they were okay and then once he asked how we all were he went on his way. We started to walk down cobblestones of the bull ring along Digbeth to Heathmill Lane and I looked at the old crown, it was an old building and I remember thinking how nice it looked. Mom and I walked along Heathmill Lane into Great Barr Street, to me it was a very long walk home.

When we got back Mom asked me to go round to Granny Pegg's and see if she could lend her a basin and any old newspaper. 'What do we want a basin and newspaper for Mom?' I asked her. She smiled at me and then said, 'We are going to have faggots, peas, and chips tonight, there's a new shop open in Cattell Road. I went running round to Gran's, when I arrived she was sitting by the wireless and asked what I wanted. I explained what Mom had said and Gran asked where Mom had got the money from to buy our dinner. 'We went to see Tommy today,' I told her, 'he gave Mom some money.' Gran slowly got up and got me a basin and some newspaper, she told me that the basin would need washing out first before we used it.

It was around five o'clock when Mom and I went up to the faggot and peas shop and when we go there was a big queue. Mom gave the basin to the bloke behind the counter and he put two faggots and one spoon full peas in there, it came to one shilling and sixpence altogether. By the time we got home I think it was about seven o'clock so Mom put the food in the oven to warm up. We didn't have any chips in the end, instead Mom toasted the stale bread and put the faggot onto the toast and few peas. It was tasty and it filled me up. I had to draw the curtains again that night and before Mom lit the candles. When I went to bed I lay there thinking about what the paper with the fancy writing on was. I must have fallen asleep, the next thing I knew I'd woken up and I wanted to go to the toilet. I got up quietly and went to the bathroom, as I went back to my room I heard Mom crying in her room. I stood there for a moment wondering what to do, but then I went back to my makeshift bed and covered myself with three heavy overcoats, the best blankets had gone to the pawnshop.

Billy had started to bully me into getting more car batteries in order for me to get more coal. Eventually I was going twice a day and I started to get coal for Mrs Bloomer, Mrs Fleetwood, and for Mrs Price. Every time I got the coal for Mrs Bloomer she gave me two shillings, Mrs Fleetwood and Mrs Price both gave me a shilling. Our coal house was getting so full the coal was getting above the wooden boards so I started to stack it neatly to the very top. The next time I went down to get some coal for Granny Pegg I filled the pram right up so that the springs were nearly touching the wheels. I went up the gully way and I just managed to get to Gran's, she was sitting by the wireless again and she looked at me when I went it. When I told her that I'd brought her some coal she came to the back door with me and she took one look at the pram and asked me where I'd got the coal from. When I explained about the railway tracks Gran asked if Mom knew about what I doing and told me that it was very dangerous. 'Wait till I see your mother,' she said, 'I'll give her a piece of my mind.' Granny Pegg wanted me to take her to the snuff shop and as we were about to leave she looked at me and asked if I'd had a wash that morning. I said yes but she carried on and said that I had a tide mark around my neck and face. Then she gave me a wet cloth and told me to wipe my neck and face properly before we went out. Once I'd finished she said I looked much better and then told me to go and say hello to my Auntie May. I went into my Auntie's bedroom to and went over to her, I said this before but she was bedridden and she couldn't speak, but she always held my hand and smiled whenever I visited her. I had to get the wheelchair for Gran out of her bedroom, it was a tight squeeze getting it out of the house and through the front door. As I was struggling with the wheelchair in came Nancy Waldron, she was going to look after Auntie May while Gran and I were out. Gran got into the chair and I had to push her, it was easy on the level and we went down the gully then down Garrison Lane to the snuff shop. Gran told me to leave her outside and to go into the shop and ask for two ounces of snuff. The lady behind the counter asked me who the snuff was for and I pointed to the window, 'It's for my Gran, she's waiting outside.' The lady went out to see if I was telling the truth and then she came went back into the shop to get the two ounces snuff I'd asked for. When the lady told me it came to a shilling and ninepence I popped my head out of the door to tell Gran who said she'd pay the lady on Friday. I asked the lady if this was okay and she nodded her head in reply and passed me the snuff. When I went outside to Gran she asked me to go back in and see if the shop had any sugar, I ended up buying a pound of the stuff.

Back outside I was about the turn the chair around when Granny Pegg asked me to push her down the lane by the park. I kept pushing Gran along by the park and we got to the end of the park across the horse road onto Watery Lane and onto the island where there was some toilets and a horse trough. We stopped for a moment so I could use the toilet then we crossed over Watery Lane again into Great Barr Street, I was pushing this heavy wheelchair with my back halfway down to the floor my bum was up in the air. I came to Great Barr bridge, it was a hump back bridge and it was hard to push the chair up and over it. We got the end of Great Barr Street and there was three blokes standing outside the Forge Tavern. I noticed they took their hats off to Gran as we passed them, we got over the horse road in Fazeley Street and got to the pavement but I was struggling to lift the chair up onto the pavement. One of the blokes came across to help me to lift it, as he did he smiled at me and he ruffled my hair. Gran and I thanked him for his help and then we carried on to Floodgate Street. I asked Gran who the blokes were and she replied, 'Never you mind who they are, I just hope you don't grow up like them Peter.' We got the end of the Street where there was a river on my left hand side, 'It's called the river Rea,' Gran told me, 'don't you ever go down there it's very dangerous and you will drown.' We turned the corner and there was a queue of people, Gran told me to leave her there and to go and get in the queue; the queue was for the sweet shop. In the shop you took a pound sugar for a half pound of fish sweets, I think there was about eight fish sweets in a little white paper bag. I thanked Gran when I got out and she smiled telling me to push her to the Acorn pub. We went the same way back and when we got back to Fazeley Street the three blokes was still standing there. They took their hats off again and the same bloke helped me lift the chair onto the pavement. He gave me two shillings and the other two blokes did the same, ruffling my hair and giving me two shillings. I got over the hump back bridge again and Gran told me to give her the money. I didn't want to at first, it was my money, but she insisted.

   We got to the Acorn pub and Gran went in for a quick half pint, I was standing outside for some time before she came back out. I had to push her up the hill and when we got into Maxstoke Street I had to stop for a rest and to get my breath back. I was about to stand by the wall when the chair started to roll back, how I managed to stop it I don't know. I think this was the second time I saw Granny Pegg laugh. We went round the back when we finally got back to her house, Gran went straight in the kitchen where she took a pinch snuff. I managed to get the chair into the kitchen and then back into the bedroom. Auntie May held my hand and smiled at me when I went over to her (I remember that she died in November 1949.) I told Auntie May I was going and she lifted her hand for me to hold and I kissed her on the forehead.

I asked Nancy if she would like a fish sweet and told her that Gran had bought me them from the sweet shop. 'He's been a very good lad!' Gran shouted from the kitchen. I asked Gran if she was going to give me the money I'd got from the blokes and Nancy asked who were they. Gran said, 'I'll tell you later,' but she did give me two shillings. 'Don't give any of that money to your Mother,' Gran told me, but I said I'd give mom the money as we didn't have any. Gran thought for a moment and then she gave me another shilling.

A little later I left Gran's and walked out of the block and up the stairs Mrs Price asked if I'd clean out the pram again. I said I would but that I had to go and tell Mom something first. 'Okay,' Mrs Price said, 'she's trying to get the gas back on you know.' I went running in, the door was open and Mom was in the kitchen standing by the stove crying. I asked her what was up and she said nothing, then she went into her bedroom still crying. I was sitting on the hard chair looking out the window wondering what I'd done.

After a while Mom came out and I asked her if she was alright, all she said was 'Yes son.' I started telling her about my adventure with Granny Peg and she said she shouldn't have taken the money off me. I asked what she meant by 'dirty money' and she said it meant that if you ever saw the blokes again I wasn't to take any more money from them. I said that they seemed like nice blokes to me and that they even took their hats off to Gran. 'They are not nice blokes,' Mom told me, 'they are like the ones who got you into trouble before.' She went into the kitchen and put the money into a jar in the pantry. I remembered what Mrs Price has asked me so I went down the stairs and knocked on the Bloomer's door and I asked if I could borrow a bucket. Mrs Bloomer filled the bucket up with warm water and she got some old rag. I cleaned out the pram and just as I finished Mrs Price came out and checked it over. When I was about to go back up the stairs Mrs Bloomer asked me if I would go and fetch her some more coal. I told her that I couldn't because Mrs Price wouldn't let me borrow the pram again so she knocked on Mrs Price' door and she negotiated the use of the pram if I got her some coal too. Mom came out to see where I was and she shouted down to me that my tea was ready. We had mash potato which was lumpy with bits of tinned meat it in, it was horrible. I had to eat it with some toast which was burnt, even Mom didn't like it but we both sat there eating because we was hungry. We sat down at the table and Mom talked to me about going to Ada Road school. 'It's not going to be easy,' she told me, 'but you need to learn more.' 'Mom, it's a long way off and I'll be leaving when I'm fourteen,' I said to her. She shook her head and said that they were putting the school age up to fifteen. I can remember saying to Mom that I could leave when I was eleven so I could help her to get some money and keep the gas and electric on. 'Not on your nelly!' she told me. 'You are going to school my lad, do understand me? And don't you go telling anyone how we got the gas and electric on will you?'

After tea I headed back down the stairs and Mrs Bloomer asked me if I could go fetch her some coal again. I collected the now clean pram and I went back down to the tracks. When I saw Billy there I said hello and he grabbed me by the collar and said I better be there on Saturday to get more of the car batteries. I promised that I would and then I grabbed a load of coal. Mrs Bloomer gave me three shillings for her share and Mrs Price gave me one shilling for hers. I carried the final two pram loads up the stairs and put the coal on our veranda. As I was finishing the second pram load Mrs Fleetwood came out and she asked me if I could get her some coal too. Off I went again to the tracks, but when I got there another bloke was at the signal box. Billy came down and he told me the bloke was coming with us on Saturday to help. I said no at first but then he grabbed hold me by the collar and dragged me round the side under the bridge where he slapped my face hard. 'You're going to do what I tell you Peter, do you understand?' I wanted to cry and how I stopped myself I don't know. I remember looking at him and saying to myself, 'I'll get you for this one day.' As I collected the coal my face was still stinging from the slap.

Despite being upset I found myself there on the Saturday afternoon, there was another bloke with a pram so off we went up the gully. I had to push the pram while the other two blokes followed behind. We got to the church and Billy unlocked the gates, he made sure I didn't run off and he got me by the arm. He pushed me and the pram inside and then he locked the gates behind us. The two blokes kept looking at me and I was getting frightened. I followed Billy and we went behind the church where he got the bar and opened the fence. I had to squeeze through opening but this time it was really hard, I managed to get through to the door where the batteries were. The door was really tough to open and one of the blokes shouted to me to hurry up. I got the door open but the batteries weren't right there like before, they was further way. It was harder for me to carry them that distance and the door banged and scared me. I stood there for a moment, the place was really dark but I started to carry the batteries to the door which kept on banging. Billy and the blokes kept on shouting at me to hurry up but it was a tough job and a tight squeeze getting through the opening with the batteries. On the way back out Billy grabbed hold of me and took me behind the church, he wanted to know where my Mom got the money from. I told him it was from my two brothers but he said he had heard different and he slapped me again. One of the blokes came round to see what was going on and asked if Billy had hit me. Billy said I deserved it for my cheek. 'I wasn't been cheeky Sir, honest I wasn't,' I told him. The bloke thought for a moment and that told Billy to let me go. Billy and the bloke away and Billy told me he'd be seeing me again when I went to get more coal. I saw them covering the batteries over, we all got out and I went and sat on the wall. The two blokes gave me four half crowns and then asked Billy if he was going to give me anything. Billy gave me four half-crowns too. I was sitting on the wall all dirty and smelly thinking about what I should do and watching Billy and the blokes walk away. Billy turned around and pointed his finger at me. I looked at the money I had in my hand, I still had three shillings from earlier and I counted it all up. It came to one pound and thirteen shillings altogether.

I ran all the way home and I was about to run up the stairs when Mrs Price came out and said, 'Peter you haven't cleaned the pram out again. What have you been doing you look filthy and you stink.' I said I'd been working over at the tip and she said she tell Mom what I'd been doing. When I got to the house Mom took one look at me and said, 'You're bloody filthy, your clothes are filthy and you've got to wear them for school! Take them off and go in the kitchen right now.' I gave Mom thirty bob and told her that I had gone tating. 'Just go in the kitchen, and take your clothes off and put them in the boiler,' she told me. I was standing in the kitchen naked and shivering while Mom got the big pot on the stove so I could wash in hot water in the sink. The kitchen started to warm up with the gas on the boiler and on the stove so Mom brought in some soap which was long and dark green, it smelt horrible. She cut some off and gave it to me to wash myself with, I remember it was rough. The water with my clothes in was starting to boil so Mom got the pot off the stove and poured the hot water in the sink while I was washing myself. She kept pulling the clothes out of the boiler with tongs up and down to get them clean, they were only clothes I had as I'd worn all my others out. Mom started to dry them by the fire, she put the jacket by the oven and hung my trousers and socks up. They must have been a little too close to the flame because they almost caught fire. When I'd finished washing all I had to wrap around me was a small towel. It was getting late in the evening when I had two slices of toast and a cup of warm milk for tea.

Come Sunday morning Mom said we'd go over to the fruit shop to see what we could get to have a nice dinner. Together we went into the shop but before Mom could say something Mr Howard told us to get out and not to come back. I was confused, but Mom and I left and instead we went to Able's. When we went around the back Mom told Mrs Able what Mr Howard had said. Mrs Able looked at me and said, 'I bet it was him who caused all the trouble.' Mom nodded and told Mrs Able that she agreed. Mrs Able went to the fruit shop and got us what we wanted. When she passed Mom the bag she said, 'You better give him,' she nodded towards me, 'a good talking to you know.' When we got home Mom cooked a horrible dinner and when we'd finished eating I remember her saying to me, 'Come on, let's go and watch your Uncle Lincoln and his band down at the Itchy Bottle, he's playing there this afternoon.' I found out later the place was nicknamed the 'Itchy Bottle' because the mothers used to feed the babies from the bottle when they were there. Bands used to play there nearly every Sunday afternoon.

A few weeks later David started to call for me again and we got into all sorts of trouble together. There was a fruit shop on the corner of Tilton Road and Garrison Lane and outside there was barrels of apples, David and I would take in turns to nick some of them. Once, when it came to my turn to nick the apples, the owner of the shop came out and caught us. We tried to run away but the owner was faster than us. He tried to scare us by taking us to the copper who was on the crossing over the horse road, the copper ended up taking David and I to Coventry Road police station. Thankfully there were different coppers at the station and they didn't know David and me. They put us in a cell and they lock the door, we pretended to cry because it was dark, but both of us had been there before. One of the coppers to the cell and opened the door, when he did we both that we were sorry and that we wouldn't do it again. They let us go after a brief telling off. A while later David and I started to nick the apples from outside the shop again. One day, when we had nicked a few each, we ran into the playground singing 'up Sam arse in America.' Where the song came from I don't know.

David's Dad was a rag bone man, he had a scrap yard in Doris Road at the top of Garrison Lane. If we couldn't get any more copper wire he told us where we could nick scrap from; at the back of Raggy Allen's. David and I took the tat we found over the tip to Raggy Allen's on several occasions, though he did fiddle us.

David's Dad told us what to do; he said that when Raggy Allen closed we should go round the back of the scrap yard. Next I had to lift David up so he could climb over the brick wall, it wasn't too high but what we didn't know was that there was a big guard dog on the other side. When we tried it David was pulling me up but the dog bit him on the arse! David let go of me and I fell down the hill. David fell over the wall and down the hill, he was really bleeding from the bit wound. Along the wall there was a small path so we climbed the hill which wasn't very steep. We went straight to David's house (he lived in Tilton Road) and his Dad started to laugh when he saw what had happened. I can remember that David wasn't too happy and that he swore at his Dad. David got such a slap around his face he was knocked him over on top of me. His Dad had to pick me up, I started to cry and I can remember saying to him that I wanted to go home. When I got back Mom told me off again because my clothes was filthy, she wasn't too happy because she had to wash them all again.

The next day David came calling for me on the way to school, he told me that if we went back again that night his Dad would give us five shillings each. So we went back again with his Dad this time. When we got there his Dad lifted me up at first, but I can remember telling him that I didn't want to and that I was afraid of the dog, David's Dad started swearing at me saying that he was giving me five shillings which was a lot of money to him. I got on top of the brick wall but I saw the dog coming towards me so I jumped down, I hurt myself doing it and I ran towards home. David's Dad was swearing at me to come back. The next day at school he was waiting for me, he told me I had to go with him tonight. I tried to say that I couldn't and that Tommy was coming to visit instead, but he told me that it didn't matter. Even though he scared me I never went that night. David fell out with me for a while but we soon became mates again. We never got into any more trouble even though he kept on calling for me till I left Tilton Road school to go Ada Road school.

Chapter 4
My first day out – Rhyl

'It was the first time I'd seen the sea and I was so excited.'

In July 1949, on Sunday 24th, Mom and I we sitting by the fire when she looked over at me and said, 'You're going to the seaside on Tuesday.' She had scrimped and saved to pay Mrs Able two shillings a week so I could go the seaside. Mom knew all the kids were going and she didn't want me to be left out. I remember the exact date we went because it was the day my Grandma Lee had passed away, she was my Mom's mother. Mom told me what had happened when I got back that day. Mom asked Mrs Exall, who became my future mother-in-law, to keep an eye on me although she already had five children to look after. Mom gave me ten shillings to spend though we still had no gas or electric, she wanted me to go see the sea and to have a good time. It was a big thing in them days going to the seaside. I think we set off around 8 o'clock in the morning. There were two charabangs and I can remember sitting by the window with Johnny Hewitt next to me. The charabangs was going up a steep hill and the road was winding, I was told the winding road was call 'Snake Pass.' When we got to Rhyl it was about twelve o'clock and Mrs Exall told me to stay with Albert and not to wander off. Mrs Able gave us all a lunch pack with one apple, an orange, and two sandwiches. Once we were all sorted we set off, Mrs Exall shouted to us to be back by four o'clock and no later. We headed to the penny arcade and I put my paper bag down, I remember been was so excited playing the penny one arm bandits. I lost the paper bag with my lunch in it and though I went looking for it couldn't find it. I went into one arcade winning odd pennies but I was starting to run out so I went back to the first arcade where I won loads. I was getting so excited but I wanted a wee and started to wet myself, so I ran off to find a toilet and forgot to take my pennies with me. When I hurried back they had all gone.

All I had left was six pennies, but I went to buy some chips which were wrapped in newspaper.

I went and sat on the beach eating my chips and watching the people bathing in the sea. It was the first time I'd seen the sea and I was so excited to sit there watching the waved and eating. When I'd finished I went back to the arcade to see if I could find any pennies so I could buy Mom a stick of rock, but I wasn't lucky. I went to find Mrs Exall, the time was getting towards four o'clock and when I found her the first thing she asked was where her three sons had got to. I told her that I didn't know and that I'd been looking for some pennies to buy my Mom a gift. and I wanted to by my mom a stick rock she said 'Come with me,' she said and we went to some sort of shed that sold rock. Mrs Exall brought me and her two daughters (one of them was about four or five at the time) a stick rock each and she also got one for my Mom. Mrs Exall was always very good to me and together we started to walk along the sea front. When we got to the meeting place her three sons was already there waiting for us. The charabangs came and we all got, but when we was about to leave the second charabang was having trouble starting up. It kept on making a loud noise, finally the driver got it started around five o'clock and we all set off. It took some time getting out of Rhyl because the second charabang kept having some sort trouble. I was sitting by the window again and I remember thinking how slow we were going.

About ten minutes into our journey home the second charabang broke down and we were stuck for here for about two or three hours. The driver couldn't get it started so the other one went to find a phone box, but he returned with no luck. The person in charge, I believe it was Dolly Able, Mrs Able's daughter, told everybody from the second charabang to get onto the first. On our seat there were three more lads and I had to sit on Johnny Hewitt's lap. One lad was sitting on half on my lap and half on the other lads other people was sitting in the aisle. It was about two hours before we got to our first stop and when we got there we stayed for about half an hour. I started to fall asleep but when we got to our second stop I woke up startled, wondering where we were. When we got home it was after midnight and all the mothers were waiting and wondering what had happened. When my Mom saw me she got hold of me and gave me a big hug, I think that's the only time I can remember having a hug from her.

When we got home she told me about Grandma Lee and I could see that she was bit upset so I gave her the stick rock. It was all broken up but Mom gave me a little smile and she asked me what I spent the ten shillings on. I told her that I couldn't remember exactly but that I'd had some chips and got her stick of rock. 'Chips?' she said, 'but what did you do with your pack lunch?' I admitted to her that I lost it but didn't exactly say how. Mom kept on at me so I told her I spent the most of the money on the one arm bandits. 'I scrimped and saved that money so you could have nice day out by the seaside, not spending it on rubbish!' she shouted, 'and I still own Mrs Able two shillings!' I could tell she was angry so I just went off I went to my makeshift bed.

A few days later I got up got ready for school and Mom gave me one piece of toast and a cup of hot powdered milk, as has usual it was lumpy. I walked into the playground and Mr Wadsworth was waiting for me. I had to go with him to the headmaster's office, I remember trying to remember what I'd done to get into trouble this time. 'You have played truant yesterday Peter,' the headmaster told me once I'd got into his office. He started to ask me some questions about a break in at the corner shop and said that I'd been seen coming around the back of the shop. 'I've got to ask you these questions before the police come,' he told me. I was being blamed for something I didn't even do! I started to cry and shout that I wanted my Mom, then I tried to run out of the office. Mr Wadsworth got hold my collar and pulled me back telling me that I wasn't going anywhere until the police arrived. I kept on saying that I wanted my Mom and I kicked Mr Wadsworth in the leg and ran out the door, I managed to get all the way to the railway where I hid.

I must have fallen asleep because some time later two kids woke me up (they thought I was dead!), I knew one of the kids his name was Tommy Lake. They asked me what I was doing, Tommy said that I must have been playing wag and when I told them I was they left me alone. I got up and went to Granny Pegg's for something to eat, when I got there she started shouting at me and saying that everybody had been looking for me. 'The school have been looking for you,' she said, 'what have you done? They said you broke into the corner shop.' I promised her that I hadn't and she must have believed me because she said she would make me something to eat and then we'd go to the police station together so that I could tell them the truth.

At Coventry Road police station Gran banged on the desk and demanded to see Inspector Taylor. The sergeant said the inspector wasn't there at the moment but said that we could wait. He asked why we wanted to see Inspector Taylor and Gran replied that, 'My grandson is innocent of what you are accusing him of. He didn't break into that corner shop.' 'We know nothing about this,' the sergeant said frowning, so Gran told him about the headmaster accusing me of breaking into the nearby fruit shop. 'I will come to the school tomorrow and I will sort out,' the sergeant promised. When we got back home Granny Pegg told Mom what had happened about the school accusing me of breaking into the fruit shop. Mom said that I couldn't have done that because I was away at the seaside on Tuesday.

Come the next day Gran came round and we all went up to the fruit shop together. I can remember standing on the corner of Tilton Road and Garrison Lane watching and listening to Mom and Gran to tell Mr Richards, the owner of the fruit shop, that he was wrong. My mate David and I were laughing at them; Mom was about to swing her handbag to hit Mr Richards when the police sergeant arrived and caught hold of her arm and then he started talking to Mr Richards about the break in. Mr Richards pointed his finger at me and said, 'Somebody told me that they saw Peter Round coming out of the back door.' The sergeant asked him who had told him that, but Mr Richards couldn't say, and then he sergeant asked what had been stolen. Mr Richards said it was about ten pounds and that it was taken on Tuesday night. Granny Pegg said that he was a bloody liar and then she slapped him across the face twice! She hurt him alright you could see in his face it was red. Gran went to hit Mr Richards again but the sergeant held her back. 'You are accusing my grandson of pinching ten pounds when he wasn't nowhere near your bloody shop!' Gran said. 'He never got home from Rhyl till midnight so how could he have broken into your shop?!' The sergeant turned calmly to Mom and asked, 'Have you got any proof that Peter went to Rhyl on Tuesday?' 'Yes,' Mom replied nodding, 'you come with me down to Mrs Able's shop.' Granny Pegg shouted to Mr Richards, 'You better come too so that you can see that my grandson is innocent.' He said that he couldn't because he had a shop to run but Gran told him to shut up the shop and to hurry up. We all got to Mrs Able's shop and the sergeant went in first telling us all to wait outside. He spoke to Mrs Able for about ten minutes and when he came out he stood on the step and looked at me. 'This young lad never broke into your shop Mr Richards,' he said, 'you better find the person who did and bring him to me at Coventry Road police station.' Gran went to hit Mr Richards again but the sergeant stopped her.

    Afterwards Mom took me back to school and we went straight to the headmaster's office. We walked in and Mom told Mr Watson that I never broke into the corner shop and the police sergeant had sorted it all out. Mom could see Mr Watson wasn't too sure that she was telling the truth so she said, 'Come with me to the shop and you can find out for yourself, or better still we will go up to Coventry Road police station.' As Mom was talking there was a knock on the door and Mr Watson shouted for the person to come on in; it was Mr Richards. He walked in and looked surprised to find us in the office. 'Now you're here,' Mom said, 'you can tell Mr Watson the truth.' 'Mrs Round is right,' Mr Richards said hanging his head, 'it wasn't Peter, it must have been someone else.' He went to walk out and Mom asked if he had anything else to say. Mr Richards quickly turned to me, said sorry and then walked out. Mr Watson turned to me and said, 'I believe it's your last day with us tomorrow Peter, us you will be going into another world. Ada Road is a tough school, I wish you good luck for the future.' As he was talking to me Mr Wadsworth came in office, Mr Watson explained that it wasn't me who broke into the shop and then he said that he thought I had something to say. 'I'm very sorry that I kicked you Sir,' I said to Mr Wadsworth. As Mom and I were leaving Mr Wadsworth put his arm around my shoulder and said, 'I will see you in class tomorrow for your last day with us.' On our way home Mom got her purse out and said, 'I only have two pence left, but we will go down to Twitter's and see if we can get you a tea cake.' I shook my head and said that we couldn't after what I did. 'He will only tell us to get out with his running nose and his dirty snotty rag with the snuff on it,' I said to her.

    The day came for me to leave Tilton Road school. David came calling for me, it was also his last day and he ended up going to Marlborough Road school. We went up to the copper on the crossing on the horse road, Mr Richards was standing outside his shop watching us as we walked passed him. On the other side of road David and I turned around and pulled our tongues out to Mr Richards and when we got to the gates we stopped and popped our heads round and pulled our tongues out at him again. We waited for a bit till he went back into his shop and then we ran over to his shop and nicked an apple each, running back to school as fast as we could go. David and I walked into the playground singing 'Up Sam arse in America'. When we got into the classroom Mr Wadsworth did nothing but talk about our new schools, both before and after break time. After dinnertime Mr Wadsworth and Mr Watson both came in and wished us all good luck at our new schools. Mr Watson said that he didn't want hear any bad news about us, only good news. 'I'm going to wish all of you good luck and that goes for you too Peter Round, you properly need it,' Mr Wadsworth said, 'okay you can go home and go straight there.' David and I was the last to leave the classroom, as we were going out of the classroom Mr Wadsworth stopped us and said, 'I saw you two nicking the apples from Mr Richards shop and pulling your tongues out to him,' he was smiling as he said it so he couldn't have been that angry at us. Only four kids went to Ada Road school me, Dennis Thomas (who lived in Tempfield street), Arthur Turner (who lived top of   Garrison Lane facing the Atlas pub), and Billy Jenkins (who lived at the bottom end of Tilton Road). I saw David for a bit during our summer holidays till we went to our separate schools. I saw him now and again over the tip looking for tat. Them towards the end of 1950 he left Tilton Road.

One Saturday I was sitting by the window thinking of what to do when Mrs Fleetwood came knocking on the door and asked me if I could go and get her some coal. I agreed so I went down to the railway tracks and at first there wasn't any coal lying about, so I went over the bridge and stood at the top of the steps thinking that Billy might let me have some of his coal. I must have been standing there for quite a while before I found myself going down the step. When I got to the stairs Billy was standing there looking at me, he frightened me and then he came towards me and I thought he was going to grab hold of me because I let him down about getting more batteries. Thankfully all Billy asked me was where my Mom got all the money from. I told him again that my two brothers got the money from somewhere in town and that was all I knew. 'Billy, we've still got no gas or electric, we had it cut off again and my brother Tommy is coming to live us next month. My Mom is worrying about getting them back on before he comes,' I told him. Billy thought for a moment and then said, 'Go on, get your coal and be quick about it before I change my mind. I borrowed Billy's bucket and filled it up as fast as I could go. When I finished I took the bucket back to Billy and thanked him, as I was leaving he shouted at me to keep my mouth shut about batteries if I knew what was good for me. I ran all the way home.

Come Sunday morning all I had was one piece of toast for breakfast, then I asked Mom if I could go out but she told me no. Mrs Fleetwood came knocking on the door, she's forgotten to give me two shillings for getting her some coal. Mom took the money off me and Mrs Fleetwood asked me when it was birthday. I said it had already gone but I told that I was eleven and that I was going to Ada Road school the next day. She asked me what my Mom had bought me for my new school and I said 'nothing'. Mrs Fleetwood smiled at me and then gave me another shilling saying I was for my birthday. I thanked her and when she was leaving she turned to me and asked me if I get her some more coal. Although I wasn't keen to I said that I would. Mom told me to be careful; I couldn't tell her what I'd been doing for Billy even though she said it was strange that he kept letting me have some of his coal.

A little later I told Mom that I was getting hungry, so she said she'd cook a stew and that I had to go over to the fruit shop to get some veggies. I told her that Mr Howard wouldn't serve me, but she said, 'Well you better say sorry to him hadn't you.' I went over to the shop but as soon as I walked in Mr Howard he told me to get out. I went to try Mr Richard's fruit shop but he took one look at me and told me to get out too. Then a lady came out from the back and she looked at me and said, 'Aren't you the one who is always in trouble with Mr Richards?' I nodded yes and she smiled to herself. She asked me what I wanted and I told her that my Mom needed some potatoes, carrots, and a cabbage. 'How much money have you got?' she asked next. I told her that I had three shillings and she said that she'd see what she could do for me. She was nice lady and she filled my bag up, it was quite heavy when she finished. It came to two shillings, although Mr Richards said it was more. The lady ignored him and asked me what my name was. When I told her it was Peter Round she said it was a nice name and then told me to go home.

I went out of the shop and Mr Richards followed me, I only got a few steps away from the shop and he shouted to me to stop. 'You owe me a shilling,' he said to me. The lady came out of the shop and told me to go home and asked Mr Richards to come back inside. When I got home Mom looked in the bag and said that I must have said sorry to Mr Richards if he'd given me all of the food. I explained that I hadn't said sorry but that a nice lady served me and that she had given me all the food. Mom started to make the stew by the fire, she got two tins of meat out and put them in the stew. The stew was horrible, but I had to eat it because I was hungry.

Chapter 5
Ada Road School

'You will receive a notification of when you will have to appear at the juvenile court.'

On 5th September 1949 I started at Ada Road school. I met Dennis, Arthur, and Billy and together the four of us walked to our new school. Come nine o'clock the bell rang and our teacher was standing on the iron staircase shouting to the new intake to get in line. He started to shout our names out and told us what line to get in, we had to get in two lines and follow him into the main hall. Then he told us new comers to go to class seven which was the one in the corner. We went into the classroom and sat down at our desks, then the teacher came in and got the register out. The teacher called our names out and when he had finished he got up from his desk and said that his name was Mr Hughes. I remember that he was tall and that he could be very strict at times. He came round with pieces of paper that had times tables on them. Some of the kids were giggling and talking as Mr Hughes walked passed them, so he got the cane out and banged it on the top of his desk. The whole class went quiet.

The lad I sat next to was called Terry Lloyd and we came lifelong best mates from the moment we met. Sadly he passed away in 2011. At break time Terry and I went into the playground and some big kids came up to us and started to take the piss because we were in short trousers. I told one of them to 'F**k off' and he grabbed me by the collar and punched me in the stomach. I bent over and then looked up at him, he was laughing at me so I gave him a good kick on the ankle. He went to grab me again and I gave him another good kick on the ankle, then his mates went to get hold of me. Luckily the bell rang so they started to walk off, saying that would get us after school. Dinner time came and I went to Granny Pegg's for something to eat. Gran moaned at me and asked why I hadn't stopped at school for dinner. I told her that I didn't have a dinner ticket and Gran got angry, asking why Mom hadn't sorted it out for me. After Gran was done with her moaning she gave me a thick sandwich and a thick yorkshire pudding, it was a bit on the hard side but I had to eat it because it was all there was. When I left a little while later Gran shouted to me, 'Don't forget my snuff!' I promised that I wouldn't and then I left to get back to school.

The big kids were hanging around the school gate when I got back. I waited till they went in but as I was going through the gate one of them grabbed hold of me and said that after school there were going to take me down the cut and drown me. Then one of teachers came out so the big lad let me go. The teacher looked over at us and said that we were late and to get back to class. Mr Hughes was standing by the door and told me that I was late and to hurry up and sit down. 'I'm going to show you lot my rules,' he said getting out his cane. 'Anyone who is late for the register or caught talking in class or not paying attention will get my six of the best.' One kid stood up and said that Mr Hughes couldn't hit him with the cane, Mr Hughes shouted for the kid to get up to the front of the class. When the kid told him to 'F**k off' Mr Hughes went to the back of the class and dragged him to the front. He got hold of the kid's hand and went to give him the cane, but the lad gave one big kick and ran out of the class and out of the school (he never came back after that).

That afternoon Mr Hughes handed out textbooks and we had to put our names in them. We did some sort of maths and I didn't understand it at first nor did Terry. He whispered to me asking if I knew what was going on and I replied in a low whisper that I didn't. At break time the big lads was waiting for me and they followed me all around the playground. Two of the big lads grabbed hold of me and took me round the side of the building where no teachers could see what they were going to do to me. They kept on saying that they going to take me down the cut and drown me. As we got round the side of the building there were other big lads smoking. One of the lads was about to hit me but thankfully one of teachers came round the corner just in time. The teacher caught the lad who was smoking, I started to get scared so I got away from the big lad. The bell rang I ran to my classroom. Mr Hughes kept on shouting at me to pay attention but I couldn't wait for four o'clock to come. The bell rang and I got straight up and was about to run towards the door when Mr Hughes grabbed me by the collar. 'Where do you think you're going my lad?' he asked me. 'I've got to get home quick,' I told him. Mr Hughes said that I needed to start paying attention the next day otherwise I'd feel his cane. 'Is that understood?' he said looking down at me. 'Yes sir,' I replied in a low and frightened voice. There was only one way out of the school and that was the front gate, the lads were standing on the other of the horse road. One of them ran across the road to get me. I started to walk quickly along Ada Road but he went to grab hold of me so I turned and gave him a good kick, then I started to run as fast as I could go. I turned left into St Andrews Street and they all started to run after me but I kept on going. I went straight across the horse road without looking and I heard someone shouting at me. I don't know what he was saying all I did was keep on running till I got to the canal bridge. They were catching me up, I went halfway across the horse road and then I ran towards the bridge and jumped up managing to get up by scraping my shoes on the bridge wall. I got to the top but one of the big lads got me by my ankle and tried to pull me down. I went to kick him in the head and lost my balance. I fell off the bridge into a load of stingers and really hurt myself. I couldn't move and the four lads got up and saw me lying there in the stingers. They all started to laugh at me but then a lady came out from a nearby house and shouted to them to get off the bridge. (The lad who lived in the house also became a great mate of mine his name is Eric Smith).

    I couldn't move for a while but when I eventually got up I started to walk along the embankment. I slipped down and managed to stop myself from falling into the cut. I got to the other bridge in Dartmouth Street but I couldn't find a way out so I tried to climb up the corner of the bridge. It was high up and I got up bit of way but then slipped and fell down hurting myself again. With my legs bleeding I started to climb up again and this time I got to the top. I rolled over and fell over the top of the bridge. I ran slowly down Barwell Road to get Granny's snuff, the lady in the shop asked what I'd been doing and I explained that some lads were chasing me. 'You're in a right state,' she said, 'you better get on home and have a bath.' She gave me the snuff and I ran all the way to Gran's without stopping. I walked in the back way, Gran took one look at me and asked what the bloody hell I'd been up to. 'You smell and you're filthy, just look at your legs! You better get on home and get the boiler on.' I told her that we didn't have the gas on anymore so she got some hot water and started to clean me up. She cleaned my legs with some stuff from a bottle which really stung. As she cleaned she asked me what Mom had been up to. I told her that I didn't know but that some big lads from school were chasing me. Gran asked me why they were chasing me and I explained that they was taking the piss out of me because of my short trousers and that I have given one of them a good kick. Gran started to laugh, it was rare to see her laugh or smile like that. 'I've got to get some long trousers for school tomorrow,' I told her.

I ran home and as I was going up the stairs Mrs Bloomer and Mrs Price came out. Mrs Bloomer said, 'What trouble are you in now you little B?' Mrs Price looked at my legs and asked what had been going on. I never said anything instead I just carried on up to my house. They both followed me up there and waited while I got the key from behind the door and then went straight to the kitchen to the pantry. I got the old eat pot out but there was only half crown in there. Mrs Bloomer and Mrs Price kept on asking me what trouble I'd been in but I still didn't reply, I just pushed through them. I ran all the way up to Oakley's second hand shop and when I got there I shouted for Mrs Oakley to come out from the back. She came out asking where the fire was and then asked what I wanted. 'I need a pair of long trousers,' I explained, 'the big kids at school are taking the piss out of me because I'm wearing short trousers.' Mr Oakley looked at me and then smiled, 'Okay lad I'll find you a nice pair.' The first pair she found for me was far too long, but after a while she finally found the right pair for me. I put them by my side and she said, 'What are you doing lad? Take your trousers off don't be shy.' The trousers I tried on was a good fit in the leg but a bit loose round the waist, so Mrs Oakley found me a snake belt. Once she'd put the belt on me I asked her how much it was. Mrs Oakley shook her head and said that she was looking for another pair of trousers for me. Once she's found another I tried them on she stood in front of me making sure they were the right fit. 'Okay my lad that will be five shillings and sixpence,' she said. 'Mrs Oakley I've only got half-a-crown,' I told her. She stood there without saying a word for a moment, then she looked like she had suddenly remember something. 'Was you here before with that old cow Pegg?' I nodded yes and then she asked, 'How are you going to pay me the three shillings that are owing.' I said that I didn't know but then I explained that I could go and get her some coal from down by the railway. 'Are you going to nick it?' Mrs Oakley asked me. 'No,' I told her, 'I know the signalman he let's me have as much coal as I want.' Mrs Oakley thought for a moment and then she said, 'Okay, go get me some coal then.' I asked Mrs Oakley if she had a pram and when she went to look I took my long trousers off and put my short ones back on. I saw a jumper I liked so I put that on too. Mrs Oakley shouted at me to come outside so I picked up the longer trousers and went out. When she saw me Mrs Oakley said, 'Oh no you don't give me the trousers.' She never noticed that I had the jumper on too. I was just about to run off with the pram when she tried to stop me and shouted that I hadn't given her the half crown. I ran down Garrison Road and went to the railway to see if Billy was there. Another signalman was at the box so I shouted up to him, 'Hey mister!' and he came down from and asked what I wanted. 'My mom is sick in bed and we've got no gas nor electric and no money to get it put back on.' I could see that he was going to tell me to 'F**k off' but then he changed his mind. 'Okay sonny, help yourself to some coal then.' I borrowed his bucket and I ran up and down the steps until the pram was full. When I was finished I took the bucket back up to the signal box and I thanked the man. He told me to wait where I was but I said that I had to go before someone pinched my coal. The bloke was quick and he grabbed hold of me, 'Was you the one who helped Billy get the batteries?' he asked me. 'No mister honest it wasn't me, it was my mate Peter Round he told me about the batteries. My name is Billy Peg.' He asked me about how I knew where to get the coal from and I explained that Peter Round told me. Finally then he let me go and I got out of there as fast as I could.

    I managed to get to Oakley's although my legs were hurting. I banged on the door of the shop and Mrs Oakley came out from the side. She looked at all the coal in the pram and asked if I'd nicked it, then one of her sons came out and asked the same question. Mrs Oakley told her son to take the pram off me and out it around the back. 'Can I have my trousers now?' I asked her, she nodded yes and then she fetched them along with the belt. She stood there looking at me and said, 'Okay my lad, you don't own me anything with all that coal you got me.'

    When I got home Mom asked me where I'd been to get in such a state. 'I was looking for tat round the tip,' I told her, 'I found five shillings worth and took it up to Raggy Allen's, he gave me the money so I went over to Oakley's and got myself two pairs of trousers and a jumper.' I explained that the kids at school was taking the piss out of me because I was wearing short trousers, but Mom didn't really say anything. She made some horrible stew again and I had to sit down and eat it again. I looked over at Mom and asked her if she was alright, she seemed a lot happier than usual. She just told me to go to bed like a good lad, but I knew that something was different.

    Come the next day Mom shouted to me, 'I'm off to work now Peter, be a good lad and have a good wash before you go to school. Don't get into any trouble and don't be late!' I did everything that Mom told me to do, I had good wash in some cold water and then I did myself a piece of toast by the fire and made a cup of hot powdered milk. I remember putting in five big spoonful's of powder and stirring it well to make sure that there was no lumps. Before I went out I made sure the fire was out and then off I went to school. As I was going down the stairs Mrs Bloomer came out and said that she'd never seen me looking so smart. 'I bet you won't come home like that will you, you little B, go on off to school and keep out of trouble,' she said. On my way through WestHolme Granny Pegg was looking through her window, she waved to and I waved back as I walked passed. I got to the school gate and Terry was waiting for me, but so were the big lads. As they came running towards me Terry big brother David Lloyd asked if they were the ones who'd been horrible to us. We nodded yes and then David went and had a word with them. The big lads never bothered Terry and I after that.

      Our first hour in the classroom was doing sums from the blackboard, Terry and I were copying each other's work and he was whispering to me asking how to do it. After we'd done our sums Mr Hughes starting talking about history and it was getting towards break time when the door opened and in came a prefect. Mr Hughes asked him what he wanted. 'Peter Round is to report to the headmaster's office at break time,' the prefect said, 'Mr Osbourne wants to speak with him.' Come break time I went to the office as I was told to, I was just thinking about whether I should run off when Mr Osbourne came out and told me to come inside with him. I went in and as I sat down I started to shake thinking about what trouble I was in. Mr Osbourne didn't speak for a moment, he was looking at some papers. 'Right Peter,' he said eventually, 'you're entitled to free dinners starting from today, so here's your ticket for today. I will give rest of your tickets to Mr Hughes.' I took my ticket and left the office. Break time was over and I had to go back to class, I sat down and Terry asked me what the headmaster had wanted. We never saw Mr Hughes get his cane out from the desk, he gave one big bang on his desk and it made us jump. 'What I have told this class,' he shouted, 'I'm going to ask you Peter Round.' At first I never said anything and then he told to stand up. He came towards me with his cane and he stood in front of me, 'Have you forgot what I told you yesterday?' I told him no sir. 'Then what are you whispering about nothing Peter?' I said, 'nothing' again and Mr Hughes said that he'd only ask me one more time. 'I was telling Terry about my dinner ticket Sir,' I explained. 'You're dinner ticket? Now tell me and the class about your dinner ticket,' he said. 'I got a free dinner ticket for my dinner,' I replied simply. The whole class started to laugh and Mr Hughes banged his cane on my desk making us all jump again. 'You lot think it's funny? Well during afternoon break time you lot are going to stay in and write out fifty lines of "I shall pay attention in class and not whisper".' Come dinner time Terry and I both stayed for something to eat and then we went into the playground. The big lads came passed us, they kept looking at me but they never said anything. Then one of big lads said to Terry, 'I didn't know that David Lloyd was your brother.'

When break was over we went into our classroom and Mr Hughes told us to follow him down to the hall. The P.E. teacher Mr Hart was standing waiting for us, we all had to stand in one big line while he walked up and down looking at us. Then he started to talking to us about what we were going to do in our P.E. lessons. He told us to remember to bring some shorts and that even if we did he'd will make sure we would still do the lesson. After he spoke he told us to go back to our classroom, we had one more lesson before our afternoon break. Mr Hughes came round with a sheet paper for us to write out our fifty lines on, we only had fifteen minutes to write all those lines down. Terry and I didn't finish, I think I managed about thirty lines in the end. There was about five or six of us who had to stay in after school to finish the fifty lines. When we had finished we gave Mr Hughes our papers then he told us to go and sit back down. He said that we had to wait till he'd counted all the papers to make sure that we'd all done the fifty lines. After about five minutes he'd finished counting and then Mr Hughes told us all to go home.

Terry and I was walking along Ada Road and when we got to the end we stopped for a bit. Terry asked me where I lived and I said EastHolme. He explained that he lived on the corner of Maxstoke Street and lower Dartmouth Street, but that he was moving to Bordesley Park Road soon. As we was talking Terry's brother came along and off they went together. I went running to Granny Pegg's, going in through the back door. Gran was sitting in her usual place between the table and the sideboard with the wireless on next to her. The first thing she said to me was that I was late. 'Now tell me why you had to stay after school,' she said next. 'We had write fifty lines out,' I told her. 'You've only been there for five minutes and you are already in trouble!' She got up and made me a sandwich. I stayed with her for a while and then I headed home.

When I got home I walked up the stairs, but got stopped by Mrs Bloomer and Mrs Price. 'How's your new school Peter?' Mrs Bloomer asked me. 'It's okay, I've met some new mates,' I replied. 'That's good,' she said, 'are they trouble makers Peter?' I told her that they weren't and she said, 'We will just have to wait and see won't we?' I didn't say anything else, I went on into the house and told Mom that I was sorry I was late. Mom made stew and as she was cooking I remember thinking that I'd never seen her so happy. The stew was horrible, but I decided not to say anything. A little later she said, 'It's time for bed son,' and off I went.

The next morning as I left for school Johnny was coming down the Holme. I walked up to him and pointed in the opposite direction, 'I'm going that way to school,' I explained. We stood talking for a while and then his Mom came over and told him to hurry up so that he wasn't late for school. We both just carried on, I went through the gully into WestHolme and saw that Granny Pegg was waiting for me. 'Don't forget to get my snuff after school Peter,' she shouted to me. I called back, promising that I wouldn't. When I arrived at the school gates Terry was waiting for me again and we went in together. The day was quiet and come four o'clock we walked towards Terry's house together. He asked me why I was walking with him and I told him that I had to get my Gran some snuff from the shop. Terry laughed and told me that the old man and woman from next door to him took snuff and that he hated the smell of it. We got to his house and said our goodbyes. I got Gran's snuff and as I was coming out of the shop Johnny was passing with two of his school mates who lived in Wolseley Street (they became my mates too).We walked up the lane together and talked about what we was all doing at school. Johnny walked up with me to Gran's house and then we both said bye to each other. Gran had already got a sandwich ready for me and as I ate she asked me how school was going and whether I'd been in trouble. I told her that it was all fine and once I'd finished eating I got up to leave. Gran told me to wait and then asked if I could come back round the next day to do an errand for her. I shrugged my shoulder and told her okay.

    I went home and found Mom in a good mood again, she got the stew on again and this time it wasn't too bad. After I eaten my dinner Mom asked if I was eating at school and I told her about my dinner tickets. Come bedtime Mom said, 'You do know that Tommy is coming to live with us at the end of the week?' I said that I knew and then I asked if the gas and electric was going to be back on by then. Mom went quiet and simply told me to get myself to bed. We did eventually get the gas and electric back on, but it wasn't until a couple of weeks later.

    The next day I went the same way to school and when I got went into Westhome Gran was waiting outside her house for me again. 'Don't forget to pop round after your dinner today,' she said when I reached her. I promised to remember and then I headed to school. I went straight to our classroom and Mr Hughes got the register out, calling our names out in turn. Afterwards he got up from his desk and came to the front of the class, he looked at all of us and said that next week there would be an exam. 'There will be changes to the classrooms,' he told us, 'there will be class 2a and 2b, some of you will go into "A" and rest of you go into a "B". There is also going to be new headmaster coming the week after next.' One lad put his hand up and asked if we would still be doing science and woodwork. 'Not until after your exam,' Mr Hughes explained, 'you'll all be doing P.E instead until then.' All we did in the morning was maths and come dinner time Terry and I went for something to eat. Afterwards I said that I was going to my Gran's and Terry said that he would come with me. When we got there I told Gran that Terry was my new mate. She looked hard at him and said that she hoped he wasn't going to get me into any trouble. Terry just stood there saying nothing. 'So what do you want me to do then Gran,' I asked her. 'I want to run over to Able's get me my loaf and a half pound of butter. Ask her if she's got any cheese and two eggs too.' I asked Gran for some money but she told me to get them to put it on the slate. Off Terry and I went through the gully to EastHolme. I showed Terry where I lived and while we were waiting to cross the horse road Terry said that Gran was a right old cow. I just laughed in reply. We went into Able's and she had everything that Gran wanted. Mrs Able asked where the money was and I asked her to put it on ran's slate. 'Okay,' Mrs Able said, 'tell your Gran she owns me a coupon for the cheese too.' Terry and I ran straight out of the shop and straight across the horse road without looking. We dropped the things off and Gran's and then left quickly so that we wouldn't be late getting back to school.

    We just about made it back on time. That afternoon we had two lessons and come four o'clock the bell went and we all went to rush out. Mr Hughes shouted at us to stay where we were, he stood by the door and said, 'When the bell goes you don't rush to get out you walk out. Do I make myself clear?' We all said 'Yes Mr Hughes' and then slowly left the classroom. Terry and I walked out together and when we got to the end of Ada Road he said, 'See you tomorrow Pete,' (he'd started to call me that). I went to Granny Pegg's and she got me a sandwich again. I ate it quickly and then left for home. When I got in Mom got the fire going and had the stew cooking. She never asked me how school was going, but at least the stew was a little bit better than the day before.

The next day Terry was waiting for me at the school gates. Thankfully it was another quiet day and nothing happened in class. When the bell went at four o'clock we all went to rush out again, but then suddenly remember what Mr Hughes had said and we all walked slowly instead. I walked as far as Terry's house with him and then I went on to the shop to get Gran some snuff again. As I was coming out of the shop I saw Johnny with his school mates again. We stopped together on the corner of Barwell Road for a while and then we walked up the lane. I told Johnny that we was doing exams the next week and he asked me why so I told him they were changing the classrooms around to "A" and "B". We got to granny Pegs he left me then he shouted I might call for you tomorrow I shouted back Gran's and Johnny said goodbye and that he might call on me the next day. I gave Gran her stuff but told her that I wasn't staying this time. She hasn't done me a sandwich but she asked if I was hungry. I nodded that I was so she got up to make me one. While she was doing my sandwich she was moaning about how hungry I always was. I ate quickly and when I got up to leave she told me not to forget to come down the next day and take her to the shop. 'What time shall I come round?' I asked her. 'About half twelve, before the pub closes,' Gran said.

Back home Mom was in a good mood again, she told me that she had some nice stew again and that it wouldn't take too long to cook. When she was done the stew smelt horrible, there wasn't hardly anything in it and I had to pick up my bowl and drink it in the end. I could feel that I was going to be sick, so I ran to the toilet. I only just about made it in time.

I went to bed with a sore throat that night. As I was getting ready for bed I asked mom if she was going to the get the gas and electric back on, since Tommy was coming to live with us. 'Never you mind what I'm going to do, I'll sort it out,' she said, 'go on now, get to bed.

Come Saturday morning Mom was up early making the fire. Once she got it going she did me some toast with a cup of lump, powdered milk. After breakfast I sat about waiting for Johnny as he said he was going to call for me, but he never did. Mom asked me if I wanted any more toast, I nodded my head in reply. As she went about the kitchen she asked me how my first week at school had gone and I explained about the exams and that we'd be split into two classes afterwards. Mom said that they were probably getting us to do the exams to see who the brainy ones were.

At twelve o'clock I headed to Granny Pegg's, when I arrived I went straight in and she told me to fetch the chair. Uncle Billy helped me to get it out of the front and then Gran followed us out. We went down the gully and over the railway bridge. Billy the signal man was standing outside the door to his signal box, he was watching me pushing Gran down the lane. At the shop Gran went in to pay for her snuff. She was in there for about ten minutes and when she came out I pushed her to the Acorn pub, when she walked in I was told to wait outside. As I waited one of Johnny's school mates came over and asked me where Johnny lived. I told him 'the top of SouthHolme.' While we were talking two lads came round the corner from Wolseley Street, they came over the horse road and headed towards us. They knew Johnny's mates and I recognised them as two lads from my school. We got to talking about the exams and when they went away one of them shouted to me that he'd see me on Monday.

A little while after the lads left it started to rain, so I had to stand in the doorway of the pub. A copper was walking passed and he looked over at me and asked me what I was up to. I explained that I was waiting for Gran and he said that I shouldn't be standing in the doorway and told me to move. Just as I was saying that it was raining Gran came out of the pub. She was obviously a bit tipsy and as she got into the wet chair she started to have go at the copper. The way that Gran was talking to the copper was making me laugh. 'You think it's funny do you?' the copper said turning towards me; he was staring to get annoyed. 'Go on,' he said to me, 'get your Gran home now.' Gran was still having a go at him as I pushed her away.

By the time we got to Maxstoke Street the rain had stopped but we were soaking wet and Gran was still moaning about the copper. Billy came out from the railway and he help me to push her up the gully. When we got to the top he helped me get her down the Holme and into the block. I thanked Billy and then he helped her out of the chair and into the house. Once Gran was safely inside Billy grabbed hold of my arm and said, 'I want to see you tomorrow Peter.' From inside Gran shouted to me to bring the chair inside. Billy started to walk away but he turned back and pointed his finger at me, 'Make sure you're there,' he called to me. When I got into the house Gran asked if I knew the man and when I told her that Billy was the bloke I was getting the coal from she told me to be careful. 'There are dangerous people out there Peter,' she told me, 'you don't want to end up in an early grave.' 'I'm keeping out of trouble Gran I promise. I've got to be good anyway, Tommy is coming to live with us next Saturday.' 'Well, well, well, we'll have to wait and see won't we Peter Round,' she said.

On Sunday I had to stay in all day and Mom made some horrible stew again. The day went slowly because I was bored with nothing to do, but I was glad I was made to stay in because I didn't have to go and see Billy. Monday morning was the same as ever; Gran waited outside her house watching me go to school and Terry met me at the school gates as usual. If my memory serves me right we had exams in both the morning and the afternoon. Terry was trying to whisper to me during the exams I was doing the same. We had exams for four days in a row. On Friday Mr Hughes told the class that some of us had done really well then he said that the rest of us who hadn't done well had better start learning fast. 'You will be told the results on Monday during assembly. The new headmaster will tell you which class you will be in.' The bell went at four o'clock and we all walked out quietly. When I got to the corner of Ada Road Billy was waiting for me. Terry and I walked passed him and he watched us and began walking along on the opposite side of the road. Terry noticed and asked if I knew 'that bloke', I didn't reply instead I just kept my eye on Billy. A little later Billy was still following so I turned to Terry and said, 'Let's run!' When we got to Terry's house we stopped to talk for a bit, but then I saw Billy coming towards me so I just ran off to the snuff shop with Terry following behind me. When we got to the shop Terry's brother David was outside. As we ran towards him David pointed towards Billy and asked why he was chasing us. I didn't reply but David ran after Billy and Terry I followed. Billy ran into the railway and David shouted to us, 'I'll get him for you!' Terry and I stopped and waited, David re-appeared a little while later, very breathless. Clearly he hadn't caught up with Billy. He asked me where I lived so I told him and said that I needed to pop in to see my Gran before I headed home. I said my goodbyes and as I walked away Terry shouted to me, 'I bet me and you will be in the same class on Monday Peter!'

  When I got to Gran's she already had a sandwich prepared for me. At first I just sat there not eating and Gran noticed that there was something wrong. She asked me to tell her what was going on and I explained that I was worried about Tommy coming to live with us as we still had no gas nor electric. 'Tommy and Albert paid for it the last time,' I told her, 'I'm worried what will happen when Tommy finds out, I think he will start shouting at Mom. He told her not to break into the meters again, I think there's going to be some trouble.' 'Look here Peter,' Gran said looking at me, 'it's not your problem, it's that bloody mother of yours. Don't you worry now, just get on and eat that. If there's any trouble in your house tomorrow you come straight round here.' 'I will Gran,' I promised, 'I just don't understand Mom at the moment. She's been in a good mood for ages now, she hasn't even shouted at me for days!' 'You must have been a good lad and keeping out of trouble,'

Gran said simply. A little later, once I was finished eating, I got up to leave. Gran waved to me from her window and told me to keep out of trouble.

When I got into the block Mrs Bloomer and Mrs Price was standing at bottom of the stairs, they watched me as I went although they didn't say anything to me. I stood at the top of the stairs looking at down and I remember thinking that something was going on. When I got into the house I told Mom about Mrs Bloomer and Mrs Price, but she didn't say anything about it. She asked me how school had been and I told her that it was fine and that we'd find out about our classes on Monday. I thought again how strange it was that she was in such a good mood. 'Peter you haven't noticed have you?' she said to me, 'go and switch the light on.' When I did I was surprised when the light on the wall came on. 'Where did you get the money from?' I asked her. Mom said that they came today and put both the gas and the electric back on, but she wouldn't tell me where the money had come from.

On Saturday morning, around eleven o'clock Tommy and his wife Irene and their baby daughter Joan arrived. He brought his own bed and a couch for me to lie on and though it was a bit hard it was better than my makeshift bed. Not long after Tommy and Irene
arrived I told Mom that I was heading out to get Gran her snuff. As I was going out down the stairs Tommy followed me out and said, 'Nip I want you to borrow Mrs Price's pram for me, collect it later tonight.' When I asked why he simply told me, 'Never you mind.' I went round to Gran's and told her that our gas and electric had been put back on. 'She might have borrowed the money for it,' Gran wondered, 'I'm going to tell you this Peter, every time you go out the house your Mom worries about you and what trouble you'll get yourself into next.' I never said anything in reply. 'Right then,' she said, 'Peter go get the chair out and take me to shop.' I got it out from the bedroom and together we went down the gully. A little ways down the lane Gran told me to stop pushing and to stand in front of her. 'I'm going to tell you this Peter,' she said looking into my eyes,

'wherever your Mom got the money from you got be grateful for it.' 'But Gran, when the meters are full she'll break into them again.' 'Not whilst your Tommy is living with you,' Gran said smiling.

    I pushed her to the shop and then when she was finished there we went on to the pub again. As I was waiting outside I saw Billy with another bloke coming up the road. When he saw me he came over to me and asked me to come and see if the next day. I explained that I couldn't because Tommy had just moved in and needed my help moving things. Billy went to grab me but just then a bloke came out of the door from the pub. When he saw what Billy was doing he asked me, 'Are you okay my lad?' 'Yes thank you Sir,' I told him, 'I'm just waiting for my Gran.' 'Which one is she?' the bloke asked, opening the door to pub. I pointed Gran out, she was sitting in the corner by the bar. 'Oh that old cow,' he said chuckling and then he ruffled my hair and said that she wouldn't be out until closing time. The bloke was right, Gran was in there for ages and when she did come out at closing time, she was a little more than tipsy. She fell into the chair and as I was pushing her up the hill she fell asleep. I woke her when we got to the block and she slowly got her and hobbled to the door. 'Peter I think I know where your Mom got that money from you know,' she mumbled, 'Peter she only did it for you. Now get that chair inside and get yourself home my lad.'

    When I got home they was all sitting round the table, Irene had Joan on her lap. I sat on the couch and Mom went into the kitchen and came out with a bowl of faggots, peas, and two slices of bread. 'Get that down you Peter,' she said, 'that will fill you up for the rest of the day.' She went back out in the kitchen and Tommy whispered to me not to forget the pram later. I told him that Mom probably wouldn't let me out again. Tommy replied, 'I'm going to give her half-a-crown so she can go and have half-a-pint. 'When she's gone out you go get the pram and meet me at the canal gates.'

    It was about 9 o'clock when Irene said that I'd better head out as Tommy would be waiting for me. I went as quickly as I could, collecting the pram from Mrs Price first and then running down the lane to where Tommy was waiting for me. I put the pram in front of him and he said, 'Okay nip go back home now.' I asked him if I could go with him but he told me to piss off home before Mom got back. I saw him go down the slope and then I ran across the horse road and jumped up on bridge top to watch him walk along the canal path. I tried to wave to him but it was dark and he didn't see me. I stood there watching him until he went out of sight. As I headed home and passed the railway I never saw Billy in the darkness. He grabbed hold of me and pulled me through the gate. I must have struggled because I fell down the stairs. I couldn't move for a while, I must have really hurt myself. Billy was shouting at me to get up, but I just couldn't move. He tried to lift me but I screamed that he was hurting me, so I put me back on the floor. I saw him run up the steps, then he came back down with a bloke and a lady, I think he was telling lies about me. Just then it started to rain and the lady said that she thought she knew who I was. The bloke lifted me up gently and asked me where I lived. I told him EastHolme and he said, 'Okay then lad, let's get you home now, I will see you there safely.' As he carried me up the steps he asked me what I was doing at the railway so late at night. I simply told him that Billy had grabbed me and pulled me through the gates, then I'd fell down the steps I explained that whatever Billy said were lies. 'I know who the kid is he,' the lady said from behind us, 'he went to Garrison Lane school with our Nancy, is name is Peter Round. Come on let's get the poor lad home.'

They got me home safely, I could hardly walk so the bloke carried me up the stairs to our front door. When we knocked Irene opened the door and the bloke put me on the couch, he told Irene what had happened as he did so. I explained that Billy had lied and that he'd grabbed me and that I'd fell down the stairs. When the bloke asked me what Billy wanted me for I said, 'I had to break into Lucas's and get him some batteries. I had to do it so I could have some coal because we had our gas and electric cut off. It was batteries for coal.' I went to tell them that I would meet Billy at the back of the Methodist church in St Andrews Street and we'd get into Lucas's that way. The bloke sighed and said that he'd go and have a word with Billy, Irene said that she'd go with him and the lady (I think it was his wife) agreed to stay and watch me.

While they had gone Mom came in and the first thing she asked was what trouble I'd been in now. The lady said to her, 'He's in no trouble Mrs Round, my husband Harry and the lady who was here gone to have a word with some bloke down by the railway. The bloke wanted Peter to go and break into Lucas's and get some batteries for him.' Mom turned and asked me if it was Billy and I nodded in reply and explained that it was how I was getting the coal. A little later the bloke called Harry and Irene came back, Harry said that Billy wouldn't be bothering me again. 'We're off now Mrs Round,' he said, 'Peter you keep out of trouble. I'll tell Nancy that I saw you, she's at Tilton Road school now you know.'

Time was getting on so Mom and Irene went to bed and I got comfortable on the couch. I must have fallen straight off to sleep because the next thing I know Tommy was waking me whispering for me to come with him. We went downstairs together and when we got out of the block by the Bloomer's window Tommy turned to me and said, 'Where's all the f****ing coal gone?' I remember that it was the first time and the last time Tommy ever swore at me. 'Tell me nip, tell me right now,' he said. I said that Mom told me not to tell him anything, but he wasn't haven't it. I explained that we'd only just got our gas and electric back on Friday and then Tommy asked where Mom had got the money from. I shrugged and said that I didn't know, but Granny Pegg said she had an idea where it came from. Tommy sighed and then said, 'Okay nip help me to get this lot up.' He had two big bags full of food and a pram full of coal. I managed to help him, although my back was still hurting. I took the pram back and then I ran home as fast as I could.

Irene did me some breakfast on Monday morning and then I got myself ready for school. When I passed Gran on my way to school she reminded me to get her some snuff. I got to the school gates and Terry and his brother David was waiting for me. David asked me who the bloke was who had been chasing us and what he wanted with me. I explained that his name was Billy and that he had been getting me to break into Lucas's to get him batteries in exchange for coal. 'Show me where at dinner time,' David told me. When we arrived at school we all had to go into assembly, Terry and I sat on the front row. Then Mr Osborne began to read out our names and what classes we were going to be in. Terry was right we were put into the same class, 2B. We had all started to chat so Mr Osbourne told us to be quiet. Next in came the new headmaster, Mr Carmichael. He walked up and down in front of us with his cane. 'I was told Ada Road school was a tough school,' he said, ' but I'm also a tough headmaster. If anybody steps out of line they will feel my cane. I hope I made myself clear.' We all shouted 'Yes sir' straightaway. After assembly off we went to our new classroom, Terry and I sat next to each other again, by the windows. Our new teacher was named Mr Sloan, I remember that he was a good teacher, fair but also strict. He got the register out and he called out our names in order of surname.

Come dinner time Terry and I went and had something to eat together and once we had finished we went to meet David and his mates at the school gates. Off we all went to the church and I showed them all how I got in. While we was standing by the gate the vicar from St Andrews Church was watching us and he shouted over to us, 'Do you lads want to go church? If so you can come join us on Tuesdays and Sunday.' He started to walk over to us as he talked, so we all ran back to school. When we got there we went into the playground together and David asked me how much I got for the batteries. I explained that Billy just gave me ten shillings and that there was two other blokes with him that he gave money to as well.

Come afternoon break time Terry and I was standing by the bike shed when one of David mates shouted over to me to go to him. I went over and together we walked to the big gates. 'Can you show me and my Dad how you get the batteries?' he asked me. I said no straightaway and he got angry asking me why not. 'I can't, if I get caught they will put me away,' I told him, 'I have already been to the juvenile court twice.' Then I walked away with him shouting at me, 'Oh go on Peter, show me!' I went back over to Terry and told him what David's mate had asked me. Terry said that it was good that I'd refused to show him. The bell went at four o'clock and I walked back to Terry's house in Watery Lane with him David's mate who had spoken to me at breaktime time was there. When Terry had said goodbye I carried on walking into Barwell Road and David's mate ran after me. He caught me up and asked again for me to show him saying that his Dad would give me a pound. I said no again and then I ran off. I got Granny Pegg's snuff from the shop and then started to walk up the lane towards her house. I heard someone shouting my name but I kept on walking and didn't look back. I went to run and as I did I looked behind me. 'Are you deaf then?' Johnny said smiling at me, 'I've been shouting you.' I said sorry and together we walked to Gran's house.

  Come the next day at school I met Terry again at the school gate and we walked into the playground together. Terry asked me what David's mate wanted and I explained that he said that his Dad would give me a pound if I showed him how to get into Lucas's. Then I told Terry that I said no because I'd have ended up back in court and then be put away for good. In the playground I saw Terry go up to his brother, David who then came over to me and said that he'd tell his mate to leave me alone. The bell went for us to go to our classrooms when we got inside Mr Sloan got the register out and called our names out. Afterwards he got up from his desk and came to the front of the class. 'There's going to be a change of classrooms,' he told us, 'I'm going to read out the names of people who are going to stay in my class. The rest of you will go back into Mr Hughes' class 1B. I'll see you next year in my class.' Terry and I found out that we were going to be sent back to the same class where we started. When we got into Mr Hughes' class the next day there were new lads in the classroom with us.

The rest of 1949 went well, both at home and at school. One day in October I went to school and when I got home Irene had given birth to a new baby girl, Dorothy, named after Mom. I was still sleeping on the couch and as I lay there one Sunday morning, Tommy told me that it wouldn't be long until I got my bedroom back. 'I'll get you a nice bed,' he promised me. This was before Christmas of 1949, Tommy and Irene were still living with us by Christmas of 1950. For Christmas 1949 Tommy and Irene bought me a jumper with no sleeves and a pair of socks. Albert he came over on Christmas Day with his wife Iris, they got me a pair of trousers and a pair of socks. I had to wait until after Christmas for my present from Mom, because she didn't have any money to get me anything at the time. I heard Albert ask Mom where her ration book for the cloths was. Mom went into her bedroom and came out with the ration book, 'Mother where have all your coupons gone?' he asked. Mom never said anything, she just stood by her bedroom door looking at the floor. 'Mother there's a shoe shop opening on the Coventry Road,' Albert told her, 'I think you will probably be alright, I've heard the clothes are coming off ration next year. You probably won't need your coupons. I'll try and get you some clothes coupons just in case you need them. I'm also going to give you five shillings, if Tommy gives you five shillings too you will have enough money to buy the nipper a good pair shoes.' When Albert and Iris had left, Mom and Irene got the Christmas dinner ready, it wasn't much but it was nice and it was the best Christmas dinner I'd ever had. Mom did get me a pair of shoes from the second hand shop that Albert told her about. The shoes were a bit tight but I managed to wear them.

In 1950 everything was still okay. We kept the gas and electric on and Tommy was bringing in food, though where he was getting it from I don't know. Everything was going great at school, most days I fetched Granny Pegg's snuff and thankfully I managed to keep out of trouble. Come September of 1950 I went back into Mr Sloan's class. In this year we got to do science with Mr Yeomans and woodwork with Mr Curtis and Mr Foster. We'd already been doing P.E. with Mr Hart. I wasn't very good at science or woodwork, in a few woodwork classes I can remember breaking the blade on the plain-saw and a few times I never got any marks. I can remember one time in woodwork I was hampering away at some wood and the next thing I knew I broke the hammer and wood I was working on. The handle slipped out of my hand and nearly hit Mr Curtis. Come four o'clock that day Terry and I was walking out the gates and Mr Curtis was standing there, when I saw him I burst out laughing. I could see that he wasn't too pleased with me so I just ran.

When I got to school the next day I had to report to the headmaster's office, I had to stand outside and wait to be called in. I must have stood there for about ten minutes before I got called inside, Mr Curtis was already in there. Mr Carmichael told me that I had to apologise to Mr Curtis. He was holding the cane so I looked at Mr Curtis and told him that I was sorry. Mr Curtis accepted my apology and then he left the office. I was about to follow him out when Mr Carmichael said that he wanted to have a word with me. 'Now Peter,' he said, 'I see you have free dinners?' I nodded in reply. 'I also see that you have no father?' Again I nodded. Then he asked me if I had any brothers or sisters and whether they lived with me. I told him that I had two brothers but that they were both married. 'Okay,' he said, 'I'm going to put your name forward to the Birmingham Mail so you can have some boots and clothing.' I thanked him and then was told to go to my class. When I got back to the classroom Mr Sloan looked at me and asked where I'd been. I told him that I wasn't late and that I'd been in Mr Carmichael's office. Mr Sloan looked at me and told me to go to my desk. Come break time we went into the playground and the first thing Terry asked me was why I was in the headmaster's office. I explained about what Mr Carmichael was doing to get me some clothes.

I can remember it was a Friday in November when I was off school for being sick. It was getting towards dinner time when Mom came in from work. A little later there was a knock on the door and in walked the gas man. Mom left the door open and the electric man followed shortly after. Both meters were full so the men emptied them and starting counting the money at the table. When they were finished counting they read the meters and one of them said to mom, 'Mrs Round this is the first time I've had to give you some money back.' The other man said the same thing and told Mom, 'Well done.' When they had gone I asked Mom how much money she'd had back, but she told me, 'Never you mind!' I asked if she was going to give some of the money back to Tommy, because he'd put some into the meters too. Mom told me now and said that I was to keep my mouth shut.

During the Easter and Summer holidays I kept out of trouble. I went over to the tip looking for tat most days, until the blokes there told me to piss off. Whenever I found some tat I took it up to Raggy Allen. I never got much money but I did I gave it straight to Mom. I never did tell Tommy about mom getting some money back from the meters. Come Christmas day of 1950 I never got any presents off, not Tommy nor Albert, not even Mom. I couldn't understand why, I knew I'd kept out trouble and was doing well at school. Albert never even came to see us either. We had our Christmas dinner together again that year, it wasn't much but it was nice.

In March 1951 a new lad started in our class and he sat next to me in the front row. His name was Peter Greening and he also became a lifelong mate with Terry (sadly Peter passed away in 1998). When Terry and I got to know Peter we realised what a character he was, you never knew what he was going to do next. One time Peter was really messing about in P.E. and he got Terry and I involved. Mr Hart was really laying into us all, he kept on telling us to jump over the wooden horse but we kept missing the jumps. All of a sudden Peter jumped on the horse and stood up on it. I was following him and I nearly bumped into him. Eventually   Terry and I ended up joining Peter on top of the horse, the rest of the class started to laugh at us, but Mr Hart didn't like it one bit.

Peter and I started to mess about in Mr Sloan's class too. Eventually he gave us the cane, we had two strokes each and afterwards we stopped messing about for a while. When it was coming up to August holidays we had our dinner one day and then we went into the playground. There was five of us altogether, Peter Greening, Terry Lloyd, Jimmy Wenlock, Albert Sanders and myself. I can't remember who it was but someone suggested that the play the wag up Coventry Road. We were really playing it up running in out of the shops until the coppers started to chase us. They caught all of us and took us back down to the school. We were made to stand outside Mr Carmichael's office and when he came out he gave us a good telling off, then he told us to report to his office at ten to nine the next morning 'You better tell your parents what has happened today,' he said to us all, 'because I will be writing to them.'

Come the next morning all of us was standing outside Mr Carmichael office and we knew we was going to get the cane. What we didn't know was how he was going give us the cane. He marched the five of us into hall where the whole school was in Assembly. He made us line up at the front and then walked up and down telling all the other kids what we'd done. 'I'm going to give these hooligans the cane and I'm going to teach them a lesson they will never forget,' he said. He came up to me first and told me to hold out my hand. I wouldn't at first but he came right up to me and said, 'If don't hold your hand out I will get one of the teachers to hold your arm out.' I did I put my arm out then and I turned my head and closed my eyes. Mr Carmichael gave me six of the best on both hands, he did it on our fingertips and I felt the sting (while I'm writing this I can still feel the ghost of that sting on my fingertips). Peter Greening was next to feel the cane and although my fingers was hurting Peter was making me laugh. In the end he took it like a man, so did Terry and Jimmy. Come Albert's turn he went to run out the door but it was blocked by another teacher. When Mr Carmichael had finished he said, 'Now you know what you get from me if you want to play truant and be a hooligan. Assembly is dismissed now go to your classrooms in orderly manner. Peter Round I want to see you in my office now!'

When we got into his office he asked why my Mother hadn't been to see him yet, he'd wanted to see her about getting me some clothes, but I'd completely forgotten. I apologised to him and explained that my fingers were still stinging. 'If they weren't I would have given you more than six,' he replied. I said sorry again and asked if I need to apologise to Mr Curtis about nearly hitting him, I said that it wasn't my fault as the handle had slipped from my hand. Mr Carmichael thought for a moment and then said, 'Don't worry about it for now Peter, but can you tell your Mother to come and see me before the school holiday?'

We went back to school on 3rd September 1951, I was thirteen and I went into class 3B. I enjoyed the summer holidays before that, during the holiday Johnny kept calling for me and we went to see his school mates who later came my lifelong mates too. We met Peter Greening and he also knew Johnny school mates because he lived in Wolseley Street. When we all met up we walked along Wolseley Street to Garrison Street and then up to the railway crossing. We watched some kids swimming in the cut, they were all naked, and all of sudden Peter Greening and other lads got undressed too. They left Johnny and I standing there and for a moment we stood there looking at each other, then Johnny started to get undressed too. I still stood there, I remember thinking that I didn't know that Johnny could swim. He ran and jumped in the cut too, all the kids was shouting at me to get undressed and join them. In the end I did but I was a bit scared because I couldn't swim. Peter Greening got out and he came towards me and pushed me in; that's how I learnt to swim and I actually became a good one.

That summer I was always excited when Johnny came calling for to go down the cut. When the barges came along we had to get out and wait till they went passed. I think it was the last Saturday of the holiday when Johnny came calling for me, he shouted up for me and I lifted the window up and said that I was coming down. When I came out of the block Johnny said that we was going hunting for tat over at the tip. When we went when we got there quite a few blokes was there too. Johnny and I got over the tip and we found some pieces of wood to move the dirt. Every time we got near to the blokes they told us to piss off. We went right over the other side of the tip towards Bordesley Green Road and we was moving the dirt away for some time when both of us hit something. We both jumped out the way and then we went back and started to move the dirt away from a bag. When we opened it we found that it was full of pennies. Johnny and I both looked around to make sure that the blokes weren't near us. Very quietly Johnny and I managed to get the bag to the canal bridge where some kids was swimming in the cut. We carried the bag across the pathway of the bridge without anybody seeing us. When we got to Sydney Road the fence was too high for us climb so we carried on up to Venetia Road. We waited for a bit and I suggested that we went to Johnny's house. He said no and that it would be better to take the bag to my house. We got the bag all the way from the top of Venetia Road to my house, we went up the stairs, but when we got to the top Mrs Bloomer's came out of her house and shouted up to us, 'What have you little B's been up to?' Johnny and I ignored her and carried the bag into my house, heaving it up onto the table. The pennies went all over the table and Mrs Bloomer, who had followed us up, asked where we'd nicked all the pennies from. Just then Irene came in and said that she didn't think we'd stolen the money. Mrs Bloomer sighed and then pointed at the money and said, 'Stack them in twelves boys.' Once we was finished Mrs Bloomer and Irene said that there was six hundred pennies altogether, that's two pounds and ten shillings. 'Now tell us Peter,' Mrs Bloomer said, 'where did you nick the money from?' I looked at Irene and said, 'I haven't nicked from anywhere honest, we found the money over the tip and that's the truth.' Johnny backed me up and said that I was telling the truth and then he asked Irene to look after his share of the money. Irene nodded and then told us to get the pennies back into the bag before Mom got back. Johnny and I carried the bag into the bedroom, we put it around the other side of the bed so Tommy nor mom could see it. After that Johnny said that he was going home, but before he left Irene gave him handful of pennies. As Johnny and I was leaving Mrs Bloomer called to me, 'Don't you forget my coal tomorrow!' We got out of the block and went round the side of the flats and Johnny started counting the pennies Irene gave him. Altogether he had one shilling and sixpence.

Come Sunday morning Johnny never came to call for me, so I had to go get the coal by myself. I went down to the railway and went through the opening. Then I slipped down the embankment and thankfully there was enough coal along the tracks to fill the pram for both Mrs Price and Mrs Bloomer. When I got to Mrs Bloomer's house she never said thank you, she simply said, 'Make sure you have a wash before your Mom sees you.'

Before our school holidays we had to take an exam to see which class we would be going into when we came back. All the kids stayed in the "B" class, I think only three lads from our class went into "A". We were in Mr Styles' class, 3B, he was a good teacher but he wasn't strict enough at times, though he did get some respect from us. During September and October I was beginning to learn something from Mr Styles, he was trying to get a chess team together and we could go along and see him during our dinner time break. I went along with Terry and Peter, but they weren't really interested. I was though so I stayed and started to go along to see Mr Styles each day after dinner. He said he could see that I was becoming a good chess player. He told me once if you played chess through a mirror I'd become an even a better player.

In November I got accused of something. I always remember it was a Tuesday and I had to run around to Granny Pegg's after my dinner to do an errand for her. I had to go over to Able's with a shopping bag to get her order. Mrs Able already knew what Gran wanted, which was good because I was running late for school so I asked Mrs Able to hurry up. 'You being late for school?' Mrs Able said, 'it's a wonder you're not playing the wag. Here you are put it all in the bag, you cheeky so and so.' As I went to leave she asked me where the money was and I told her to put it on Gran's slate. I went running back to Gran's, went straight in to drop off the bag, and then I ran all the way back to school.

When I got back I looked through the window of the class to see if Mr Styles was in there, then I went running round to the iron stairs and up to the staff room to see if I could find him. As I was passing the science class something must have caught my eye because I went inside towards the desk. I heard something so I turned around and I saw something that I shouldn't have seen. I was told by the teacher to stay where I was, then they asked the lad in the room to go and fetch Mr Carmichael. When he came in Mr Yeomans told the headmaster he saw me trying to steal his wallet. I promised that it wasn't me, but the headmaster told me to go with him to his office. Once we sat down he asked me to tell him the truth before he called the police. I knew he wouldn't believe me if I told him, I never did tell him what I saw.

A little later the police came and again I had to tell them that it wasn't me who'd been trying to take the wallet. 'You better come with me to the police station,' the copper said. At the station we went into a room and the copper started to ask me lots of question, I kept quiet and said nothing. The copper kept going out of the room and coming back in, all the time he was asking me the same questions. I was in there for a while before he came back in and asked me again if I'd tried to take the wallet. I swore yet again that I hadn't and I told him that I hadn't eaten since dinner time and that I was hungry. The copper brought me a sandwich which was horrid so I didn't eat it, instead I threw it on the floor. The copper came back into the room and when he saw the sandwich on the floor he told me to pick it up. I didn't move so he said, 'I won't ask you again, pick it up.' I just sat there so he grabbed hold of me by my collar and threw me to the floor by the sandwich. I still didn't pick it up, I just sat there. Just then Mom and Irene came in. The first thing Mom said was, 'This time they will put you away!' Then she turned and left, but Irene stayed with me. 'Irene please believe me, I never stole the wallet,' I told her. She asked if that was the truth and when I promised that it was, Irene nodded and said that she believed me. Next the copper came into the room and told me to come with him. I followed him to the desk where the sergeant said, 'Right Peter we are going to charge you with stealing a wallet from your teacher Mr Yeomans. Soon you will receive a notification of when you will have to appear at the juvenile court.'

The next day I went to school and Peter and Terry was waiting for me at the gate, both of them asked what had happened and I told them the whole story. Peter asked me if I'd looked in the wallet and I explained that I never even touched it. The bell went so we went to our class. When we sat down Mr Styles got the register out and he called our names out. He got up from his desk and came in front of the class, then he called me to go out and we left the classroom together. We went into the corner of the hall, all the kids were looking out of the classroom window to see what was going on. Mr Styles looked down at me and put his hand on my shoulder. 'Peter I believe you, I know what happened,' he told me, 'I still want you in my chess team because you're a very good player. I'm going to make you the captain after you beat Deakin.' I thanked him and then we went back into class. As I sat back down at my desk Mr Styles told the class that he didn't want to hear anything about what had happened the day before.

At dinner time Peter told me that he was going to play the wag and he asked Terry and I if we wanted to join him. Terry said no and while I was thinking about it Mr Styles came into the hall looking for me. 'Go back to the classroom Peter,' he told me, 'I want you to play me three games of chess and three games for the captaincy with Deakin, because I want you to be captain.' I'm not being   bigheaded but I did win all six games and I did come captain of the chess team.

One Wednesday when I had to go and fetch Gran's snuff I walked down to the shop with Terry after school. When we got to Terry's house I carried on walking, went to the shop, and got Gran her usual. When I arrived at her house she was sitting in her favourite place by the wireless. When I passed her the snuff she turned to me and said, 'I believe you Peter. Everything's going to be alright.' 'Gran, I was told I will be put this time,' I said to her. 'Well, if they do put you away it won't before long,' she told me.

I can remember our first chess game was at Marlborough Road school in December 1951. Ada Road won 6 games to four, I won mind beating there captain. When we had a chess game we always had to go to the other schools, they wouldn't come to Ada Road. Come Christmas of 1951 Tommy and Irene and their two daughters were still living with us. For Christmas Mom got me a new pair of shoes and a shirt, Tommy and Irene got me pair of trousers. When Albert and Iris came on Christmas Day they brought me a pair trousers and a jumper with no sleeves. Mom and Tommy never told Albert what had happened with me at school. Albert told Mom that him and Iris would probably be moving out of Sydney Road because they had to go to the council after Christmas. Before Albert left he asked Mom, 'What's the nipper been up to now? I've heard he'd been in trouble at school pinching a teacher's wallet. Is that right nip?' he looked right at me. I shook my head and told him no. Mom said, 'He's been charged and is waiting to go to court. I'm afraid they will send him away.' 'It will probably will teach him a   lesson,' Albert said. At that time I jumped up from the couch and said, 'I didn't nick that f**king wallet!' 'Then why have they charge   you Peter? The police wouldn't have charged you if you hadn't try   to steal it,' Albert said. Then Mom asked him who told him about what had happened and Albert replied that it was one of the Collins' kids, they went to Ada Road school too.

I went back on the 7th January 1952. I was trying to stay out of trouble and Terry was helping me, most of the boys in our class played the wag but we tried not to. A couple of weeks after we went back after Christmas we were in class listening to Mr Styles going on about the sums when there was a knock on the door. In came a prefect who asked Mr Styles if I could go to the headmaster's office straightaway. I followed the prefect to the office and when I got there and knocked on the door, Mr Carmichael shouted at me to come in. Inside there was a copper waiting for me, he looked up when I entered and told me that I had to go with him to the police station. 'I want my Mom to be there too,' I said. The copper said that Mom had already been told to make her way to the station.

When we arrived Mom was already there with Granny Pegg. The sergeant on the desk said to me, 'Peter, I'm going to help me if you're honest and tell me, did you steal that wallet?' 'No Sir I didn't, but I can tell you about what I saw.' Just then Mr Carmichael came into the station and when I looked over at him I hung my head and said nothing. Then I the sergeant told me that I had to appear in the juvenile court on Thursday 21st February at 9 o'clock. We left the station not long after that and as we was going out Gran turned around and she had a right go at Mr Carmichael. 'My grandson wouldn't steal that teacher's wallet!' she shouted at him, 'I believe Peter and you should too!' She still shouting at him going half way down the Coventry Road, she even tried to run after him. When we got back to Gran's Mom said that they were going to put me away. Gran told her not to be silly, that they weren't going to put away her grandson.

When I got to school the next day Peter and Terry was waiting for me by the school gate as usual. I told them about my court date and then we headed into school. Terry turned to Peter who was still hanging around by the gate and asked if he was coming with us. 'No I'm off, I'm going to meet my Mom and Dad in town.' When we got into class Mr Styles pulled me aside and said that he'd heard about my court date. He also told me that he believed me and I thanked him.

I carried on keeping out of trouble with Terry's help. Meanwhile we had two chess games both at grammar schools, one at Bordesley Green and the other was at Camp Hill. Ada Road won both and I won both games playing both captains. On the Tuesday 19th February, at break time I pointed to a lad in the playground. 'That's the kid that got me into trouble,' I told Terry and Peter. Come the next day Wednesday, again at break time, I finally told Terry and Peter what I really saw. When I'd finished Terry and Peter ran up to the kid and him into the toilets. I followed them as they pushed him into the cubicle and told me to wait outside. I heard the kid crying and then he told Peter and Terry everything that really happened. They knew the truth then and so did Mr Styles. At least some people believed me.

On the Sunday before I went to court I went round to Granny Pegg's. Violet Peg was there when I arrived and she said that she was coming with us to court. I looked at her and asked if I could tell her what really happened, she said of course I could. I asked her to come back with me to my house so that I could tell her and Irene together. I trusted them both. I ran back towards home and Violet followed me. I went running into the house and shouted to Irene that Violet Pegg wanted to see her. Together Irene and I went downstairs and outside the block I told them both. As I was talking Mrs Bloomer came out and Irene explained what was happening. They both called the lad a dirty little 'B'. 'Do you know this lad's name Peter?' Mrs Bloomer asked me. 'Yes,' I replied, 'his name is Allen Edwards, he lives in Arthur Street. I know him, but he's not in my class at school.' When Gran found out the story later that day, she turned to me and nodded, 'I knew you was hiding something Peter,' she said.

When Thursday arrived I got ready to go to court. Irene helped and got me 'looking smart' as she put it. We got there for 9o'clock, only Irene and Violet came with me. Mr Carmichael and Mr Yeomans was already when we arrived and Mr Carmichael came over to see me. He asked me if I was alright and Irene and Violet shouted that of course I wasn't, that they hoped the dirty 'B' over there (pointing to Allen Edwards) was going to tell the truth and that I shouldn't even be there. Eventually it was time for me to go in. I had to stand in front of the bench where there were two blokes and a woman. The woman was Mrs Cadbury, she was in the middle. Then the police sergeant read out the accusation about me stealing the wallet. Next Mr Yeomans got up and told the court about what happened, how he saw me going to his desk and taking the wallet. All the time Mrs Cadbury was looking at me and the two blokes. As Mr Yeomans was talking I shouted over to him that I never even touched his wallet. Then Mr Carmichael got up he spoke up for me a little bit not much. I appreciated it all the same. After about hour they went out the room and I had to go sit by the police sergeant. A little while later they came back in and I had to stand up and face Mrs Cadbury. 'Peter you leave me no alternative but to send you away to a special school for 8 weeks,' she said, 'take him away please.' Irene and Violet shouted at Mr Yeomans that he was a horrible man and that he knew I was telling the truth. Mr Yeomans hurried out the room but Violet went running after him. I heard Irene telling Mr Carmichael the story I'd told them. I had to go with the police sergeant to another room, inside there two lads. One of them asked me if I'd been sent down 'for a first.' I didn't know what he meant so he explained it to me. After about hour Irene came into the room and told me not to worry, that they were going to try and get me out of there. 'Irene that Allen Edwards, I think he should have been here,' I told her. 'It's alright Peter,' she said, putting her arm around me, 'I have spoken to Mr Carmichael, I've told him what you told me and he said he's going to look into it.' Finally, it was time for me to go. All together there was six kids going to the school on the Moseley Road.

      I don't want to write too much about the school on Moseley Road, all I can say is it was very strict and horrible. I got beaten up twice because I stuck up for myself. The second time I was beaten up they held me down. I went to the school on 21st February and I got released on Friday 7th March, on the night before my release one of the strict teachers came into the dormitory. He pointed his stick at me and said, 'You will be going home tomorrow.' At first I didn't believe him, I just lay there most of the night wondering if what he said was true. After breakfast I had to report the head teacher, when I got to the office I knocked on the door and he shouted to me to come in. Inside he gave me a good stern talking to and when he'd finished he got up from his desk and walked round to me. 'You're one lucky lad Peter,' he told me, 'you are being released today.' Outside the school I never saw them at first but Tommy, Albert, and Violet Peg was waiting for me. I was so glad to see them all. Tommy, Irene, and their two daughters moved to Owen Street up by the accident hospital. Albert and Iris had also moved up to Owen Street, both Albert and Tommy were in back-to-back houses. I had a week off when I get home before I had to go back to Ada Road school. When I went back I had to report to Mr Carmichael's office, he told me that he wanted to apologise to me on behalf of the school. I didn't say anything in response I just asked him if I could go. I walked into the classroom and Mr Styles said, 'Glad to see you back Peter, we have a chess game tomorrow and you're still my captain.' I smiled and thanked him.

When I finally found out who was behind my release I never got to say big thank you to him. It was Mr Styles. When I spoke to Terry I found out he was the one who had gone to Mr Styles and told him the whole story about Allen Edwards. I told Terry that Allen Edwards had never turned up at the court, then Terry told me he had left the school. Apparently Mr Styles had always believed in me, according to Terry. Although I never got to say thank you, I think I made it up to Mr Styles by winning my chess games as captain. After the Easter holidays I started to play the wag, a few times I went down to the cut and went swimming, other times I went over to the tip looking for tat. On a few occasions while I was playing the wag I went looking for Allen Edwards, but then I found out that his family had left Arthur Street. Tommy once caught me nicking one off his cigarettes, he said to me, 'Okay nip if you want to smoke you smoke like a man, now take a big draw.' I did as I was told and I took a big draw in. I couldn't stop coughing for a while and it even made me sick. From that time to the present I have never smoked. I didn't just misbehave playing the way, on some occasions when we had science lessons Terry, Peter and I would play it up, we wouldn't listen to Mr Yeomans and one time I told him to f**k off. Once the three of us even tried to set fire to the science room with the bunsen burner. Mr Yeomans threatened to fetch Mr Carmichael if we didn't stop playing up.

During the summer holiday that year I kept out of trouble a little bit. Johnny and I would sometimes go down to the cut in the afternoon, after searching the tip for tat in the morning. I also went nicking the coal for Mrs Bloomer, Mrs Price, and Mrs Fleetwood, I even went down to Wilson bakery one time to see what I could nick. I got there and the gate and the door was open, I stood there for a moment and then I went in. I saw some tea cakes and I looked around to see if anybody was about. It was quiet so I grabbed two cakes and ran out as fast I could go. I went hurrying along Montague Street and I saw George who I'd met some time before down at the cut, he was with his other mate, Jack. George told me that he knew where I'd been and that him and Jack were heading there now too. We carried on walking up to Wilson bakery and when we got there the gaffer was standing outside the gate. 'Hello Peter,' he said to me, 'what brings you round here?' I told him that were just walking round, he laughed at that and said, 'I think you three was about to nick some bread wasn't you Peter?' We shook our heads, but then he said, 'Come with me you three.' We followed him inside the gate and he told us that if we wanted some bread, we needed to work for it. The gaffer told us to start by cleaning out some wooden trays. We all looked at each other and agreed to help him, so the gaffer got us some scrubbing brushes, green soap, and some buckets filled with water. I think there were fifty or sixty trays to clean, so we got scrubbing straightaway. We were there for a while and the gaffer kept coming out to see if we were still working. It was Jack who finished the last tray, when he saw the gaffer said, 'Well done, better than nicking the bread right?' Then he went back inside and came back out with six paper bags, he gave us two each and inside were three loafs and three tea cakes. As the gaffer passed us the bags he laughed and said we'd saved him from burning all the trays, he obviously didn't want to have to clean them himself. Finally he gave us five shillings each and said, 'Go on hop it and if I catch you lot round here again you know what to expect; some hard work.' As we was walking away from the bakery George told me that he'd joined the boxing club in Gem Street, up by the Coleshill picture house. George Ridley went on to win the A.B.A. boxing final. The next time I meet up with George after that day he was working in the fish market. Before I headed home I went to Granny Pegg's. When I went inside Gran looked at me and said she hoped that I hadn't been nicking anything. I explained that I'd been made to work for the money and food I was carrying. Gran smiled and I told her, 'I'll take you down there, then you know I was telling you the truth Gran.' 'Well aren't you going to give me loaf?' she asked. I gladly passed her one and then she told me that she hope that Mom appreciated what I'd done for her. When I got home I told Mom about my day and at first she didn't believe me. She stood looking at me for a moment and then told me 'Well done.' I smiled and gave her the five shillings.

On my fourteen birthday I never had any presents off my brothers nor off Mom, the only present I got was from my Gran, she gave me one shilling. Time was getting on and before I knew it I was going back to school. I went into class 4B and Mr Thomas was the teacher. He was really good, all the time I was in his class he only gave the cane to one person and his name was Arthur Hewitt. He was playing it up all the time so Mr Thomas gave him the cane. Mr Thomas hardly ever got up from his desk, he even got one of the lads up to write on the blackboard for him. He had the nack of throwing a piece of chalk at a lad if he heard him talking during class. Mr Thomas never missed, he had a line of pieces of chalk on his desk ready to throw at you even you was sitting right at the back of the room. If you had a problem you could go to Mr Thomas and he would sit and listen to you, he'd try solve it for you.

It was my first day back at school and after break time, Mr Thomas came in. He sat down and he looked straight at me. 'You're Peter Round?' he asked me, 'you've got to go report to Mr Carmichael's office after dinner.' All through the rest of the lesson and during dinner I kept thinking about what I'd done this time. When I'd finished eating I went to the office and I knocked on the door. I went inside and I stood there looking at Mr Carmichael. I was shaking and said to him, 'It's my first day back at school Sir, I haven't done anything wrong.' He looked at me and said, 'I want to see your Mother this week Peter, it's about you getting the
Birmingham Mail boots.' I was so relieved! I thanked him and left the office. Mom did go see Mr Carmichael that week and he gave her a letter telling us to go to Digbeth Police Station. Mom and I went on Friday afternoon, when we got there Mom asked if I remembered coming here before. I hung my head and told her 'Yes.' The people who gave us the clothes were very helpful and they gave me two pairs of trousers, two shirts, and a pullover. When I got to school on Monday I looked around the playground and noticed that there were a few kids in the same clothes as me.

I'd been behaving for a while, going to school and not missing any lessons, but then I got fed up and I started to play the wag. This one time I went over the tip and I saw Mr Kettle over there, he asked me if I could go with him down the railway to see if we could get some copper wire. I said no at first but he kept on at me, so in the end I went with him. When we got there Mr Kettle knew the signalman on duty and he let us pass. I collected a bag of wire and when I handed it to Mr Kettle gave me was two shillings for the hard work I'd done for him. Afterwards I ran home and when I got towards EastHolme I saw Mr Harvey, the school boardman standing on corner. When he saw me he shouted to me come to him. I ignored him and instead I ran towards NorthHolme. Mr Harvey ran after me so I headed to Granny Pegg's. I hurried into Gran's and saw another lady (I found out later that her name was Sadie) was there too. I explained that the school boardman was chasing me and Sadie told me to go and hide in the toilet. From behind the door I heard Sadie telling Mr Harvey off, she was really having go at him and I couldn't not stop laughing. Even though it was funny at the time that day scared me a bit. Afterwards I started to go school quite regularly.

It was getting towards Christmas and Mom told me that she was going to get me a nice present that year. Later that day when Mom went out to go to the toilet, I looked at the meters and saw that she'd only gone and broken into them again. I don't know what made me look in the first place, I suppose I just had a feeling. When she came back inside I was standing by the cupboard and I asked her what she'd done. 'I'm not having no gas and electric for Christmas,' she told me. 'I'm getting fed up with this,' I said, 'I'm going to find where Tommy and Albert live and I'm going to tell them what you've done.' I went to leave but Mom was standing in the way of the door and I couldn't get passed her. It got to stage where we were shouting at each other and I was throwing things about. Suddenly there was a knock on the door; it was Mrs Bloomer. 'Dorothy what's been going on here,' she said, 'look at the state of the place!' I saw my chance to get passed Mom and I ran out of the house, I went to Gran's. I told her and Sadie (who was there again) what had happened and she asked me to and get the chair and to take her to my house. Sadie came along with Gran and I and when we got back they went inside while I waited out by the door. I heard Mom shout, 'Look what your so-called grandson has done to this place!' Sadie said that Mom must have given me a reason to mess up the place. Sadie called me inside and when I got into the living room she put her arm round my shoulder. I told her that I must have lost my temper; Sadie said that we'd clean it up together. Once we'd cleaned up the mess, with Mr Bloomer's help, Sadie told me that she wanted a cup of tea. I went into the pantry to get the tea, but just then Mom called out that we didn't have any money. Mrs Fleetwood was hanging about and she went to get us some tea from her house. She also had to find us some cups because I had smashed up the only cups we had. Later that night, when everyone had left, I did say sorry to Mom for losing my temper. I will promised her that I would never lose my temper again; and I never did.

Christmas went by and for a while Mom and I still had the gas and electric on. One Wednesday, when we was back at school, I was sitting by Albert Sanders; Terry and Peter were both off that day. Albert told me that he was going up the Coventry Road after dinner and asked if I wanted to go with him. Together Albert and I went into Woolworths, I stood by the counter nearer to the door. I was just looking around and then I saw Albert suddenly running out while lady behind the counter was looking at him. I didn't know what was going on, but I grabbed hold of some earrings and then I ran out after Albert. I caught up with him and we hurried back into school together. We said nothing to each other until the end of the day when we showed each other what we'd nicked. Albert and I walked out of the gates together and then went our separate ways.

When I arrived at Gran's, Violet was there. I passed Gran her snuff and then I gave Violet the earrings I'd taken. There were five of them altogether and Violet burst out laughing. Gran looked at the earrings in Violet's hand and asked me if I'd nicked them. I tried lying, but Gran knew the truth. There were five earrings and not one of them matched.

On Thursday morning we had go straight into assembly. Mr Carmichael was standing in front of the whole school and there was also a copper waiting for us. Mr Carmichael told us that he wanted to know who was the two lads were who went into Woolworths and stole some items. 'I will find those two lads,' he said, 'I'm not going to have this school getting a bad name.' Thankfully he never found out that it was Albert and I. After school that day we had a chess game at Camp Hill grammar school. When we got there this bloke came to watch Deakin, Albert, and I. At first I didn't know that he was from the Birmingham chess club. We won all our games except one, Deakin and I had to play again. I played captain again and won all three games, then I had to play the bloke. It was three hard games, but I won all of them. When we'd finished the bloke got up and shook my hand, then he went over to Mr Styles. While he was talking the bloke kept looking over at Deakin and I. Later, came up to us and told us 'Well done.' I forgot to tell Mom that we had a chess game after school that day, so when I got home she was crying; she thought I'd run away. I told her that I was fine and said that I'd won my game and that a bloke from a big chess club had come to watch me. Mom was pleased for me and asked when my next game was. Coming up to Christmas we still got the gas and electric on. I think we were at school for two days only.

    Come the next Christmas Mom did get me some nice presents. I got a lovely shirt (which unlike the Birmingham Mail shirts it wasn't itchy), some trousers, a pullover, and pair of shoes and socks. On Christmas Day morning I had a nice wash in hot water at the sink, then I tried on my new clothes, I was pleased to see that they fitted me quite well. Mom told me that I looked nice and smart. There was a knock on the door; Mrs Bloomer, Mrs Price, and Mrs Fleetwood brought Mom some cups, saucers, and some plates, they even brought me a nice shirt and a pullover with sleeves like the one Mom had got me. There was no sign of Tommy and Albert that day they never came to visit us. I went round to Gran's to show her what Mom had given me, she smiled and told me that I looked smart and clean. Gran's was busy that day, they was all there. Billy and his Dad, Violet and her husband Tom, and Sadie. I stayed for a little while and when I said that I was going everyone started to give me money, I came away with five shillings and sixpence. As I walked out of the door Gran told me to remember her snuff. When I got home Mom and I had dinner together. It wasn't too bad and she did her best to fill me up. I gave Mom the money telling her that it was what the Pegg's had given to me. When I handed it to her she started to cry. 'Mom I'll be leaving school soon,' I said to her, 'and I will look after you I promise you.'

Chapter 6
My Last Year in School

'I went to bed lying there and thinking I that I should start nicking the coal again.'

We went back to school on the 5th January 1953. By the end of January the gas and electric was both cut off again and we never had them back on until the beginning of June. I'd come home from school one day to find the gas and electric blokes at our house. They had been trying to break in to cut us off, if weren't for Mrs Price running up to get the caretaker, the blokes would have broken our door down. When I got to the top of the stairs they asked me who I was and if I had a key to get in. I told them they I didn't and that I had to wait for my Mom to come home. They kept on at me, asking if any of my neighbours had a key, Mrs Bloomer shouted to them come away and Mrs Fleetwood went back into her house and came back out with the broom. She started hitting the blokes with the broom! Mrs Bloomer collected her broom too and Mr Bloomer followed up back up the stairs. After Mr Bloomer had spoken with the blokes they finally went downstairs and waited outside the block for Mom to come home. I went into the Bloomer house and after a while Mom came back. Before she could say anything the two blokes came up the stairs and asked her, 'Are you Mrs Round then?' As soon as Mom opened our door they pushed passed her, nearly knocking her over. They cut us off and told Mom that she owed British gas and British electric quite lot of money, they never said how much. Mom done some horrible stew for dinner that night, I ate it though and then I went to bed lying there and thinking I that I should start nicking the coal again.

One Monday in February Mr Styles came up to me at dinner time and said we had a chess game on Wednesday at Cockshot Hill School. 'You'll have pay for own bus fare,' he told us lads that was going to the game. Albert Sanders and I told Mr Styles that our Mothers had no money, 'Surely you're Mothers can find four pennies for you both?' he said. On the Wednesday I had my dinner and as soon as I finished I never stop for my pudding I ran all the way to the snuff shop, I didn't even stay for pudding. The lady at shop asked me why as was there in the middle of the day. I explained that I had a chess match after school and that I was the captain of the team. She smiled, telling me that it was nice, and passed me Gran's snuff. I ran all the way to Granny Pegg's and when I went inside she looked at me and asked if I was playing the wag. I told her about the chess game after school and then she asked me if I'd run over to Able's for her and fetch loaf, a quarter pound of butter, and a bottle of milk. Once she'd given me two shillings I ran over to Able's and got Gran's things. When Mrs Able asked me for the money I hesitate for a moment, then I told her to put it on Gran's slate and I pushed the shillings deeper into my pocket. I ran back to Gran's and put the shopping in the kitchen, then I shouted to Gran that it was all there and that I had to hurry back to school.

    I went back to school and straight to the toilets. I shut myself in a cubicle and stood there thinking, 'What have I done? I've pinched money off my Gran.' I won my chess game that day, the same bloke from our earlier game was there with another bloke from the Birmingham chess club. This other bloke played the captain of Cockshot Hill and one of his team, Deakin and I all at the same time. Next he played us all individually and, I'm not being bigheaded but I was the only one who beat him. Mr Carmichael wasn't interested in chess, though he did ask how the school got on. He was interested in football, if the school football team did well he would tell school while we were in assembly, he never mentioned how the chess team got on.

    Towards the end of February I got a boil on my back, I told Gran and when she had a look she told me to wait until it came to a head and then she'd have a cure for it. If my memory serves me right it was the last day of the month when I went to Gran's and, when she had a look at it, she told me it was ready to burst. I sat down at the table while she got an empty milk bottle, she told me that it wasn't going to hurt. Turns out it did hurt a lot and I screamed the place down. Gran sorted me out though and told me that I'd never get another one and she was right about that. While she putting some blackjack ointment on me, I said, 'Gran I have something I need to tell you. I've pinched four shillings from you?' 'How come four shillings?' Gran asked me. 'Two last week and two this week,' I told her, 'I took the money you gave me for your shopping and then I told Mrs Able to put it on your slate.' Gran sighed and said she actually knew all about that and that she wanted to know what I wanted to money for. 'We had to pay our own bus fares when we was going to the other schools to play chess,' I explained. Gran nodded and then told me to get the chair out so that I could take her to the snuff shop. As I helped her into the chair I told her I was sorry and she said, 'I know you are Peter. When is your next chess game?' When I told her that it was the following Thursday Gran said that I should ask Mom for some money. I hung my head and explained that Mom didn't have any and that we'd had our gas and electric cut off again. Gran got angry, 'Your Mother needs to get herself a job and stick to it!' 'I'm going down to the railway later to see if I can get some coal,' I told her. Gran told me to be careful, if I caught again she said they would put me away and through away the key. Then she smiled at me and told me to get her to the shop.

    As usual we got Gran's snuff and then we headed to the Acorn pub. While Gran was in the pub I went up to the canal and jumped up on the bridge. There was a barge full of coal on the canal so I quickly hurried away and collected Mrs Price's pram, I just took it without asking. I ran back to the canal and found that the gate was closed but not locked. I pushed one gate open and hurried down the bumpy slope, I got to the barge and I shouted but nobody was there so I starting to help myself. I filled the pram up as much as I could. It was really hard work getting the pram up the slope and I kept slipping and hurting my knees. I finally got it to the gate and managed to push it all the way home. When I got there I shouted up to Mom, she looked out of the window and called down to ask where I'd got all the coal from. 'I'll explain later,' I shouted back, 'I've got to go and get Gran now.' I ran back down to the Acorn pub and Granny Pegg was waiting for me outside. 'Where the bloody hell you been?' she asked. 'I went and got some coal from the canal for Mom,' I said. As I pushed her home Gran told me that I'd have to go and get her some coal, but that I must be careful when I did.

Later that night, after a dinner of horrible stew, I had a wash and then went to bed. I was asleep for a while but then I woke up and crept out left the door, leaving it on the latch. I went running round the back and got Mrs Price pram then I ran down the lane with it, going all the way to the cut. No one was about so I filled up the pram with coal from the barge again. Once I was finished I got the coal back home and headed out again; that was only my first pram load. When I got back there I saw a few people nicking the coal, there was two kids from my school pinching it too, all filling up prams like me. I got a second load of coal to take home and then I got two pram loads for Granny Pegg. After I left her coal outside her back door I decided to get one last pram load for Mom. When I got back to the canal the barge was nearly empty, but I managed to fill the pram up all the same.

On Sunday morning at 2 o'clock Mom came into my bedroom with two pieces of toast and a cup of hot powdered milk. She said that I must have had a good sleep and then thanked me for getting all of the coal. I told her that I managed to get Gran two full loads of coal too and that there were a few other people nicking the stuff when I was down there. As we was talking there a knock on the door, it was Mrs Price shouting for Mom to come and see what I'd done to her pram. Mom told Mrs Price that she'd get it sorted and then asked me to get it cleaned. What I did I went round to Granny Pegg's with the pram as it was easier for me clean it round there. When I got there Billy, Gran's son, was carrying her share of the coal in. He asked me if I'd got the coal and when I nodded he said, 'All I can say is a big thank you

Peter.' Billy helped me to clean up the pram and then he also fixed it, he told me, 'That will stop the old cow moaning at you when I said that it belonged to Mrs Price. Once we were finished I took the pram back to Mrs Price, the door was open and I shouted in that I'd cleaned it up for her. Mrs Price came to the door and asked what I'd been doing with the pram anyway. When I explained about the coal she told me that I should have got her some too, especially if I was going to borrow her pram. Off I went down to the canal again, when I got there there was a queue. In front of me was Mr Cox and his son Brian, in front of Mr Cox there was two kids with their prams. In the barge there was a bloke shoving the coal scraps into the prams. When it was Mr Cox's turn the bloke told him that the barge was full of coal the day before but that now it was empty. The bloke filled up Mr Cox's pram up then he turned to me, giving me a very strange look. 'Okay bring your pram closer to the barge,' he said. Every time the bloke shovelled some coal into my pram he gave me a hard look. He filled the pram up to the top and then said, 'Go on, now hop it. I don't want to see you down here again.' I turned the pram round and went as quickly as I could go to Mr Cox who was waiting for me at the bottom of the slope. He helped me to push the pram up the slope and when we got to the top I asked him who the bloke on the barge was. 'I don't know,' Mr Cos said, 'I think he works on the barges.' I thanked Mr Cox for helping me and then I got back to Mrs Price and shouted out that I had her coal. When she saw the pram she said, 'Is that all you managed to get?' You could see that she wasn't satisfied, she never even said thank you so I didn't dare ask her if I could cut through her house.

      Come Monday school was the same has usual. I was getting on with my school work at dinner time when the two kids I saw down the cut on Saturday night came up to me and asked me how many pram loads of coal I got. They told me that they'd managed to get ten, I didn't know whether they was telling truth or not, I just carried on what I was doing. The following day at dinner time Mr Styles came up to me and said that he'd put my name, and Deakin's and Albert Sanders' down to join the Birmingham chess club. He explained to me that you had to be a very good chess player to join the Birmingham chess club, 'Peter you're are a very good player,' he told me. 'I have every faith in you to join the Birmingham chess club.' We had our usual chess games at the same schools, Camp Hill, Bordesley Green, and Cockshot Hill. Ada Road School had one chess game at a very posh school in Solihull. We lost nine games one time, I was the only who won by beating the other team's captain. I can remember their captain he thought he'd won the game before it even started. When I won my three games he never shook my hand, all he did was get up and leave. That was my last game for the school.

After dinner Peter Greening and I went up on the Coventry Road, I saw Sadie pushing Granny Pegg so I went running up to them. The next thing I know this copper grabbed hold of me by the collar and asked what I was up to. Before I could say anything Sadie started shouting at the copper and he eventually let me go, telling Peter and I to get back to school. Instead of doing as we was told Peter and I we started to push Gran home, so the copper followed us. When Sadie noticed she went back up to him and shouted again telling him to leave us alone. He stopped following us and Peter and I got back to school just before the bell was about to go. The prefect by the gate was about to take our names when Mr Carmichael came out and saw what we was doing. I introduced Mr Carmichael to Gran and he told me that I could take her home, that I had to hurry back to school. He told Peter Greening to tell Mr Thomas I would be late.

I helped Sadie get Gran home and hurried back to school. When I got back into our classroom Mr Thomas shouted to me get up to his desk. 'Where have you been?' he asked me. I looked over to Peter Greening, he was laughing his head off. He got me into trouble because he never told Mr Thomas that I would be late. 'You will stay in after school, now get back to your desk.' Just before the afternoon break Mr Carmichael came into the classroom to speak with Mr

Thomas. He looked over at me and asked if I got Gran home okay. I stood up and said, 'Yes sir,' then I explained that Mr Thomas wasn't told that I'd be late so that I was been kept in after school. Again I looked over to Peter Greening, he was still laughing. Mr Carmichael told Mr Thomas what had happened and then Mr Thomas asked Peter Greening to stand up and explain why he hasn't said anything. All Peter said was that he was sorry and that he'd forgotten.

When we got out of school Peter started to laugh saying that he wanted to get me into trouble. I just laughed. Then Peter said we should go and have a swim so we headed down to the cut, but it started to rain so Peter headed home instead. I stopped at the shop for some snuff then I went to Gran's. Sadie was there when I arrived and she asked if I knew that it was her birthday. I told her I didn't and then she asked what I was going to get her as a present. All that night I lay awake thinking about what I could get Sadie. Come the next day at dinner time I ate quickly and then I got up, not waiting for pudding again, and I ran out of school. I hurried up the Coventry Road and went into Woolworths. I waited until the lady working on the counter wasn't looking the other way and then I grabbed some earrings. I ran back to school, getting back just in time for the bell. After school I went to Granny Pegg's and gave Sadie the earrings. She looked at them and started to laugh. 'Peter, these don't match,' she said, 'I'll keep them though.'

Chapter 7
My Introduction to Market Life

'That was just one of the many lessons I learnt at the market.'

In the week before Easter Peter Greening and I were playing the wag again. We went down to the town to see Peter's Mom and Dad who worked on the barrows. I never saw my Uncle Harry there until I heard him shouting. I went up to him and he asked me why I wasn't in school. I don't know what made me say it, but I told him that I was looking for a job. Uncle Harry looked down at me and then asked if I could get up early. I nodded yes and then he said for me to meet him outside St Martin's pub at 9 o'clock, he pointed out where the pub was and told me 'Don't be late.'

The next day I waited a little while once Mom had gone out then I ran all the way to the bull ring. I skipped school again and I got to the right place for 9 o'clock. Uncle Harry was waiting for me and he asked me when I left school, I lied and said that I already had. We went into the main market entrance together, I was amazed at what I could see. Uncle Harry took me to a few firms such as George Jackson's, the Randle brothers, Parsons and J.V. White, and Francis Nicholls. As we was going down towards the end of the market we passed Thomas Platt pitch and the bloke on the stall looked at me and said that I didn't look strong enough to work in the market. Next we headed to the Arthur Brett pitch, Uncle Harry was looking for someone called Steve Fisher. When he saw him Uncle Harry shouted, 'Have you got a f***king job for my nephew.' I'd told Uncle Harry that money was scarce in our house and that anything I could earn would help Mom out a lot. I had a brief 'interview' with Steve Fisher and the first thing he asked was if I could get up early, by early he meant 4 o'clock in the morning! I was very nervous and in a low voice and with shaking hands, I told him that I could. I was fourteen at the time and Steve never asked me if I'd left school nor how old I was.

At about 9 o'clock on Friday morning and I spent an hour with Steve who explained to me what I'd be doing, I think he was trying to put me off a bit. I was still nervous, and I think Steve noticed, so he asked me to do an errand for him. The errand was to fetch him jug of tea from the Star Café nearby. He gave me two shillings and told me where to go. I ran there as fast I could go and came back with the jug of tea. He asked me to do one more job for him and that was to sweep the ground and tidy the empties at the back of the ground. I did what he asked and then he told me I'd got the job and I must be back there for 4 o'clock in the morning. He told me that I could leave then and that he'd see me in the morning. As I was walking away Steve shouted to me to come back and said, 'I never asked your name.' I told him it was Peter Round and then he passed me 5 shillings. I went to find my Uncle Harry, he was selling his 'handy carriers' outside Woolworths (Harry Round was the first to sell handy carries outside Woolworths). I went up to and told him about the job, I said thanked him for his help.

I walked all the way home and stopped on the way for Gran's snuff. I couldn't wait till Mom came home to tell her that I'd got a job. At first she didn't like idea of me going out that early in the morning and then she asked me how I got the job. I told her it was Mrs Greening who Mom knew from the Acorn pub. I couldn't tell her it was Uncle Harry who got me the job because I'd played the wag from school. I went out again and took Gran her snuff. When I told her about my Saturday job she said, 'That's very good Peter, you've still got to take me down to the snuff shop you know.'

Come Saturday morning Mom got me up at 3 o'clock. She had a piece of toast and a cup of oxo waiting for me. I left home at about twenty-five past three and as I was coming out the block Mom lifted the window up and shouted to me to be careful. I ran all the way to the market, stopping for a short time at the Old Crown to get my breath back. As I went through archway at the main gate of the market there was a copper standing there. When I passed him he shouted,

'Come here sonny boy!' He asked me where I was going and told him that I was off to work. Then asked who I worked for and I said, 'Arthur Brett'. He marched me straight down to the right place. Arthur Brett was standing there, he was a giant of man. He looked smart with silver, grey hair. The copper asked if I worked for him and Arthur said, 'I don't know you'll have to ask Steve, he may have taken him on when I wasn't here.'

My first job was to go the farmer's avenue to fetch ten cabbages and ten cauliflowers. The farmer was called Saxon and when I approached him he asked me what I wanted. 'I've come for Arthur Brett's order,' I told him. Saxon nodded and pointed to some cabbages and cauliflowers, so I started to take the cabbages out of the boxes and put them on the barrow one at a time. I thought Arthur had only bought singles and not boxes. The farmer shouted at me, 'What do you think you're f***king doing?' He looked at me and started to laughed. 'Okay son, I can see that you're new.' Saxon helped me to put the boxes of cabbage onto the barrow, he told me to come back for the cauliflower. When I got back to the pitch Arthur showed me where to put the boxes of cabbage. I went take the boxes from the front of the barrow when Arthur suddenly shouted at me really loud, I just stood there. Steve came to my rescue, 'Peter you load from the front of the barrow and you unload from back,' he told me. He showed me how to do it the right way and then sent me to collect the cauliflowers. This time I made sure to load and unload the barrow properly, just like Steve showed me.

My next job was to go and fetch ten carrots and five parsnips, I knew what they meant although it was bags instead of boxes this time. I had go to J.V. White in 3rd Avenue, when I got there I couldn't see anybody about. Eventually a bloke appeared and I asked him for the carrots and parsnips for Arthur Brett's order. The bloke pointed towards some bags and told me to help myself. I put the carrots on the barrow first and then the parsnip on top. I must have put all the weight on the front because I was struggling to lift and pull the barrow. I only got a few yards when the bloke came up to me and said, 'I'll help son, I can see that you've only just started.' He sorted the barrow out so I could and pull it without any trouble. As he walking away the bloke asked me if I could count properly, at that time I didn't know what he meant. When I got back to Arthur he looked at the barrow and told me to get a bag of the carrots and a bag of the parsnips and hide them quickly. While I was hiding them the bloke who'd helped me came running up and shouted to Arthur, 'How many carrots and parsnips have you have got?' 'A five and a ten,' Arthur said, 'Billy you can count them they are all there.' I found out later that the bloke was called Billy Cartwright, I had to go to his pitch quite often after that day. It was then that I realised what Billy meant about counting. I put the carrots and parsnips on the barrow without counting them properly. Arthur told me to fetch a jug of tea and some 'holy ghost.' I stood confused for a moment and then asked which church I should go to. Arthur looked at me and laughed, 'Peter I can see you are going to fit in at the market very well.' Then I realised it was toast that he'd asked me to go fetch. I was standing there waiting for the money when Arthur asked me what I was waiting for. 'Go to the Star Cafe and ask for Hilda, say the toast and jug is for Steve Fisher and hurry up.'

    At the cafe I asked for Hilda and told her that I'd come for Steve Fisher's order. She came round from behind the counter and asked me my name. I told her it was 'Peter' and then she looked at me and said that I had a nice bum, feeling it at the same time. I couldn't get out the cafe quick enough! When I got back to the pitch there was a customer waiting for me to take his fruit and veg to his van. Steve had already loaded produce onto the barrow for me, he'd done it just right so that I could lift it and pull it without any hesitation. I had to follow the customer to is van, his name was Arthur Pallet, he was always one of my first customers in the morning. When we got to his van I helped him to unload and pack the produce into his van, then I had to bring back the empty boxes. As I was walking away Arthur shouted to me to come back. 'I know it's your first day,' he said, 'but you must always wait for your tip.' He passed me five shillings and I told him, 'Thank you Sir.' 'Just call me Arthur,' he replied.

My next customer was a woman, Mrs Cooke. During the morning I must had about fifteen customers altogether and I loaded two vans that came alongside the pitch. I struggled to lift the big cases of oranges so Steve showed me the way to lift them without hurting myself. 'You need to lift properly otherwise you'll ruin your married life,' he told me with a smile. At first I didn't know what he meant then I caught on and smiled back. It was getting towards the end of the day, I think it was about eleven o'clock, when Steve told me to start tidying up. When I'd finished Arthur said, 'Let's see how many tips you've earned Peter.' I started counting for a few minutes and then said, 'You've done really well Peter. You're going home with two pounds and eighteen shillings.' Both Arthur and Steve told me that I'd worked really hard and that they'd see me on Monday. Arthur left shortly after that and then Steve pointed to a nearby bag and told me to bring it to him. He filled it up with fruit and veg and then passed me the bag back and told me to get myself home.

As I approached home I saw coalman in the Holme, so I ran up to him. 'Got any coal to spare mister?' I asked him. He said he had and asked me how much I wanted. I told him three shillings worth and then said which block I lived in so he could bring it to us. I went running up to the house, I remember feeling really proud as I went up the stairs. I went inside and gave Mom the bag with the fruit and veg and told her that I'd asked the coalman for some coal. Mom looked in the bag and said, 'That's nice Peter. How much have earned today?' I got two pounds and eighteen shillings?' I told her. 'And how much did you pay for the coal?' It told her it cost me nine shillings and then she said that I had to give her two pounds and nine shillings 'for my keep.' 'No Mom I'm keeping the nine shillings for myself,' I said. She started to argue with me, so I gave her the two pounds and ran out the house. As I was going out the coalman passed me on the stairs, I opened the coalhouse door for him then I ran out of the block. I went straight round to Granny Pegg's and the first thing she said was that I was late. 'Come on, I'll miss my half pint otherwise.' The chair was already out and Gran got in, so I pushed her to the gully and then stopped. 'Gran I want to pay you back the money I pinched off you,' I said passing her the coins. 'That's a good lad,' she said smiling, 'now get me to the Acorn before they close.' I ran all the way there, even though I was knackered, I knew Gran wanted her drink. When we got to the Acorn Gran went in while I waited outside. I was getting tired so I sat in the chair, I must have fallen asleep because next thing I knew Gran was shaking me awake and asking me to take her to the snuff shop.

Once she was finished in the shop I started to push her back home, all she did was moan about how she'd only had time for two half pints and that she'd had to drink them up quickly. When we got to the top of the gully she told me to stop on the bridge. I went round to the front of the chair and Gran said, 'Peter I have all the faith in the world in you. You're a good lad giving me the money back, I knew one day you would give it back to me. How much did you give to your mother?' 'Two pounds,' I said, 'and I bought her some coal as well.' Gran nodded and then said, 'She should be pleased with what you have done for her and I hope she appreciates what you will do for her in the future.' After that we went on and I got Gran home.

Mom had something nice to eat waiting for me on the table when I got back. There was two sausages, mashed potato, and two carrots, I had it with two pieces of bread and a cup of hot powdered milk. I asked Mom when she got the sausages from and she told me they'd come from Able's. 'Mom you haven't got any coupon left have you?'" She shook her head and said that the food was coming from the ration book, but I knew that they weren't been used   anymore. After dinner I told Mom that I was going to bed and she said that I should go and get some rest. Lying on my makeshift bed that night I couldn't believe the money I'd earned. I remember thinking that I wouldn't have to wake up to find and nick some coal. That was my last thought as I fell into a deep sleep.

The next thing I heard somebody was shouting my name. I lay there for a bit all confused, then I heard it again. Somebody was shouting, 'Roundy Roundy!' I got up and went to the window, it was Johnny shouting up to me. I lifted the window up and heard Johnny shout up to me to come down to the cut for a swim. At first I said no but then Johnny shouted up again, so I thought about it and then told him I'd be down in a tick. I went into the living room and told Mom that I was going out to the cut with Johnny. 'No you're not,' she told me, 'it's dangerous.' I told her that I'd been there before and I could see her thinking about it. She eventually said that I could go, but warned me to be careful.

Johnny was waiting for me at the bottom of the block. As we walked down to the cut I told him I'd got a part time job down at the wholesale fruit market. 'Wow,' he said, 'how much money do you get?' I told him and he was really impressed, though I told him that it was really hard work. I also told him about my part-time job and that I had to get up and 4 o'clock in the morning for it. 'My dad won't let me go out that time in the morning,' Johnny said. When we got to the cut there was loads of other kids swimming around, they were all naked again nobody took any notice. We all playing around splashing each other and having a great time, we must have been there for a while. There were kids from Johnny's school and from my school so we got to know each other a bit. That's how we all came lifelong mates. On the Sunday we did the same thing, went down to the cut had a good swim all us kids together.

Come Sunday evening Mom told me that I should get myself to bed early because I had such an early start the next day. At 3 o'clock Mom came into the bedroom and gently woke me up. She'd already got me two pieces of toast and a cup of oxo ready. While I was eating my toast Mom told me that I had to make sure I had something to eat and drink every morning. I nodded and promised her that I would. It must have been twenty-five past three when I left home, as I was going out the block Mom lifted the window and told me to be careful. Off I went running down the lane, as I was going over the hump back bridge at the bottom of Great Barr Street I heard someone shout, 'Hey you, sonny boy! Come here!' When I looked it was a copper so I went over to him and he asked me where I was going. I said that I was going to work but he replied, 'You're not, you're coming with me.' The blue light started to flash on the nearby police phone box, the copper told me 'wait there', but as soon as he turned his back I ran. I didn't stop until I got to moat lane where I saw a line of lorries waiting to go into the market, then I was walked up the lane where loads of the market lads were yelling at me to get out of the f***king way. I started to run again and as I went through the main gate another copper shouted at me to stop running and walk. I got to the pitch and I looked at Arthur telling him that I was sorry I was late. He told me to follow him and together we went into the middle of the avenues. Arthur told me to look up at the big clock, as he pointed he told me that I wasn't late, that the clock was always right and that I was right on time. When we got back to the pitch I was given my first job; to go to Saxons and get the cabbages and cauliflowers, 10 of each as instructed by Arthur. I went straight to Saxons, remembering the way from before. I also remember how to load the barrow and where to put the veg back at the pitch. 'Okay Peter,' Arthur said when I'd finished, 'your next job is when the gates are starting to open, go and fetch the jug of tea and the toast. You can have what you want too.' The fifth avenue gate was open so I went that way, I walked all the way round the side of the market and towards the Star Café. 'Here comes the good looking lad,' Hilda said when I went inside. She came right up close to me and started to feel my bum again. She asked me what I wanted and I asked for some toast and a sausage sandwich. The reason I asked for a sausage sandwich was because I could smell them. After Hilda had finished serving me she came to the door with me, still feeling my bum. I had my hands full and I was getting frightened that I might drop I was carrying. When I got back to the pitch I told

Arthur that Hilda never asked me for the money. 'Never mind about that Peter,' he said, 'now get the barrow and go to Frances Nicholls. Get 50 oranges, they're all different, counts ten grapefruits, and ten lemons. Ask for Paddy he will put you right and he knows what you got to bring round first.' I went to France Nicholls and when I got there I found that Paddy was really helpful. He showed me how to take the produce off the stack without hurting myself and how to lift them just like Steve did. I was still struggling to lift things but at least now I was doing it the right way. As time went on I was lifting everything without any trouble, it started come to me automatically. I couldn't believe how much the customers was giving me in tips, ranging from two shillings to ten shillings. It all depended on what work I had done for them. My quiet days were Mondays and Wednesdays, they were what we called empty days when the customers brought back the empty boxes. On Mondays and Wednesdays I sometimes only earned 15 shillings or less compare to the market days where I could earn up two pounds ten shillings or even three pounds depending on the customer and what they wanted.

      One night, at the end of a weekend holiday, I was lying awake thinking about how I'd get to work without Mom knowing. She went out at 7 o'clock in the morning for her cleaning job. The time came for me to get up and I had get ready. I had to creep out of the door and quietly put the key back from the letterbox then I ran down the stairs and of the out the block. I ran all the way to the Old Crown where I sat on the window ledge for few minutes till I got my breath back, then I carried on running till I got to the market. As it was a Monday Moat Lane was quiet and there weren't many lorries about. I got to the pitch and Arthur said hello and told me, 'You know what you're first job is Peter.' That day Steve went round to all the big firms buying the fruit and filling the pitch up ready for the next day. Then the customers started to arrive bringing back their empties. One customer called Chas Wilkinson asked me to go and get a jug of tea and some toast. I asked Steve if I should go to the Harrison's Cafe, but he laughed and, passing me back to cups and jugs to be washed, told me to go to the Star Cafe. So off I went to the cafe, when I got there I gave Hilda the cups and jugs and asked her to give them a good wash as Steve instructed. 'You can go through to the back and wash them yourself,' she said to me. Although I was busy I went through to the back and started to wash the cups and the jugs myself. Hilda followed me and came right up close to me, she was feeling me all over and even put her hand down my trousers. I couldn't move and I was shaking a bit. She must have noticed because she told me not worry and that she'd 'Look after me.' After that I grabbed my order and got out of there as quickly as I could go. As I walked back to the pitch I told myself that I wasn't going back there again. 'How's Hilda?' Steve asked when I got back, I didn't reply, instead I just carried on with my day's work. little while later it started to go quiet and it was time for me to take the empty boxes to the firms. The firms charged for the empties if you didn't return them; 5 shillings for the boxes and 15 shillings to a pound for the banana boxes. Come one o'clock the gates was closing so I headed up towards the main gate. I couldn't go straight home so to kill time I went to the rail embankment and just sat there till it was time to go and fetch Granny's Pegg's snuff.

    This went on for a few weeks with Mom and Gran not knowing that I was playing the wag from school. One day I must have been a bit early getting Gran's snuff, because when I got to her house she looked at me and said, 'You haven't been to school my lad.' I promised her that I had, but she pointed to the clock saying that it was only just 4 o'clock and that she hadn't seen me cutting through the Holme on my way to school. 'No Gran,' I told her, 'I go and call for a mate of mine from Wolseley Street.' We went back and forth for a while and eventually I told her that I'd been playing the wag and working down the market. 'I've been getting some money so I can get the gas and the electric back,' I explained, 'I have to hide the money from Mom. I'm frightened in case she finds it.' Gran sighed and then said, 'I know what you can do. Go see if they'll let you pay a bit off the bill each week, I bet they will if you pop to the office. I'll ask Violet or Sadie to go with you on Monday shall I?'

I carried on doing the same thing, creeping out of the house in the morning and running all the way to the market. I always stopped at the Old Crown to get my breath back on the way. One Tuesday it was market day and Moat Lane it was packed with lorries. Some of the lads would go up the lorry drivers and ask them what firms they were delivering to and what they had in their lorries. Then the lads, when the driver wasn't looking, would nick some of the boxes of produce off the back. When the drivers would get to the firm they would sometimes be short on their delivery. The lads would sell what they nicked to customers or they would get the salesmen to sell it for them. You'd be surprised what went on in the wholesale fruit market at that time in the morning, not only in Moat Lane but all around and inside the market.

One Thursday, towards closing time, I had to go with Steve to a firm call J.V. White and get 100 tomatoes. We called those boxes boats because of the shape of them. Steve show me how to stack them on the barrow so we could get all 100 boats on there and then we went back to the pitch together. Arthur was still there to unload the tomatoes to the back of the pitch. After I finished helping with unloading, Arthur told me to head off home. I took a slow walk home and went to Gran's, it was nearly 4 o'clock and she'd made me a sandwich. As I ate Gran started to have a go, 'It's alright you helping your Mother,' she told me, 'but it's a wonder the school boardman hasn't come looking for you. He will eventually Peter and you will get yourself into a load of trouble. I know trouble is one of your names.' I just sat and listened to her and when I'd finished eating, I thanked her for the sandwich and said that I was off home. I'm going now gran see you tomorrow thanks for the sandwich. When I got home Mom made the horrible stew again and when we sat down together she told me that she is going to look for a job in a factory. I said it was good and asked where, but Mom said that she wasn't sure yet.

Come the next day Friday I crept out to work, but this time I had to get dressed on the landing. After running all the way to the market I found Arthur at the pitch with his usual white coat on. He told me that the gates would be open soon and that a certain customer (we'll call him Mr 'A') would be coming for the tomatoes. Arthur wanted me to get the tomatoes loaded into Mr A's van quickly. Once the gates opened Mr A pulled his van alongside the pitch, I heard Arthur say that there was 110 altogether. As I loaded the van, Mr A gave Arthur 5 shillings. As I loaded I noticed that the numbers went from 110 to 120, so I asked Arthur how, if I'd fetched 100 tomatoes the day before, there were more now. Arthur simply smiled at me and said, 'I'm going to teach you how make 100 tomatoes into 110 or 120 Peter. What you had to do is, you turn the bottom of the tomato box over and open it very careful so you don't break the wood. Then you take a layer out and pack it with straw very tight and so on till you get the number you want.' That was just one of the many lessons I learnt at the market.

One of my regular customers was Vera Pickering, she always gave me ten shillings as I did a lot of running round for her, going to different firms and getting the produce. One Saturday towards the end of May Vera sent me to a firm call Bousfields at the top of the market by the main gate, I can remember it was for 20 pears. When I got to Bousfields I went up to the salesman and asked for what Vera wanted. He pointed to the pears and as I was loading them onto the barrow a group of woman came up to the pitch, I think there was about ten of them altogether. I pointed to women out to the salesman and he smiled at me. 'They are here to get their husbands wages before they go in the pub,' he told me, then I heard him talking to himself saying, 'two for the gaffer and one for me.' All of a sudden he said, 'F**k the gaffer,' then he started saying, 'Two for me and one for the gaffer.' Come the end of the day Steve gave me my wages, two pounds and ten shillings.

I had   trebled my wages over the week in tips alone. As we were clearing up the horse and cart came into the market. The bloke jumped off his cart and the horse carried on up to the coloured bloke who was waiting for him. The coloured bloke gave the horse his carrots and then he started to walk away and the horse followed him, knowing that he had more carrots.

When I got home a little later Mom was waiting for me and the first thing she asked me was how much money I was going to give her. I passed her all of my wages but she asked if that was all I was giving her. 'Yes,' I told her, 'I'm going to buy the coal and I won't give you that money, I'll see the coalman myself.' As we was talking the coalman came into the Holme so I ran down to him and gave him nine shillings, it got us enough coal to last the week. Later on I ran round to Gran's, she was waiting for me and had a little moan when I arrived, saying that we'd have to hurry to get to the Acorn pub in time. When we arrived at the pub Gran got out of the her chair and as she was walking to the door I gave her a half crown, saying that she could get a half pint on me. Gran never thanked me and when she came out later she went over to the snuff shop. By the time I got Gran back to her house I was knackered. I told Gran that I was heading home but she told me to wait. She told me that Violet and Sadie were going with me on Monday and that they'd meet me by the church where the buses stop at one o'clock.

Come Monday Violet and Sadie were waiting for me and off we went to the electricity office together. At first the manager wasn't going to let me pay so much each week, but Sadie had go at him and then Violet started on him too, so eventually he gave in. He wanted a full payment plus charges for putting the electric back on. Violet and Sadie nodded and told me to agree with this. Then the manager asked how much I'd be giving him that day and I passed over two pounds and ten shillings. The manager nodded and said, 'Okay we will take it from here,' then he gave me a card and told me not to lose it and that I needed to bring it with me every time I visited the office. The same thing happened at the gas office and I had to pay a certain amount every week, they also gave a card. Afterwards when we was coming down the bull ring, we got to Woolworths and I asked Sadie and Violet if they wanted me go and nick them some earrings. They both said no, not while I was with them, I laughed and said that I'd never have done it anyway.

I did go and buy them some earrings the next day Tuesday, I went to Woolworths after work. The lady at the counter helped me to match the earrings, I remember that they were about sixpence each or one shilling each. Earlier that day at work I did my usual jobs and come 5 o'clock in the morning the gates was opening and Steve shouted to me to get the barrow and go to Randall Bros. and Parsons. I was told to fetch ten boxes of bananas so off I went, when I got there I went through the archway. It was dim and dark and there was railway carriages lined up by the side of the bays, I remember that it was a bit scary. You could see the railway blokes pulling the carriages along with a hook. This big bloke standing outside the banana room looked over to me and asked me what I was doing there. I told him that my name was Peter Round and that I'd come for ten bananas for Arthur Brett. The bloke told me that the banana weren't quite ready yet, so I stood by the bay looking into the
banana room. The bloke could obviously see that I was interested in what was going on, so he let me climb into the bay and enter the room. I later learnt that the bloke's name was Big Jim. As time went on he taught me everything about bananas from taking them of the railway carriage to packing them. Big Jim showed me how to ripen them with the gas temperature and how to cut them off the stems. 'When you pack the best ones,' he told me once, 'you have to put mauve paper for the best and blue paper for the seconds and pink paper third.' He also showed me how to take a hand out from the middle of the banana box and pack back without anyone noticing. When Steve found out I could do that it was my first job every morning go to the banana rooms and fetch ten bananas and make ten into eleven. The

railway blokes knew what I was doing and they always told me that I'd get caught one day, but I never did.

Once I'd got the earrings after work, I headed to Granny Pegg's. Violet and Sadie was both there and when I gave them the earrings they asked if I'd nicked them. 'No I didn't,' I told them, 'see they match this time.' They just laughed while Gran sat there. I looked over at Gran and told her, that I'd always look after her, I did I give her 5 shillings every Saturday when I look her to the Acorn pub. She told me that she was proud what I was doing, but that she also worried about me.

During the last week in May I had a good week in tips and I also found three banana boxes lying about with a pound deposit on them. I picked them up and took them back to the pitch where Steve gave me a pound for them. All the things I did for the firm Arthur never gave me anything, but Steve gave me ten shillings now again in my wages.

At the beginning of June 1953 after work one day I went to the gas office and paid two pounds and ten shillings off the gas bill. When I came out of the office I walked up Newhall Street and I heard someone shout my name. It was Steve and he asked me what I was doing that side of town. I told him the truth, that my Mom and I had no gas or electric as we'd been cut off, but I also said that I was paying so much each week off the bills. Steve looked at me for a moment and then said, 'Okay Peter you come back with me.' Together Steve and I went back to the gas office and he asked to see the manager or whoever was in charge. Within a few minutes the manager came out and Steve went with him into the back room. They came out after about twenty minutes and Steve said, 'You're going to have your gas back on Wednesday morning, isn't that right?' He turned to the manager who nodded in reply. As Steve and I walked over to the electric office he asked me about my home life. I told him that it was only my Mom and I and that I didn't know where my father was. Steve nodded and said, 'Come on, let's get your electric back on too.' He did the same thing at this office, talking to the manger and getting the electric put back on for me.

248

When we was walking out I asked Steve how much I had to pay each week and he simply said, 'Nothing Peter.' I thanked Steve for his help and then said goodbye.

When I got home at 4 o'clock I told Mom that I had great news for her. When I said that our gas and electric would be back on by Wednesday, she asked me how I'd managed it. 'I borrowed the money off my the gaffer,' I told her, 'I've got to pay him back so much each week.' 'How are you going to pay him back if you only work Saturdays?' she asked me. 'Mom you have to trust me,' I replied, 'just really trust me this time.' I told her that my gaffer was really good and that I wouldn't be getting into any trouble. Then Mom said that she had good news too, she'd got a job at Warne, Wright, Rowlands on Keeley Street. I told her that day that I hope she'd stick to it, and she did until she retired in 1960.

One Wednesday was a very slow day at work. Steve bought 100 cases of oranges and they had to be sorted and, because it was a slow day, he told me to tidy the pitch up. At about 12 o'clock Steve, Arthur, and I went to the railway goods yard. When we got there the bloke in charge showed us where the 100 cases oranges were and the trailer for us to put them on after they'd been sorted. We started to sort the good from the bad and Arthur and Steve showed me how to open the cases and take the bad out from the side and then repack the bad into the middle so they didn't show from the side. We never took any bad oranges out, when the railway blokes was right up the other end of the railway yard I had to swap them over for the good ones. After about two hours we'd finished and Arthur gave the bloke in charge a tip, then he looked at my hands and told me to come with him. 'I'm going to get that grime off your hands Peter,' he told me. While nobody was looking Arthur opened one of the cases and we swapped out some of the bad oranges. Then Arthur took me off to the toilets, which were filthy and smelt horrid. He got the bad oranges and, by rubbing them into my hands, he got all the grime off them. He told me that next time I'd know how to get my hands clean.

Before we left Arthur told me to get down there early the next day and make sure that we had the right amount of oranges. I took a slow walk home and to kill time I walked down Montague Street. I thought to myself that if I went passed the bakery I'd see if I could get a tea cake. I was a bit hungry and although Hilda would give me a thick sausage sandwich every time I went in the café, she always felt my bum. I let her do it because I knew I could get what I wanted. I passed the bakery but the gate was closed, so I carried on walking home. When I got to the snuff shop I went inside to get Gran's usual. When I got to her house to give her the snuff she moaned at me for playing the wag, but I promised that I'd be fine.

When I got home Mom told me that the gas and electric had been put back on. I could tell that Mom wasn't too happy about it. 'I can't see the gaffer lending you money,' she told me, 'you only work part time on a Saturday. I think you're in some sort of trouble.' I shook my head, 'Mom please trust me,' I said, 'I'm in no trouble.' We never had the gas and the electric cut off again till Mom passed away in 1974 at the age of 74. Later that night I asked Mom when she started work at her new job, she told me it was Monday. I thought to myself, 'Good I can come straight home, go to bed and get some sleep before she gets home.' Mom told me that she wanted a nice tidy home when she got back from work, I told her, 'Okay.'

I got up a bit earlier the next day and crept out of the house, getting dressed on the landing again. When I got to Allison Street I was just in time to see the railway driver hooking up the trailer. He said 'No' at first till I said that they were for Arthur Brett. 'Okay son,' the bloke said, 'go get them then.' I went over to Big Jim and asked him if the bananas were ready. 'Yes Peter,' he told me, 'they're ready.' Together we walked away from the banana room and along the bay. 'Here they are Peter,' Big Jim said pointing, there was eleven of them altogether. Big Jim looked at me and with a smile and a wink, I knew what he'd done for me. I put the bananas on the trailer and when I'd finished the bloke got in the lorry and drove away. I went up Moat Lane pushing the barrow passed the lorries and a couple of the drivers followed me, asking me what I was up to. When I got to the pitch Arthur was waiting for me and he helped me to unload the produce. 'Well done Peter,' he said, 'I will make you a good market man. You listen to me and Steve, we won't put you wrong, we think lot of you.' I thanked him and I thought to myself, 'I wonder if he is right?' Steve and Arthur never did put me wrong and they was always helpful. I'd done my usual jobs that day when Steve arrived, he went straight up the back to put his white coat on. I followed him and said, 'Steve my Mom said thank you for helping us. I promise I'll keep working for you to pay you back.' 'Okay Peter,' he said, 'next Wednesday there will be only 50 oranges, you can do them on your own.'

On Monday Mom went to work and when I'd finished I caught the bus home. When I got back I tidied up the house and then went to bed to get some well-earned sleep before Mom got home. It was the Wednesday when I had to go down Allison Street to sort out the 50 oranges. Arthur came with me but he only stayed for a while to help me get started. A little later he said, 'I'm going now Peter, don't get doing any swapping over will you?' He smiled and then he jumped off the bay. Before he walked off he turned around and shouted 'Don't lose that hammer or I will lose you.' He'd given me a pound to pass on to the bloke in charge. I did swap all of the oranges over when nobody was looking, I covered them up in the big stacks so nobody would notice what I'd done. I only sorted a few out and then I put them onto the trailer. I sat with a couple of good cases for about hour when somebody came my way I make believed I was doing my work. After I'd finished I went looking for the bloke in charge, I had to go right up the top. He was there in charge of the carriages coming down on the lift from Moor Street train station. I watched him and saw how he brought the carriage down onto the lift then the railway porter got his hook and pulled the carriage to the turntable to whichever bay the carriage had to go on. I gave the bloke in charge the pound and then I caught the bus home again.

As I was going up the stairs Mrs Bloomer came out of her house and said, 'Come here you little B, I want a word with you. You've been playing the wag again haven't you?' When I told her that I hadn't she replied, 'Yes you have, the school board man has been here looking for you. Tell me the truth to your auntie Bloomer, and don't lie to me.' She looked down at me and I sat on the stairs. 'Yes Mrs Bloomer I have been playing the wag, but I haven't been getting myself into any trouble. I've been working down the fruit market and money so I could get the gas and the electric back on. I've been paying a bit off the bills each week.' Mrs Bloomer sat down next to me and said, 'Peter all I can say is that you're a good lad, but you are taking a big risk. You can get yourself into big trouble. Does your Mother know?' I shook my head. 'You be careful Peter,' Mrs Bloomer said, 'if the school board man comes round here again leave him to me, I'll deal with him and just be careful. I won't tell your Mother as long as you keep out of trouble.'

The next day I ran all the way to the banana rooms just in time to catch the railway driver. Big Jim had done it again for me, I had eleven all together. The first thing Arthur asked me was, 'Where's my hammer?' I passed it to him and he told me that I'd done a really good job and to keep it up. I did my usual jobs first and then I went to get the jug of tea, the toast, and my sandwich. When I got to the cafe Hilda called me to the back again. I went through and she grabbed hold of me and started kissing me. I tried to push her away but I couldn't, she was holding me tight. Then she started to undress me but I eventually managed to push her away. I rushed to the door but found that she'd only gone and locked it. The other woman who worked at the cafe (I think her name was Ann) as was knocking on the door, I was glad to see her. Soon Hilda opened the door and I was out like a shot, I collected my order and I left.

In July 1953, I think it was the first Friday of the month, and I was working. It was getting towards closing time when Steve asked me to run over to the Drovers pub with this swag box and ask for Big Harry. I was to give him to box and he'd give me some meat in return. 'Go now and get back before they close the gate,' Steve told me. I stood by the door of the pub, it was full of all the meat market workers. I shouted out 'Who's Big Harry?' and the pub went quiet for a few seconds. Turns out Big Harry was standing right by me, with a point in his hand he turned and put his face right by mine. He lifted his hand up, I thought he was going tip his beer all over me, but instead he burst out laughing and the whole pub also too. (As time went on Big Harry turned out to be another bloke I got on well with.)

The next Saturday it was a really busy morning and come 12 o'clock I was waiting for Vera Pickering to come back and give me my tip, I'd done a lot of running around for her. Arthur and I stood together, he was also waiting for Vera to come back. While we waited and asked Arthur something I'd been thinking about. 'I was on Bousfields pitch,' I told him, 'and the salesman was saying "2 for the gaffer and 1 for me", then he said never mind the gaffer and he starting saying "2 for me and 1 for the gaffer" instead. What was he doing?' I asked. Arthur replied, 'He is fiddling his gaffer and I know you won't do that to me. I've got every faith in you Peter.' Vera came back and paid Arthur, she also gave me 15 shillings, then she went and got in her lorry. 'She's in a very good mood giving you that much money,' Arthur told me, then he asked me if Steve gave me my wages. I said that he did and then I thanked him. I went to walk away when Arthur shouted for me to hang on and that he'd walk with me. He went up to the back of the ground to lock the little shed up where the phone and his other stuff was kept. He noticed that Steve hadn't taken Hilda's swag bag so he asked me to take it to the Star Cafe. 'The cafe will be closed by now, but you can get in round the back,' Arthur told me.

I walked up to the main gate and could see all the market workers carrying their swag bags. I went down Jamaica Row where all the barrows were lined up with the hawkers shouting their produce. My mate Peter Greening's parents works on those Barrows. I passed Mrs Greening and she shouted to me. 'Don't forget Peter Round you own me a half pint for me not telling your Mother what you've been up to and Arthur Brett too. You haven't left school you're only fourteen and he doesn't know does he?' I stopped and walked over to her. 'Okay Mrs Greening here you go' and I gave her 5 shillings. I carried on down Jamaica Row until I found the entry, I turned left then right till the cafe door was right in front of me. I walked straight in and I stood there for a few seconds, I couldn't believe what I was seeing. Hilda was lying on the floor naked and Steve he was on top of her with his trousers down and his bum in the air. They looked up at me and all Steve said was, 'Put the bag down Peter, see on Monday and don't be late.' I didn't know what to think, I just walked away.

As I was running down the lane on Tuesday morning Mr Greening saw me and shouted, 'Roundy take my barrow to the market.' I took his barrow on a few occasions after that day, one time I was stopped by a copper who thought I'd nicked it. It wasn't until I explained that I worked for Arthur Brett in the market that he let me go. I carried on running with Mr Greening's barrow and then I left it outside once I got the fifth avenue. When I got the banana rooms I apologised to Jim for been late. 'Don't worry Peter,' Big Jim told me, 'and if Arthur starts moaning at you for being late, tell him that the bananas wasn't ready when you got here. If he keeps on moaning at you tell him to get in touch with me okay Peter?' I smiled at him and said, 'Thanks.' When I arrived at the pitch I said sorry to Arthur for my lateness too. 'You know what you've got to do Peter so get cracking,' Arthur told me.

That day and the day before Steve went and got the tea and the sandwiches from the cafe, but he never said anything about what I'd seen on Saturday. I had a good day in tips and left the market at 1 o'clock. I went round to Gran's to get a sandwich and Sadie was there. All of sudden there was bang on the back door and when Sadie went to answer it and saw there was a bloke standing there she asked who he was. 'I'm the school board man. I saw a young lad of school age come in here a moment ago,' he said. 'There's no kids live here, now piss off,' Sadie told him angrily. 'I saw the kid,' the bloke said, 'I've been looking for him and I know that he came in here.' Sadie shook her head, 'I'm going to tell you again there's no kid in here.' Then Granny Pegg went to the door and asked the bloke the name of the kid he was looking for. When he said 'Peter Round' Gran told him to try the next Holme, that he might find me there. Then she told him to piss off. Gran shut the door and she said to me, 'Peter you've got to be very careful otherwise you are going to get yourself into trouble again,' Gran said, 'they will put you away.' 'Gran I'll be leaving school in about two weeks' time,' I told her.

It was a Thursday when I asked Mom if I could go the pictures, she said yes straight away and I ran out the house, happy to be out. It was my first time going to the pictures and I was really excited. I went round to the Kingston, there was a long queue waiting to go in. In the queue was Jimmy Wenlock and Albert Sanders, they let me in queue by them and they asked me if I'd been playing the wag as they hadn't seen me in ages. 'Mr Styles has been looking for you,' Albert said, 'he's been round your house and Mr Thomson too. I bet the school board man has been looking for you has well.' I said that he had, but that at least we all only had a couple of weeks until school ended. Albert and Jimmy told me that they had got the afternoon off the next day to go round to Jenkins Street school to collect their national insurance numbers.

The next day at work I asked Steve if I could leave at about one-thirty. When he asked me what for I told him that I had to go somewhere for my Mom. I got onto the bus and asked the conductor if the bus was going up the Coventry Road and by Jenkins Street. She told me that it was and I asked her to let me know where to get off. When I got to Jenkins Street school all the kids from my class was there too. I got my national insurance number and then I left. Walking back down the Coventry Road I saw Sadie and I told her where I'd been. She replied that she'd have to go down there herself one time to get her number too. Sadie and I carried on together and walked passed the Barns furniture shop, I stopped to look in the window and told Sadie that I'd love to buy a bed. 'Come with me then,' she said, 'and we'll see what we can do.' We went inside and Sadie got talking to the bloke in the shop. After a little while the bloke turned to me and told me to come back the next day. 'We will see how much you can pay and sort out the money you'll need to pay each week,' he said. When we got outside I thanked Sadie and she said that she'd get Violet to come with me the next day.

When I got home I tidied the house up and at about four-thirty Mom came back early. I asked her if she'd got the sacked and she shook her head. 'I went passed your school,' she said, 'I've been speaking to Mr Carmichael, he told me you haven't been to school for the last four months.' I hung my head. I knew she'd find out eventually. 'What have you been getting yourself into Peter? You've got be in some sort of trouble.' I promised her that I was in no trouble and said that she had to trust me. 'I've been working at the market the whole time, that's why I haven't been in any trouble,' I explained. 'Look what I've done for you, I got the gas and electric back on, I'm buying the coal, I haven't had to go out and nick any. I'm also buying a bed for myself tomorrow.' Mom looked at me and then she started to cry, at the same time she was really having go at me. She kept having a go at me for most of the night. Before I went to bed she said to me, 'You're going to school on Monday.' I tried to tell her that I only had a couple of weeks left before school ended, but she wasn't having any of it.

Mom got me up to go to work on Saturday and before I left she asked me what I was going to tell my gaffer about going back to school on Monday. I simply told her that I was going to tell him nothing. It was a normal Saturday. I worked hard and then I took gran to the pub followed by the snuff shop. That night I gave Mom the money for my keep. Mom told me that if I'd been working all week I should be giving her more money for my keep. I gave her an extra 5 shillings and she said, 'That will do for now.' Violet went with me to the furniture shop and when we arrived Sadie was already there. She sorted me out a bed, a wardrobe, and a dressing table. I remember buying four blankets, some sheets, and two feather pillows. I paid thirty shillings every Friday for everything, I remember they delivered the furniture the following Tuesday.

When I got up early for work on Monday Mom was already up, she was standing by the door and told me that I was going to school. 'I told your Mr Carmichael that you'd be there today,' she told me. 'Mom if you don't let me go I'll play the wag anyway.' After another argument in which she said that she'd fetch Tommy and Albert to talk to me, she eventually let me go.

When I finally got out I ran all the way to the bananas rooms without stopping for my usual rest. I was really late but neither Arthur nor Steve said anything to me. I'd been worried in case they'd tell me off, but actually I think they was glad to see me, knowing that I'd never let them down.

When the furniture was delivered on the Tuesday Mrs Bloomer, Violet, and Sadie tidied my room and made my bed up for me. Every day Mom got me up for work with some toast and a hot drink, she also made my bed for me. It was nice to have a proper bed, but some morning I didn't want to get up I was so comfortable. Come the end of the July I'd left school and though Mom never said anything, I knew that she was proud of me. After I finished paying off my furniture I also bought Mom bed, which made her cry.

I had the pleasure of working with Arthur Brett till he retired in 1954 or 1955 from ill health. He taught me all about life in the market and the back slang. He'd come to the market every Friday for his birds and cages, slang for his wages. I remember I had to get him a box to sit on. We always had a chat the first thing Arthur would always ask me how I was doing and if Steve was treating me right. I believe he passed away in 1956. He only had one daughter who married into the Atkins family who owned the Rowbottoms cooked meat shops. Steve came to work for Arthur Brett in 1948 when he came out the R.A.F. and he came a partner in 1949. I had the greatest pleasure of working with Steve Fisher from April 1953 till 18th July 1958. For the five years I worked with Steve he treated me like a son. He never had any children, only a niece. When Steve found out that I ran to work every morning he bought me a bike.

I should have left school at end of July 1953 not in April that year. The day before I left to go in the army, Steve told me, 'Peter I knew hadn't left school when you came to me for job. I thought you wouldn't last a week, but you lasted five whole years and I'm proud of you.' Though the market was hard work I loved every minute of it. I liked getting to know the all the salesmen, the groundsmen, and the porters. Towards August 1953 I was getting to know in's and out's of the market and also how to earn money on all the empty boxes and the potato sacks. I was speaking the back slang that Arthur taught me. What went in the market was nobody's business, it just went on.

When I had my call up papers to do my national service in May 1956 Steve told me what to do and I did it. When they finally caught up with me I had to go in on the 19th July 1958. The day before I left to go in the army Steve gave me my week wages and more on top. My good customers gave me extra tips when they knew I was going in the army. After I'd done my six weeks training at the end of September 1958 the platoon had a weekend leave and I came home on the Friday. The first thing I did on the Saturday morning was go down to the market to see Steve. When I got the pitch I asked where Steve was and was told that bad news that he'd passed away early on in September. I was devastated. I went over to the Star Cafe to see Hilda, when I walked in we went through to the back and she put her arms around me and gave me a hug. We sat down and talked, she told me that Steve thought the world of me and that he was going to make me a junior partner in the firm. 'He was hoping you'd come back to work for him when you left the army,' Hilda told me, 'I think he had three or four lads after you left but none of them stuck at the job.' As I was leaving she hugged me again and then walked me to the door. Thankfully she never touched my bum. When I got home I told Mom that Steve had died. 'You've lost a good gaffer and a friend,' she said. Later that day I had a moment in my room and lay on bed thinking about Steve.

Photographs

Mom & Me

Tommy Round

Albert Round

Eastholme

St Andrews Church

The Hen and Chickens Pub

Willson's Bakery

Coventry Road Police Station

GPO in Garrison Lane

The Snuff Shop

Garrison Lane

Garrison Lane School

Teachers at Tilton Road School

266

Ables Corner Shop

The Acorn Pub

Printed in Great Britain
by Amazon